# URBAN POLITICAL ECONOMY

3

*For Tom*

Leonie Sandercock
Michael Berry

# Urban political economy

## The Australian case

GEORGE ALLEN & UNWIN
Sydney London Boston

First published in 1983 by
George Allen & Unwin Australia Pty Ltd
8 Napier Street, North Sydney, NSW 2060 Australia

George Allen & Unwin (Publishers) Ltd
Park Lane, Hemel Hempstead, Herts HP2 4TE, England

Allen & Unwin Inc
9 Winchester Terrace, Winchester, Mass 01890 USA

National Library of Australia
Cataloguing-in-Publication entry

Sandercock, Leonie, 1949-.
Urban political economy.
Bibliography.
Includes index.
ISBN 0 86861 095 x.
ISBN 0 86861 103 4 (pbk.).
1. Sociology, Urban-Australia. 2. Urban
economics. I. Berry, Michael. II. Title
307.7'6'0994

Set in 10/11 pt Plantin by Setrite Typesetters,
Hong Kong

Printed by Bright Sun Printing Press Co Ltd,
Hong Kong

# Contents

# Tables

# Acknowledgments

Chapters 1, 2 and 11 have not been published before and most of the remaining chapters have been modified or reworked in the light of recent developments. We gratefully acknowledge Oxford University Press for permission to reprint Chapter 3, which first appeared in Patience & Head (eds) *From Whitlam to Fraser* (1979); to Hill of Content Publishing Co. for Chapters 8 and 9 which first appeared in Hay, Ward and Warhurst (eds) *Anatomy of an Election* (1979); to the editors for permission to reprint Chapter 6, which appeared in *Antipode*, vol. 13, no. 1, 1981; to Hale & Iremonger for permission to reprint Chapter 5, which appeared in P. Troy (ed.) *Federal Power in Australia's Cities* (1978); to the editors for Chapter 10, which appeared in *The Australian and New Zealand Journal of Sociology*, vol. 13, no. 1, 1977; to the editors for Chapter 4, which appeared in *The Journal of Australian Political Economy*, no. 3, 1978; to Stephen Murray-Smith for permission to use material in Chapter 2, a longer version of which appeared in *Melbourne Studies in Education (1982)*; to Silverfish Books for Chapter 7, a version of which first appeared in L. Sandercock, *The Land Racket* (1979).

Our special thanks to John Iremonger for constructive criticism and Pat Gillard and Jane Price for typing, cross-checking and supportive skills.

# Introduction

In the study of urban problems various thinkers such as Jane Jacobs, Margaret Mead, Louis Mumford, and the Australian Hugh Stretton have transcended traditional disciplinary boundaries and applied a kind of humanist perspective to the study of cities. More recently, a new kind of trans-disciplinary approach—that of the political economy movement—has been applying its perspectives to urban issues (or, 'the urban question', as the leading theoretician of this new wave, Manuel Castells (1972a), was to call his seminal book).

Many Australian students of cities have been trying to come to grips with the relevance or otherwise of this French-led school of urban Marxism. Their interest has been fanned by the fate of the Whitlam government. Both the manner of its dismissal and, more specifically, the attempts it made at urban reforms through the Department of Urban and Regional Development, seemed to reveal to some Australians the structural limits to (urban) reform in a property-owning or capitalist democracy. It was a time when they became all the more susceptible to the fresh interpretations emanating from French and English Marxist urban research. Thus, for many who had been immersed in the heated urban policy debates of the Whitlam years it was a time to return to basic Marxist Theory and/or the basic questions of political economy.

It was hardly surprising that political economy was enjoying a revival by the mid-1970s. Orthodox economics had relieved politics and property of any responsibility for the existing division of earnings and patterns of consumption. Political economists maintain that property and power are the essential elements in class struggles and sectional conflicts. From their vantage point, the production and division of society's annual product among the members of society is *the* central question.

Those who have sought to understand these problems have been led to a revival of political economy, with renewed focus on the class system which structures and constitutes the economy. By way of contrast, for the orthodox economists the problem of *allocation* stood at the centre; their questions were how the members of society choose to spend their incomes, and how suppliers adjust to this (Nell, 1972). Orthodox economics tries to show that markets allocate scarce resources according to relative efficiency; political economics tries to show that markets distribute income according to relative power. The heart of the matter is the concept of 'capital' and its relation to social class and economic power.

Now, how is this relevant to cities? The key contribution of the new political economy to the urban question is its stress on urbanisation as a process of capitalist development. The new urban sociology is essentially a political economy of space. It is concerned with the causes and consequences of the social organisation of space by private capital, the working class and the state. It analyses urban and regional development in relation to the process of capital accumulation, stressing that such development plays an important role in generating the conditions for continued accumulation by opening up new markets, drawing on further supplies of labour, helping in the reproduction of the social relations of production, and so on.

Szelenyi (1977) has documented the transformation within urban sociology, from the old concern with ecological factors (stemming from the dominance of the Chicago school) through the social democratic concerns of the mid–late 1960s with social inequality and the role of urban planning in the allocation of urban resources, to the current concern with class analysis, the structural sources of social inequalities, and the nature and historically changing role of planning and state intervention in the urban system. He argues that the publication of Castells' *The Urban Question* demonstrated that the application of the conceptual tools of Marxist political economy opened both new dimensions for, and unresolved problems of an urban class analysis (Szelenyi, 1977).

Thus, while the social democratic debate about urban problems over the past ten years has been conducted in terms of unequal accessibility of and to scarce urban resources (the philosophy of locational inequality), the new urban political economy stresses that the 'urban crisis' is an economic and financial one, a product and central element of the generalised crisis of advanced capitalist societies. In this sense, the urban problem is more and more identified with the inadequacy of 'non-productive urban infrastructure'. Castells (1977), O'Connor (1973) and others have argued that in advanced capitalist societies the flow of capital into the spheres of transport, schools, housing, water and sewerage and so on is breaking up, and consequently the infrastructural means necessary for the reproduction of labour are not delivered automatically any more. These insights clearly need to be explored and developed in the Australian context, in the light of successive Federal budget cutbacks to allocations for urban and regional development. A start is made in this direction in this book.

Many students of Australian cities, who have ploughed their way through the European theoretical literature, may yet remain puzzled as to how to pin down and apply that body of theory to the Australian situation. These essays—written between 1977 and 1982, some previously published, others not—have been collected with the intention of providing some *Australian* focus to the urban political economy debate. Attention is drawn to recent Australian scholarship in this vein (Aungles and Szelenyi 1979; Stilwell 1980; Larcombe 1981; Logan 1980; Beed 1981) while noting the disparate methodologies and language. What is significant is the new commonality of starting point—the question, who's getting what out of the urban economy and the urban planning system, and why? That is the authors' general definition of urban political economy. Attempts to establish the content and develop the questions suggested by this starting point have raised important and productive conflicts of a methodological, as well as theoretical nature (Harloe, 1977). Therein lies the promise of urban political economy.

For some years now, planners and planning students have been told by a succession of radical texts that, as state employees, they are simply performing as the agents of capital, or as the personification of a logic of capital, or at best as the bearers and expression of the objective class relation at any one time (Castells 1977b: 77). The authors are unhappy with this position and prefer to agree, with Saunders (1981), that urban planners, like other 'urban managers' are standing on the major fault line of contemporary capitalist societies between what may be crudely expressed as a 'logic of capitalism' (social investment, the ideology of private property, etc.) and a 'logic of socialism' (social consumption, the ideology of social need, etc.). In Australian society this contradiction is beginning to be expressed institutionally—in the growing tension between central (federal) and local (state and local) government agencies—as well as functionally. In such a situation the role of planners, and of those who educate them, can be nothing other than contradictory, at least for those who care about the distribution of this country's wealth, for they will experience problems in reconciling their role in mediating between the interests of private property and the criterion of social need.

Room for manoevre will clearly be limited, but it helps to know what questions to ask and where to look for answers.

# Part One  THEORY

MICHAEL BERRY

# 1   The Australian city in history: critique and renewal

## The city in Australian historiography

How have urbanisation themes figured on the research agendas of Australian historians? The answer must be—'barely at all'. Until the relatively recent work of some economic and social historians, urbanisation or, more generally, the spatial dimension to social life, has appeared as no more than a background factor in historical studies which focus instead on the initial dominance of the pastoral industry, the drama of 'key events'—Goldrushes, Federation, World War, Depression, etc.—the achievements of 'great men' and the search for the great Australian character.

The apparent exceptions—the plethora of local and regional histories compiled piecemeal over the past half century—have been dismissed as '. . .overwhelmingly council-commissioned works of the "scissors and paste" variety, owing more to antiquarianism than to analytic historical investigation' (Glynn, 1970a:5). Moreover, the few historically competent studies of particular towns or regions offered little understanding of urbanisation themes in general: 'Even if such studies were multiplied many times they would constitute little more than an amorphous mass of *ad hoc* commentary' (Glynn, 1970a:5). This sweeping generalisation is, perhaps, unfair to some of the best histories with a strong regional focus—say, for example, Kiddle's (1961) study of the Western District of Victoria and Bate's (1962) study of the Melbourne suburb, Brighton. However, Glynn's twin criticisms stand. The urban question has consistently maintained its marginal status in Australian historiography and where individual histories have focused on particular cities, towns and

My thanks to Peter Williams, Frank Williamson, Graeme Davison, Andrew Wells and Chris Paris who read and commented on parts of an earlier draft of this chapter. A draft of the third section of this chapter appeared as part of a paper presented to the Urban Research Unit Seminar, ANU, in August 1981.

3

regions it has not been possible to generalise from their results. In the latter case, 'space' has been used as an arbitrary selective mechanism, a means of distinguishing local from outside factors, endogenous from exogenous variables, so that description and analysis can focus on the former; exogenous events or processes were important only to the extent that they had noticeable local effects—for example, on the biographies of particular individuals, families or institutions. This spatial fetishism still largely characterises the work of urban historians in the ten years since Glynn wrote.

Why have Australian historians lacked a spatial imagination, why did they not develop a theory of the urban as an integral part of their projects? There are at least four possible answers to this question.

In the first place, it must be admitted, most twentieth-century Australian historians have not been interested in developing a theory of anything; their empricist methodology did not allow it. *History*, for the dominant pre-war school of Australian historiography [termed by Pascoe (1979) 'the liberal patriots'] meant the collection and substantiation of 'facts', their situation within a broader social context and the superficially idiosyncratic explication of this dialectic between fact and context. History consequently emerged as part-science, part-art, and Gareth Stedman-Jones' comments on British historians seem to apply equally to many of their Australian colleagues:

> History was a science because it was composed of 'facts'. 'Facts' were events, and events resulted from the action of individuals producing them through the framework of institutions. All these were verifiable empirical realities, and once they had been established and confirmed, it was the task and duty of the historian to judge them. At its most elevated level therefore, history could attain the status of a scientific sermon. (Stedman-Jones, 1972:98)

The dual approach to history, with its suggestion of a craftlike life for the historian, most clearly characterised the work of historians loosely gathered around R.M. Crawford at Melbourne University in the period just prior to and after the Second World War; Crawford's famed 'moral conception of history' neatly summed up the second half of the traditional liberal project. 'Cities', or more accurately, particular cities at particular points in time, appear naturally in this view, when they appear at all, as bundles of facts about population levels, economic activities, cultural pursuits, social values and built environment manipulations, all carefully documented and 'verified' by painstaking searches of primary sources and welded together in the historian's particular contextual world view, on the basis of a generalised though loosely defined commitment to some notion of 'progress in history'. *The* city, as an analytical concept, dissolves into countless, unrelated, historically specific and arbitrarily delimited backdrops to empirical studies of other things. *A* city, say Ballarat in the 1860s or Wollongong in the 1930s, is synthesised through the edited outlooks, preferences and prejudices of selected contemporaries who, in each case, left the primary source material mined by the particular historian concerned. Such exercises in 'urban biography' (McCarty, 1980) offer no basis for comparison or generalisation, either at the level of primary sources or at the level of interpretation. Criticism here gravitates to often interesting, certainly important, but, in the end, limited disagreements over the authenticity and veracity of sources.

Of course, this is not to claim that idiographic historical studies with a particular spatial (or any other) referent cannot be compared in terms of the interpretative principles at work. Recent developments in the philosophy of science have made most people aware of the selective mechanisms which structure social enquiry. 'Facts' don't select, organise and relate themselves. Modern historical criticism can and does attempt to place historical research in terms of the background assumptions (often implicit) about human nature and how society works, the epistomological and metaphysical positions held, and the dominant material and cultural features and concerns of the society in which the historian works.

This latter point leads to the second explanation for the late and stunted development of Australian urban history. Historians, like all people, are time and space bound; their work will reflect the particular concerns of the society they are a part of. Thus, the absence of urban or spatial themes in historical scholarship might stem from the absence or systematic distortion of such themes in the wider society over the period in question. Glynn favours this explanation. He begins his case for an urban approach to Australian history by summarising the now familiar story of a country characterised by a sparsely distributed population concentrated into (designated) 'urban' centres, metropolitan dominance and city-first development, and then states that: 'The avoidance of such an approach by so many for so long, can be attributed to that El Dorado of Australian culture and historiography—the search for distinctively national characteristics and character' (Glynn 1970a:8). The uniquely Australian character, given classic statement and dissection by Russell Ward in *The Australian Legend*, has all but stolen the attention of Australian historians away from other problematics. In attempting to answer why this happened, Glynn offers an 'urban interpretation' of the Legend itself; in other words, he attributed the latter's significance and dissemination to the dominant rhythms of urban life—a neat trick since it combined a critique of a substantial body of traditional Australian historiography with the establishment of yet another rationale for an urban focus to future work.

Ward's thesis has been the focus of intense controversy since its appearance more than twenty years ago and a number of criticisms have been levelled against it (Davison, 1978a). At the very least, most accounts can be criticsed for an inadequate specification of the mechanisms and success of diffusion. However, regardless of how the legend originated and spread, regardless of its historical accuracy, to the extent that it concentrated the minds of subsequent historians it provides a possible explanation for the anti-urban bias observable in Australian historiography.

Thirdly, it can be argued that the absence of a spatial problematic is tied up with the conventional treatments of social class in Australian history. Connell (1977) and Connell and Irving (1980) have recently argued that historians have either ignored or trivialised the process of class formation in Australian history. This outcome has resulted partly from the dictates of method, particularly in the case of ultra-empiricists for whom 'class' is an illegitimate abstraction, and partly from the static, ahistorical sense in which 'class' has been used in much historical (and social scientific) research. For many historians 'class' has become a background, sorting category against or through which the central themes can be drawn; in Connell's illuminating terminology, this signals the choice of a 'categorical' rather than 'generative' approach to class analysis. Thus, for example, most labour historians from Childe (1923) onwards focus on the emerging political organisation of the working class rather than on the emergence (making) of the working class itself; the latter is taken for granted. Similarly, because the labour movement arose and developed *in* particular cities and towns, the latter could be accepted as simple historical facts, a backdrop against which historical analysis proceeded—in short, a series of discrete glass bottles into which the wine of historical scholarship could be poured and through which it could be observed to mature. Any concern with the historical factors conditioning the emergence of Australia's spatial development and with the relationship of those factors to the development of class structure, has fallen well beyond the historian's reach.

Interestingly, Connell (1977: 13–14) points to some labour and regional histories which do seriously attempt to treat class as a relation rather than an hierarchical organising principle. However, in each case analysis has been contained within a localised spatial framework in which attention has concentrated on the developing relationships of particular pastoralists and pastoral workers or mine-owners and miners, to the exclusion of national and international processes. For example, Gollan's (1963) study of coal mining in New South Wales, according to Connell (1977:13), is limited to industrial relations and pressure group politics as they unfolded in the isolated mining settlements and the capital city of the State. An inadequate conceptualisation of 'class' coheres with an inadequate conceptualisation of 'space'.

For other 'old left' historians, space serves as a substitute for class analysis. Thus, Connell (1977:16) suggests that Ward's tendency to slip from an ambivalent (and simplistic) class model to a reliance on 'environmental determinism' (the natural vigours of bush life) in order to explain the Australian Legend, in effect links him to a similar tradition strongly entrenched in mainstream Australian historiography. Brian Fitzpatrick (1941), on the other hand, did marry class to spatial analysis.

However, here a simplistic class model coheres with a simplistic theory of imperialism, one which threatens to confine causal analysis to the conspiratorial agency of élites frequenting Whitehall and 'the City' (of London)—an implication which N.G. Butlin (1964) was later to stress with devastating consequences.

Why, then, have successive generations of historians failed to seriously address themselves to spatial and class themes? For Marxists of vulgar bent the answer is clear-cut. Historians and academic social scientists in general are apologists for the ruling class; their work forms part of the dominant ideology, an integral element in the reproduction of ruling class hegemony. This particular stance, common enough on the left, has usually served as an excuse for ignoring or dismissing the scholarly output of bourgeois social scientists *en masse* (a complement repaid in kind by the latter who are then relieved of the duty to consider *any* Marxist analysis). This position is, at base, methodologically self-contradictory, it often being pointed out that Marx himself was concerned to develop his analysis of capitalism through an extensive critique of the categories and theories of classical political economy. More than that it simply begs important questions with respect to, firstly, the nature of the correspondence between the structure of bourgeois thought and ruling class interests, and, secondly, the historical conditions constraining and institutional means shaping academic production as an element in an over-arching bourgeois hegemony.

These large questions lead on to a fourth and final explanation for the virtual irrelevance of the urban problematic in Australian historiography, one which complements in some senses (rather than contradicts) the previous two. If the rapid developments in urban social theory over the past twenty years, and their application in a number of different fields, have arisen as a series of complex responses to real historical forces, then the absence of an urban focus among earlier historians is hardly surprising. Other themes reflecting the dominant concerns of their time would naturally have concentrated their attention: war, nationalism, Depression, Federation and, as already stressed, the search for the Australian character served to fire the historians' imaginations. The recent developments referred to, concern the qualitative leap in urban political action and violence, associated state intervention and urban research characterising North American and European countries from the early 1960s onwards. Paralleling these political economic and applied research developments, urban social theory has undergone a radical transformation (Szelenyi, 1977), due to the work of sociologists (for example, Rex and Moore, 1967; Pahl, 1975), radical geographers (for example, Harvey, 1973; Walker, 1978a, 1978b), political economists [for example, see the various contributions to the special issue of the *Review of Radical Political Economics* (Vol. 1, No. 3) devoted to uneven regional development], and the French urban Marxists (for example, see Pickvance, 1976; Harloe 1977; Castells,

1977a, 1978). In spite of the large theoretical and methodological differences dividing contributors to this 'new urban sociology', they are agreed on several basic points, namely, the increasing social importance of urban questions and the need to develop a macro- rather than micro-sociological perspective with which to analyse the social-structural determinants of pervasive social inequalities and social conflict.

Only when the time was ripe, apparently, did urban concerns surface and draw a definite, albeit somewhat grudging, response from historians. Interestingly, when this occurred, especially in the work of economic historians like Butlin and McCarty (discussed below), the new urban problematic was largely dissociated from the rekindling of interest in questions of class structure and conflict and, as such, diametrically opposed to the contemporary developments in urban sociology. In discussing the relationship of the historian to his society, Carr comments: 'When you take up a historical work, it is not enough to look for the author's name on the title page, look also for the date of publication or writing—it is sometimes even more revealing' (Carr, 1964:42). Carr's observation certainly applies to the roughly simultaneous interest in urban questions sparked off among both sociologists and historians over the last decade; however, it offers little or nothing in the way of explaining why the latter should ignore or downgrade the question of class inequality and conflict which the former highlight. This, in turn, should warn us away from overly simplistic and functionalist explanations of the emergence of the new urban concerns.

In summary, until the 1970s Australian historians were relatively uninterested in the urban problematic. Although, as Davison (1979) has argued, the rumblings of the emerging British school of urban history were beginning to reverberate in the colonies during the 1960s—indeed, one of the major contributors to the British debates turned his sights on Melbourne's past (Briggs, 1963)—urban themes continued to be marginal to the traditional concerns of Australian historiography. It is indicative that, by 1970, the two major Australian works with a central urban or spatial theme, Geoffrey Blainey's *Tyranny of Distance* and Hugh Stretton's *Ideas for Australian Cities*, were written by the two great loners in Australian historiography, to be met by active hostility, on the one hand, and studied neglect, on the other.

**Discovery and reification of 'the city' in the 'new urban history'**

In 1964 Noel Butlin published his pathbreaking book, *Investment in Australian Economic Development*. This book, more than any other, has been responsible for legitimising the historical study of Australian urbanisation, although Butlin's particular concerns and methods of analysis have had far less influence.

Butlin focuses on the period from 1860 to 1900, as the decisive phase in Australian economic growth, the period in which Australia supposedly cut free from British domination to set the foundations for independent economic and political development in the twentieth century. He reaches this position by way of two major conclusions, based on interpretation of the fruits of a massive exercise in statistical compilation. In the first place, he argued, this period was characterised by a long boom driven by extensive investment in urban productive and infrastructural assets. In the second place, the colonial governments were the largest investors, accounting in total for almost half of gross capital formation in the period, largely financed by public loans raised on the London money markets.

Both conclusions encouraged Butlin to call for historians to grant priority to urbanisation over rural development in order to understand Australian history from 1860 onwards. The first conclusion provides direct support for this interpretation, the second conclusion does so indirectly, since the intended and unintended effects of public investment overwhelmingly fuelled urban development. In this latter context, provision of social overhead capital (water, sewerage, local roads, public buildings) was much less important than public provision of communications networks, especially railways. Railway building in the capital cities encouraged urbanisation and massive residential construction, while regional railways pushing out radially from the capitals reinforced their economic domination over their respective hinterlands.

Butlin's position is open to attack from two obvious directions. It might be argued that Butlin's own statistics demonstrate the reestablishment of wool as Australia's main export after 1870, accounting for two-thirds of total export income by 1890 (Butlin, 1964:30). However, as Butlin also shows, the export sector declined in aggregate terms over the entire period, from a little over a quarter of gross domestic product to less than one-seventh (Butlin, 1964:28). Moreover, in the latter part of this period, from 1876, pastoral production grew at a much slower rate than construction, manufacturing and railways, and slower than gross domestic product in total (Butlin, 1964:19). In other words, Butlin argues, during this period the structure of economic activity was progressively re-oriented away from the international to the domestic sector, and in the latter, away from the pastoral industry to the city.

Secondly, how does Butlin handle the central importance of overseas investment in Australian economic development, a 'fact' also established by Fitzpatrick who used it as the empirical basis for a diametrically opposed interpretation—namely, the dominance of British imperial interests? Overseas capital flowed predominantly into two areas, pastoral investment and the public sphere. Butlin has already established the declining overall importance of the former in relation to urban-concentrated residential construction which was financed largely by domestic savings. Public investment, according to Butlin, far from passively reinforcing the interests of British capital in turning Australia into a quarry for raw materials, resulted from the independent and aggressive borrowing policies of colonial governments which facilitated the construction of domestic urban-centred communications and social overhead networks, and underwrote rapid economic growth.

Critical reaction to Butlin's work has focused on the reliability of his statistical series; the peculiar force of quantification—in particular, its mesmeric effect on literary historians—threatened to carry the day on numbers alone. However, as Clark (1975, 1976) notes, there are questionable theoretical assumptions underpinning Butlin's approach, both with respect to his statistical compilations and their interpretation. From the Marxist perspective, Butlin's approach can be criticised both for its empiricistic methodology and its fetishistic treatment of space—that is, for its tendency to treat 'space' as a separate and theoretically prior category of analysis.

Among economic historians, Butlin's arguments and statistics have been subsequently debated, modified and refined. However, theoretical fashions change and the implicit Keynesian growth theory informing his work has fallen from favour to be replaced by a general commitment to neo-classical growth models. Even Butlin (1970), in his later work on twentieth-century economic development, has opted for the latter approach. In a review of five Australian economic history texts published since Butlin, Schedvin (1978) stressed their basic agreement over subject matter and interpretation:

> the motor of economic growth is rational economic man (REM) who acts continuously through time in log-linear fashion independent of culture, social structure or the physical environment. As REM is constant, the key variables are natural resources, population, trade and investment; money and government activity are minor variables, the latter usually acting to retard the efficiency of REM. For the most part there is a one-for-one relationship between measured growth and 'material well-being'. There is a strong preference for the establishment of simple mechanical relationships between a small number of easily quantifiable variables. Social conflict is out; income distribution is either unimportant or assumed to be reasonably favourable; technology (surprisingly) has a minor role; there are no business organisations of any consequence and other institutional arrangements are regarded as dependent variables; except at the purely mechanical level, international comparison is at a discount. (Schedvin, 1978:183)

When such an approach is wedded to orthodox international trade theory, imperialist exploitation becomes a logical impossibility. The past materialises as the harmonious outcome of individual initiative displayed by domestic REMs engaged, as Butlin demonstrates, in urban activities. Butlin's vision placed less emphasis on the stability and efficiency of Australia's development and rather more emphasis on the progressive and initiatory role of rational economic government; nevertheless, the common message is clear: concentrate on domestic, especially urban events and processes. It is this message or legacy bequeathed by Saint Noel which has created the 'ideological interest' [to use McCarty's (1970:10) term] necessary to sustain the new urban historians. A ritualistic reference to Butlin's book is now, it seems, sufficient justification for a single-minded urban focus.

A crucial point in the emergence of the new approach came with the publication in 1970 of a special issue of the *Australian Economic History Review*. McCarty's article, probably the best known single piece on Australian urban history (outside Bultin's), focused on the functional similarities and differences of Australia's capital cities. Davison and Bate contributed articles related to larger research projects which later resulted in the publication of extremely influential books on Ballarat in the second half of the nineteenth century (Bate, 1978) and Melbourne in the 1880s (Davison, 1978b). The final article in the collection, by Glynn (1970b), considered the prospects of an Australian urban history in the light of recent developments in Britain. In doing so he uncovered a second source of (possible) inspiration and legitimation. Glynn gave an account of contributions to a 'Round-Table Conference' on the study of urban history held at the University of Leicester in 1966. British historians had already discovered the city, though according to Glynn's account there was little agreement as to the delimitation and definition of their subject matter or on the methods appropriate to its pursuit.

In the 1970s, a number of book-length studies of particular Australian cities were published, in addition to those by Davison and Bate mentioned above; for example, on Sydney (Spearritt, 1978; Kelley, 1978), Brisbane (Lawson, 1973) and Perth (Stannage, 1979). It seems likely that the 1980s will witness an explosion of similar studies as the new sub-discipline of urban history reinforces its institutional position and wins academic acceptance. However, what really needs to be done, beforehand, is an evaluation of the theoretical assumptions and limitations characterising and guiding this growing current of thought. The following remarks are hardly exhaustive, but are meant to advance the discussion in that direction.

There are, in this author's view, three competing approaches to the theorisation of the urban visible in the new work. In the first case it is pretty much, 'business as usual', a particular city serving as a convenient container in which to distil other essences; the contributions to Kelley's (1978) collection on nineteenth-century Sydney illustrates this tendency with articles on individual topics (like transportation and women in the workforce) designating the several, independent, focii. The conception of the city as smorgasbord does not arise only in edited collections of readings: Spearritt's (1978) study of Sydney also heads off in several unrelated directions (for example, his description of the failure of town planning, his obvious interest in slum life and popular culture, and his oblique interest in the social role and status of women), though in other respects it straddles the second approach discussed below. The best (and most single-minded) example of this genre is provided by Sandercock (1975) in her historical study of town planning in three Australian capital cities. Historical narrative—the careful placement of events and people in chronological order—dominates the book, although there are clear but tentative signs of an attempt to develop a structural political theory in order to explain the failure of town planning as a social movement. The cities chosen on arbitrary grounds are, for Sandercock, geo-political frames helping to delineate the object of analysis. As with all histories written from within this perspective, 'the city' (or region)—as opposed to particular cities or regions—does not exist as a coherent theoretical construct. This approach does not strictly entail a theory of the urban at all, but its negation.

Conversely, in the second approach a deliberate effort is made to construct an ideal type of the (modern) city, often termed the 'metropolis'. Particular features of social life are abstracted from their concrete historical contexts (usually related to North American cities in the early part of the twentieth century) grafted together and used to organise observations on and suggest explanations of life in the city under review. It has been argued elsewhere (Berry, 1980) that Davison's study of *Marvellous Melbourne* can be viewed in this light.

Davison is primarily concerned to trace the emergence of Melbourne as a modern metropolis during the last two decades of the nineteenth century. This metropolitan type integrates elements of Wirth's theory of urbanism, the economic historians' concern with changing economic and population structures and even Weber's analysis of bureaucracy. These 'internal' factors provide a base from which to consider the impact on social life of 'external' market factors—continuing capital and labour inflows, the accelerating penetration of technological innovations, etc. 'Class', conceived in stratificationist terms, appears as a secondary or intervening variable through which to explicate the spread of a pervasive urban ideology among the middle and working classes (no upper or ruling class being in evidence), increasingly committed to or aspiring after domestic respectability in owner-occupied suburbia. Class-based conflicts are restricted to particular industries undergoing rapid transformation and depersonalisation on the factory floor; however, mass internalisation of the urban ideology outweighs these divisive forces, at least until the material rock on which it depends crumbles with the onset of depression in the 1890s.

There are real difficulties with this approach. It implicitly depends on a Weberian methodological position. Concrete reality is so infinitely complex, according to this approach, that it can only be grasped by the construction and application of ordering concepts which, nevertheless, have no essential connection with reality and cannot be empirically verified in that sense. They do, however, provide benchmarks against which concrete reality is compared and particular cause–effect relations empirically established, albeit on provisional grounds. Moreover, this approach is implicitly dependent on Weber's division of labour between sociology and history as separate but complementary disciplines (Whimster, 1980). For Weber, sociologists provide the concepts and models which historians use to 'cut-up' and interpret past reality as a collection of particular cause–effect relations. There is nothing, other than the sociologist's value-orientation, to guide the process of constructing concepts nor any possibility of the historian's establishing higher-order, law-like generalisations as opposed to an essentially unrelated collection of particular cause–effect linkages.

Weber was concerned, above all, to establish the absolute non-comparability of ideal-typical categories and concrete historical reality. To confuse the two was the prime methodological sin and one which characterised most macro-theories of societal development (especially the Marxist). The appeal of such a stance to Australia's sociological historians is obvious. They, too, according to Pascoe (1979:126), were attempting to distance themselves from the over-arching, deterministic explanatory schemes of 'new left' historians and syncretic conservatives alike. A high price, however, was paid for this independence. History-writing was turned into an exercise little more heroic than the documentaries of committed empiricists; no grand integrating themes, no large-scale generalisations and no overall understanding of the past were possible. In the clash between methodological purity and the pursuit of history as an art form, the latter usually wins and the ideal-typical constructs gradually assume more and more realistic forms as the narrative unfolds. *The* city or metropolis loses its conventional status and becomes the particular city under review; the key characteristics defining the former become the real historical forces conditioning the latter's developments. In other words, the city is *reified*: an abstract entity is treated as a concrete thing.

By adopting and reifying the metropolitan type, the new urban historians have been able to develop overall interpretive and explanatory accounts of their subject. Davison, Spearritt, Bate and others have achieved this by stressing the independent and theoretically prior force of cultural factors over class structure and conflict. Urbanism (and suburbanism) as a way of life in the emerging metropolis appears disconcertingly like the picture of reality favoured by the wealthy and powerful citizens of the city themselves; life is increasingly 'middle class', progressive and harmonious. From a different epistomological and metaphysical position, Castells (1977a) has attacked just this emphasis in the work of the Chicago urban sociologists, by stressing the theoretical primacy of class, conceived in materialist rather than culturalist terms. As Harloe has argued (1977:10–13), the contrasts between Castell's approach (and Marxist theories of urbanisation in general) and Weberian analyses hinge not just on the particular theoretical emphases propounded and value-orientations implied, but also on the philosophical bases informing each. By choosing one approach over another the historian or sociologist is, explicity or implicitly, subscribing to the epistomological and metaphysical assumptions entailed.

The third approach discernible in the new urban history is comparative in scope and method. Real cities are compared in order to establish defining characteristics and patterned relations between them along lines suggested by a priori models. Thus, McCarty (1973) has suggested that the colonial capitals in nineteenth-century Australia fulfilled certain 'commercial' functions with respect to the (capitalist) world and each other which largely determined their development. These functions were related to the colonisation of Australia as a 'region of recent settlement', and hence are also discernible in the development of other countries falling into this category (for example, Canada and the United States in the eighteenth century and Latin America in the previous two centuries). Similarly, historical geographers utilising the models of urban geographers and economists—central place theory, location theory, growth pole and related models, Rostow's stages of economic growth, etc.—attempt to specify invariable spatio-temporal patterns of development equally applicable to virtually all historical contexts, differentiated mainly by the empirically estimated values given to the parameters of the model(s) in question (Cloher, 1975; Burnley, 1980).

This approach, in effect, reifies the urban in a narrower, more specifically Marxist sense. The city is conceptualised as an arena for the interplay of designated urban roles rather than as one structuring element in the determination of social relations between real people; functions may change through time, becoming more complex and differentiated [as in McCarty's (1970) distinction between the walking and public transport cities], but the city remains, as ever, a complex of designated roles and functions. Needless to say, 'class' disappears beneath the feet of maximising REMs operating in relatively competitive market situations. The alternative strategy of tying a historically contingent definition of the urban to the dominant social structural features of the society in question (as, for example, Castells' suggests in the first part of *The Urban Question*) is ruled out of court in a double-edged sense: firstly, the city is deliberately defined independently of social structure and, secondly, any sociologically conceived notion of social (especially class) structure is dissolved into the atomistic neo-classical economic world of competition, market flows and the free exchange of equivalents. This allows Glynn (1970a:4), for example, to claim that Australia's urban development had been irreversibly cemented by the end of the nineteenth century, with the implication that twentieth-century development has simply been 'more of the same'. In this mechanistic and profoundly unhistoric view, the emergence of advanced capitalism on a global scale has done nothing to alter Australia's urban structure.

## Towards a theory of dependent urbanisation

It was argued in the preceeding section that the recent upsurge of interest in the urban among historians and economic historians has either resulted in little or no progress beyond the 'biographical' outputs of earlier local and regional historians, or has led to the reification of the urban in a manner which dissociates the urban problematic from the (class) structural determinants of social life and social change. As always, an inadequate historical conceptualisation of 'class' coheres with an inadequate analysis of urbanisation.

It should be clear that these conclusions are not theoretically innocent. The arguments on which they rest have been organised from within a perspective forged by contributors to the 'new urban sociology', more particularly by Marxists like Manuel Castells. The author also accepts the imperative directing the work of Connell and Irving (1980): Australian history must be approached through class analysis and the latter can only be carried out by confronting historical reality. This position demands an historical study of urbanisation in class terms. However, the reverse side of the same coin requires class analysis to develop a spatial dimension. In commending the relevance of modern urban social theory to historical research, an American historian has concluded:

> Recent writings by geographers, architects and urban planners . . . all suggest that the historians may be missing something important in the process. Space is socially produced, they say, and for this reason is not politically or socially neutral. The shape of urban and regional space, they insist, not only reflects the nature of class relations in any society, but also powerfully determines new social outcomes. The quality as well as the shape of urban space, for example, is also held to be historically specific. The nature of public space in the late medieval or early modern city, therefore, will differ from public space shaped, for example, under a system of monopoly capitalism. This is because in a regime of commodity production, space too is a commodity in a way that it was not before, and this is seen to have crucial economic and political consequences. (Amsden, (1979:13)

In this passage there is still a tendency to oppose class and space as independent categories. Nevertheless, it does stress the need to relate the spatial organisation of society to its class structuring. The urban is not a trans-historical category frozen in meaning; cities evolving in a world increasingly dominated by advanced capitalism are not simply more populous and densely packed versions of medieval cities. Castells (1977a) has offered a useful starting-point for an historical analysis of urbanisation. Redefining the urban question in an historical context entails, he suggests, conceptualising the spatial arrangements or organisation of social life as a product of (or basic element in) the development of social structure. For Castells the spatial distribution and concentration of populations, and their production, consumption and cultural activities (including the production, consumption and symbolic valuation of the built environment), are only explicable in terms of the dominant social dynamic which, as a Marxist, he identifies as the uneven global expansion of the capitalist mode of production which emerged, historically, in Northern Europe.

Thus, for example, the process and pattern of urbanisation associated with the emergence of the first capitalist nation, Britain, do not provide an historically invarient series of developmental stages, equally applicable to all countries and all periods. The British experience essentially entailed the economic destruction of the peasantry and its relocation as a proletariat in the rapidly industrialising cities; externally, British economic and naval power forged a world market largely in a vacuum, (the Dutch trading empire apart) prior to the competitive thrust of later starters. When other European countries and the United States did industrialise in the second half of the nineteenth century, they faced different constraints and opportunities to those conditioning British development a century earlier. Not only could the later developers benefit from the technological advances of the intervening period, they had to overcome the economic and military might of a well-entrenched rival. This latter fact necessarily influenced the structure and pace of their development, not least its spatial expression. This is most clearly seen on the international stage during the classical age of imperialism, when competing capitalist countries set about the colonial partition of the underdeveloped world. At the national level, emerging German and French capitalism did not entail the massive rural dislocations and internal migrations characterising British development, while American urbanisation depended far more on booming international, rather than internal, migration. These and other differences are to be expected, argues Castells, since they express changes in the rhythms of capital accumulation—developing forces of production and class relations giving rise to new structural contradictions—on a global scale.

The constraints posed by the rise of capitalism in Europe and America loomed largest in the Third World where new patterns of dependence complemented and underwrote development in the advanced countries. A dependent society is one in which the economic, political and cultural structures express and reinforce the class interests of the ruling class(es) in another, dominant society (Castells, 1977a:44). Clearly, dependence is a matter of degree and can only be established, in any instance, by concrete historical research into the mode of, and success with which, dominant structures have been imposed or, alternatively, repulsed. In order to explain the particular patterns of urbanisation visible in the Third World, it is therefore necessary to analyse the forces for expansion in the dominant societies, the pre-existing social structures of the dependent societies, and their 'mode of articulation', that is, the main forms and processes of domination linking and modifying both structures.

Castells distinguishes three forms or types of domination. *Colonial domination* involves the direct political subjugation and administration of dependent territories in order to secure valued resources for the dominant society. *Capitalist-commercial domination* is imposed through trading relations; manufactured goods (and invisible services like shipping and finance) are exported from dominant to dependent societies in return for raw materials, the rate of exchange or terms of trade expressing an unequal exchange by which value is transferred from the latter to the former, as manufactured goods sell above and raw materials below their respective values. *Imperialist industrial and financial domination* arises when capitalists in the dominant society export capital as well as goods to the dependent society. Control is exerted indirectly through the provision of loan capital and directly through the creation of local industries in order to exploit low wages in the dependent societies and circumvent tariff barriers. The precise form which dependent urbanisation assumes will depend on the type of domination ascendant in the context of the particular, historically specific social forces structuring the dominant and dependent societies in question.

Castells attempted to apply this general framework to Latin America, creating obvious difficulties for anyone interested in applying this approach to other historically specific situations—in this case, the Australian. With the partial exception of Argentina, Latin American experiences differ significantly from those characterising and driving Australian development. Australia industrialised earlier, more extensively, but at a smaller scale, prior to the massive internationalisation of production and intensive international division of labour dominant in more recent times. Similarly, the current explosion of Third World industrialisation is reflected in the spectre of de-industrialisation in Australia, most apparent in the decline of traditional manufacturing industries concentrated in the large capital cities (especially Melbourne, Sydney and Adelaide). This suggests the need for caution in attempting to apply the substance of Castells' analysis to the Australian situation; in particular, it suggests the probability that the urban typology he used to guide his analysis of Latin American urbanisation will have to be qualified, supplemented or even replaced for Australian purposes.

Just as an adequate analysis of Australian urbanisation cannot be based on a wider theory of *dependent underdevelopment*, neither can it be easily related to theories of *dominant development* in the advanced capitalist countries or, at least, not without substantial qualification. Thus, Castells' central proposition, namely, the fact of structural changes in advanced capitalism displacing basic contradictions from the sphere of production to the sphere of consumption, and the implications this has for spatial organisation and the politicisation of urban life, may not shed much light on contemporary Australian urbanisation and is irrelevant to a study of urbanisation in earlier periods. What is needed is an approach which allows one to grasp the total or global process of capitalist development from the perspective of a theory of *dependent development*. In effect, this calls for a third or 'mid-way' view which would 'fill out' Castells' abstract framework by shifting the focus from the First and Third Worlds to the particular experiences of a small number of societies like Australia, for which development was limited, uneven but present. This entails a focal shift, not a completely different view: *dependent* development implies the existence of relations of domination.

It must be stressed that the category of 'dependence' or 'dependent development' used here in no way relates to Latin American dependency theory but to the continuing theoretical debates among more orthodox Marxists concerning the analysis of global situations characterised by the articulation or inter-relation of societies structured by different modes of production (or stages of a mode of production) in which one mode is dominant.

In order to advance this analysis in this direction, it is necessary to start at the most general level of abstraction—the relationship between the process of capital accumulation and the production of spatial forms. In effect, this entails specifying those pre-conditions which must be met if production is to continue on a capitalist basis—that is, if production is to be primarily carried out by a class of property-less wage earners who must sell their labour to capitalists in order to survive. In this context Stilwell (1978) has delineated four functional conditions for continuing accumulation and sought to relate each to the problematic of spatial organisation.

Capitalism requires an ever-expanding market for the increasing volume and variety of the commodities it produces. The incessant competition of individual capitalists leads to continual intensification of the division of labour and the increasing application of technological advances to the production process, which leads, in turn, to a progressive cheapening in the cost of producing commodities and a rapid increase in their output. In order to realise their investments and reap a profit, capitalists must be able to sell their commodities. Historically, one major solution to the problem of markets has been the geographical expansion or penetration of capitalist relations of production and exchange from the few original centres of capitalist production in Northern Europe. This has clearly been an uneven process, both with respect to its form and pace, on the one hand, and its geographic spread, on the other hand. At the level of exchange, the most dramatic and far-reaching manifestation was the construction—first under British and later German and American hegemony—of an international economic order during the eighteenth and nineteenth centuries. The scale of this expansion can be gauged by the fact that, for the period from 1750 to 1913, the total value of international trade increased fifty-fold (Woodruff, 1973:658). However, capitalist penetration also occurred within the borders of the first capitalist nations. In Britain, for example, the new, cheap, factory-produced textiles cut the local (and external) market from underneath the feet of traditional cottage producers in the countryside. Together with the progressive and massive expropriation of tenant farmers and labourers from the land (and, hence, from the means of domestic production), this led to an increasing commercialisation of rural life, culminating in the near-total dissociation of production from the home and reinforcing the drift of the displaced peasantry to the factory towns. This latter point leads to consideration of the second functional requirement for accumulation, namely, the creation and maintenance of a pool of surplus labour power which acts as a restraint on wage levels. The lower wage levels are, the greater the profits (always assuming that commodities can be sold and profits realised) and the greater the rate of accumulation or growth. Some guarantors of a relative surplus population or 'reserve army of unemployed' are inherent in the dynamic of capitalist development itself—for example, the tendential displacement of labour power resulting from the competitive application of new technology to production, and the temporary waves of unemployment brought about by recurrent economic crises. Other forces leading to a similar outcome are historically contingent or specific to a particular situation or stage of development—for example, the recruitment of female and child labour during the early phases of English industrialisation. Into this second category may be placed those spatial rearrangements with have encouraged the creation and geographic concentration of surplus population at appropriate places for capitalist production. Examples of this type have already been given: the expulsion and drift to the cities of the agricultural population in industrialising England, and the massive waves of European emigration to America during the eighteenth and nineteenth centuries. Stilwell (1978: 23–4) offers two more recent examples—the pervasive 'guest worker' system in Western Europe and the post-war influx of non-English-speaking migrants to Australia, where they have become concentrated in the lowest-paid jobs and the most disadvantaged industrial suburbs of the main capital cities. The direct impact of a continuing flow of temporary or permanent guest workers is to keep unskilled wage levels lower than they would have been had local workers been recruited. More indirectly, the existence of a growing mass of unskilled, disorganised and desperate workers provides an incentive for capitalists to redivide and refine the production process in order to de-skill previously skilled occupations, which, in turn, acts as a general break on wage levels throughout the home economy.

In addition to adequate labour power, capital accumulation requires secure sources of raw materials and produced means of production. In particular, it requires the satisfaction of a complex and expanding ensemble of *general preconditions of production*, including the provision of extensive and integrated communications and transportation networks expressing, in Marx's terms, capital's attempts to annihilate space by time (Harvey, 1975:11–13). The form, level and spatial patterning of these networks historically reinforced the emerging geographical circulation and concentration of capital, tending in the nineteenth and early twentieth centuries to result in clear-cut patterns of regional and international specialisation. The earliest, most visible and far-reaching examples of geographic specialisation saw key industrial sectors like steel-making, textiles, armaments and ship-building tightly concentrated in a relatively small number of centres in the major imperialist powers—that is, the north of England, the Ruhr in Germany and the north-east of the United States—and the complementary concentration of raw material extraction in the periphery. More recently, as Stilwell stresses, the multi-nationalisation of capital has resulted in large, qualitative changes in the geography of accumulation. The production process has been reconstituted and subdivided on a world scale. Instead of being geographically concentrated within a single factory, as in the early stages of capitalism, the division of labour has become international. Raw materials extracted in one country are refined in a second, enter as semi-finished products in the production processes of a third and are sold in a fourth. In each country, multinational capital faces local workers organised along national lines and the Nation State, playing each country off against the rest through the ever-present threat of capital flight. No one group of workers or state in isolation, can exert control over the entire production process. The actual global pattern of production which emerges will reflect the efforts of each multinational corporate group to maximise total profits within the group, whether or not this entails real or book losses on operations in a particular country or region. This, in turn, will depend on the differential prospects for exploiting low wages, loose tax laws, generous subsidies, free infra-structure and a 'favourable' political climate in each country.

A spatial reorganisation of production is also taking place in some advanced capitalist societies. In the case of the United States, Walker (1978a) has argued that regions in the traditional sense—that is, spaces within which most economic decisions are made locally, in the light of local conditions, and most economic consequences are contained, through interlocking linkages or multiplier effects—are fast disappearing. They are being replaced by an uneven 'spatial mosaic' of specialised activities ranged or segregated across space and integrated through the internal administrative control of the large corporation. However, this does not lead to rigid or permanent patterns of regional specialisation. The heightened mobility and penetration of capital leaves it less dependent for profit on any one location. The disruption to accumulation posed by striking workers or an unsympathetic local state in one place can be resolved by shifting production to similar plants located elsewhere. Capital circulates through the institutional form of the large corporate conglomerate, flowing into and out of specific locations according to the profit situation of the group as a whole. The increasing degree of capital mobility, therefore, increasingly secures the necessary delivery of processed raw materials and intermediate (producer) goods within the corporate group; to a lesser extent, it also increases the reliability of supply of basic producer goods to other capitalists outside the group.

The fourth and most basic functional requirement for accumulation is the reproduction of capitalist social relations, notably, the capital–labour relation in production. Social conditions must be generated which ensure that sufficient workers deliver themselves up to the point of production, resigned to selling their labour-power in exchange for a money wage— willing, therefore to give up control over the uses to which their labour-power is put and, consequently, to give up any claim on the product of their labour. The main spatial dimensions to this problem (for capital) have already been noted in the discussion above of the geographical creation and concentration of a relative surplus population and the multi-regionalisation of production on the intra-national and international scales. However, the movement of labour and capital across space does more than keep wage levels down and the means of production secure. It also strategically weakens any group of workers or state authority bound to a particular territorial base *vis-à-vis* capital, thereby removing or reducing the economic and political basis for a society ordered by alternative—that is, non-capitalist—relations of production. The outcome of the abortive socialist experiment in Chile is only the most dramatic example of this situation. At the economic level, to the extent that multinational corporations successfully maximise profits, they impoverish local and national economies: successful exploitation tends to absorb or remove the locally generated investible surplus which could, under different socio-political conditions, have been directly applied to improving the material welfare of local populations.

The geographic generalisation of capital also allows capitalists to prey on the parochial, racist and xenophobic sentiments of different cultural groups. Inter-regional and inter-national differences and conflicts among workers (often stemming from pre-capitalist times) mystify the nature of capitalist exploitation and further weaken working class consciousness and unity. It is precisely the capacity to forge working class co-operation across space, in order to oppose the multi-nationalisation of capital, which these divisive ideological currents help destroy.

In summary, *places* are locationally specific ensembles of 'usual effects' or 'use-values', differentially effective with respect to the process of capitalist production:

> *From the perspective of capital*, concrete places contain a specific ensemble of the material of nature, a built environment, labour power, members of other classes, various commodities, etc., as well as the specific constellation of social relations into which these spatially-situated people have entered amongst themselves and with their environment. These social relations are conditions and forces of production as far as capital is concerned, i.e. they affect labour productivity, time of circulation, and so forth. [(Walker, 1978a:29), italics added]

There are two related problems inherent in any attempt to directly apply analysis pitched at this high level of abstraction to concrete instances. Any such attempts almost inevitably assume a functionalist cast: what is good for capital comes to pass. Moreover, a consideration of functional

imperatives does not automatically lead to an understanding of historical
sequence or development, rather the reverse. Functionalism, especially
when linked to a structuralist perspective—the normal form in which it has
emerged in modern social theory—threatens to obliterate historicity,
confining analysis to the synchronic or static level (Hobsbawm, 1972:277;
Giddens, 1979:3). What is needed is an analytic approach which derives
the changing spatial forms of social organisation from the nature of
capitalist relations of domination or exploitation but in a way which ties
the determination of particular, historically contingent spatial outcomes to
the crisis-ridden, class-structured process of capital accumulation. This, it
was suggested earlier, was the promise (if not the product) of Castells'
work.

In capitalist society, exploitation or the continuing appropriation of
surplus product does not require the direct, repressive use of force or the
maintenance of personal relations of dependence, both characteristics of
feudal society. The emergence and reproduction of the capitalist mode of
production logically entail the permanent transcendence of relations of
direct force and dependence. Clearly this process has a spatial
dimension—for example, the creation of a class of formally free and
independent wage labourers in Europe required the demise of customary
ties which bound serfs to a particular locality. However, analysis at this
level tells one little about what actually happened. Spatial reorganisation on
a large-scale is necessary for capitalism to develop, but the extent to which
such reorganisation is forthcoming is precisely what has to be established
by concrete historical research, and not settled in advance by falling back
on functional imperatives based on some crude notion of historical
inevitability.

In order to move from a static consideration of functional requirements
to an understanding of historical process, one needs to concentrate on the
dynamic of capital accumulation, the object of Marx's mature work. The
bare outline of this dynamic is as follows. Individual capitalists are
constrained by the logic of their position to 'accumulate or perish'. In an
unregulated, competitive world, each capitalist is forced to defend his
profit margin by changing the labour process in order to improve labour
productivity, which, in turn, is generally secured by the ever-increasing
application of machinery and other forms of fixed capital at the expense of
workers. The unintended, overall outcome of this competitive war is a
chronic tendency for the general or average rate of profit to fall. This
tendency results in recurrent economic crises whenever the actual rate of
profit falls below a level sufficient to encourage individual capitalists *en
masse* to re-invest profits already realised. In other words, the historical
process of capital accumulation is inherently discontinuous or crisis-prone.
However, the very process which creates this tendency also calls forth
various 'counter-tendencies', making the actual historical career of the
average rate of profit—and, hence, the overall process of capital

accumulation—highly problematical and uneven in time and across space. This suggests that it is necessary to conceptualise historical development in terms of the crisis-prone process of capital accumulation grasped as a contradictory unity. Spatial reorganisation is a necessary and central element in this overall process: for instance, most of the examples relating social structure to spatial form noted above can be treated as counter-tendencies. However—and this is crucial—there is no logical connection between (or institutional mechanism ensuring) the historical unfolding of the restructuring process and the satisfaction of the functional imperatives discussed above. In fact, the reverse is true; there is a logical 'disconnection' which strongly predisposes the system to historical malfunction. This follows from the two basic contradictions inherent to the capitalist mode of production (Harvey, 1978, p.102–3), namely, the production of unintended and dysfunctional (from the point of view of capital in general) aggregative effects of competition *within* the capitalist class, and the tendency towards intensification of conflicts *between* the dominant capitalist and subordinate working class. These are explicable at the most abstract level of analysis in terms of the over-riding opposition of the increasingly social or co-operative nature of reproduction of material life and the private appropriation of the product (as profit). Individual capitalists are 'encouraged' by the coercive force of the law of competition to act primarily in terms of their own, particular, often short-term, interests. The overall and unintended outcome of this war of all against all will often be unfavourable, sometimes disastrous, for the common or joint interests of all capitalists. Thus, if left to themselves, capitalists as a group will tend to overwork workers to the point of physical extinction (so destroying the very basis of their profits and social dominance), chronically under-house them, provide inadequate medical care and education, and by geographically concentrating large numbers of workers in factory towns or port-cities, provide favourable conditions for the emergence of increasingly large, well-organised and militant working class organisations.

This last point reflects the force of the second contradiction. Capitalism is a system of social reproduction in which a small group who collectively own the means of production effectively control the process of (re)production and are thereby able to appropriate an increasing proportion of the material product of the direct producers (the workers). The fact of exploitation—or to use Harvey's words again, the continual infliction of violence on workers—pervades all spheres of social life, severely constraining the overall life-chances of workers and partially, unevenly, but inexorably filters through to the level of individual consciousness—a necessary but not sufficient condition for emerging class consciousness and action. Thus, in any concrete historical instance, capitalists as a group may not be able to organise the necessary structural readjustments to ensure future capital accumulation and continuing profit, either because they do not know what adjustments are necessary or cannot co-operate in bringing them about, or because workers stop them from so doing. In the latter case, disruptive or 'dysfunctional' opposition may break out in the workplace, at the communal or domestic level, within the political sphere (that is, through the concrete interventions and non-interventions of state agencies) or at the ideological level.

Glimpsed as an overall process, and within broad constraints, capital accumulation proceeds with a certain law-like regularity expressed through the irregular, anarchic, seemingly random recurrence of economic crises. The actual form assumed by the crisis-prone course of capitalist development depends on the manner in which intra- and inter-class struggles unfold. At the global level, the uneven spatial and temporal penetration of capitalist relations of production in the face of persisting pre-capitalist modes of production has resulted in the emergence of highly complex and differentiated patterns of class struggle which must be grasped through careful historical analysis guided, but not determined *in toto*, by an understanding of the logic of capitalist development in general. This task necessarily leads to a consideration of the successive stages of capitalist development and raises the vexing problem of periodisation.

Most contemporary Marxists distinguish between the earlier appearance of competitive capitalism and subsequent emergence of advanced or monopoly capitalism, however much they disagree over the specification of each form and the manner in which the former developed (or degenerated) into the latter. Wright (1978) has recently advanced an influential analysis which further subdivides this basic distinction into six developmental stages: primitive accumulation, manufacture, machino-facture (or 'modern industry'), monopoly capital, advanced monopoly capital and state-directed monopoly capital. Each period or stage is characterised by a dominant form of class structure—a dominant articulation of the forces and relations of production—which establishes structural limits or constraints within which the accumulation process proceeds. Progressive developments in the forces and relations of production, the outcome of incessant competition between individual capitalists (or capitalist blocs in the later stages), on the one hand, and the development of class struggle, on the other, raise obstacles or impediments to the smooth reproduction of conditions necessary for accumulation to proceed in its existing form (stage). However, the very contradictions which give rise to impediments also (gradually) induce structural changes in the form of accumulation itself, which temporarily move the process of accumulation back within the structural limits to reproduction imposed by the *new* forces and relations of production. Accumulation can then proceed in its restructured form until new impediments threaten chronic crisis, and force restructuring to a higher phase, and so on. Wright suggests that the basic impediment which arose in the period of modern industry was the tendency of the rate of profit to fall, brought about by a rising organic composition of capital and an increasingly well-organised and militant working class. The 'structural solution' to this impediment was the increasing concentration and centralisation of capital (facilitated by recurrent economic crises) which ushered in the monopoly stage of accumulation. The impediment with increasingly came to dominate this later stage, according to Wright, was a strengthening tendency for the mass of surplus value extracted in production to exceed the prospects for profitably reinvesting it, manifested in increasingly prolonged crises of realisation or 'underconsumption', which resulted, in turn, in the growth of state intervention in the economy (at this stage, primarily in the sphere of exchange).

Wright's analysis clearly focuses on developments internal to the capitalist 'centre'—that is, to those nation-states which first underwent capitalist development—and especially on British and North American experiences. However, he explicitly integrates the analysis described above with an historically grounded theory of the changing forms of imperialism. Thus, the restructuring forced by developing impediments is necessarily seen to 'spill over' the national boundaries of the capitalist centre and involve the integration and reorganisation of peripheral societies in the light of the crisis tendencies driving the former's development. The success of restructuring at the centre will critically depend on the manner and extent to which the periphery can be integrated into the capitalist world system. In short, Wright's framework allows us directly to address the problem with which we started, namely, how to grasp the historically specific development of dominance–dependence relations on a world scale. Wright explicitly restricts his attention to developments in the centre (Wright, 1978:167, fn.59). He is concerned, above all, to distinguish and historically situate the different forms of imperialist domination of periphery by centre by relating them to the staged unfolding of crisis tendencies in the latter; each stage of capitalist development calls forth 'emergent' or typical forms of imperialist domination which reflects the dominant impediment, state of class struggle and evolution of state interventions which characterise life at the centre. Thus, Wright is able to argue that in the stage of modern industry, the high tide of competitive capitalism, the tendency of the rate of profit to fall—fuelled by a rising organic composition of capital and rising wages in the centre—led both to an increasing concentration and centralisation of capital and the intensification of labour-saving innovations within the centre *and* the increasing export of capital to the periphery in order to secure cheaper raw material supplies.

As a total theory of dependent development and underdevelopment Wright's analysis falls short. It offers only half the story, a framework by which to understand the external forces which constrain but do not totally determine peripheral development or lack thereof. The other half of the story would require us to shift our vantage point from centre to periphery, to focus on internal developments there in the light of the historically specific impact of external forces originating in the former. The individual histories of particular dependent societies will, therefore, differ according to the stage at which, the manner in which, and the degree to which they were integrated into the capitalist world system. This raises the possibility of accounting for widely differing forms of dependence and, therefore, widely differing degrees of development and underdevelopment outside the capitalist centres of Northern Europe, the United States and Japan—a vital advance if one is to understand the peculiar developmental trajectory of Australia.

If it is properly interpreted and extended, therefore, it is Wright's framework, rather than his substantive analysis, that provides a suitable basis from which to apply and develop the general and highly abstract approach to dependent urbanisation. However, it must be admitted that few attempts have actually been made to *apply* such an analysis, to relate, consistently and coherently, evolving spatial form to the staged development of capitalism. Gordon (1978) and Walker (1978b) are exceptions. Since their analyses focus on processes of urban and regional development in the United States, they provide only comparative benchmarks for other analyses which must focus on the social production of space in relatively dependent societies like Australia. In the latter context, only Mullins (1981) and Stilwell (1980) have begun to discuss the questions raised here.

One can now develop the analysis of general stages of capitalist development into a tentative periodisation as a prelude to its application in the case of Australia, by relating Wright's framework to the recent resurgence of interest among Marxists in 'long waves' of development. The stages of capital accumulation pertaining to the capitalist centre could be interpreted in terms of the four long waves of expansion and decline propounded by Mandel (1975). The latter's explicit periodisation can then be used chronologically to locate these stages, thereby orienting analysis of the manner in which crisis tendencies have actually unfolded in the dependent society in question. It is also tempting to interpret the expansive phase of Mandel's long wave as the period in which the structural adjustments forced by the dominant contradictions or structural constraints characterising the previous stage are relatively successful in reestablishing the conditions for intensified accumulation; conversely, the declining phase of a long wave can then be seen as the period in which new contradictions intensify to the point of forcing new readjustments which (can) eventually lead to the emergence of conditions favourable to a new long-term upswing.

It is now possible to specify—albeit schematically—the necessary framework for a Marxist analysis of Australian urbanisation. This framework is more fully developed elsewhere (Berry, 1983).

Figure 1.1 draws together the elements discussed above, in the context of—and from the point of view of—the development of Australian

**Figure 1.1  Stages of Australian urbanisation**

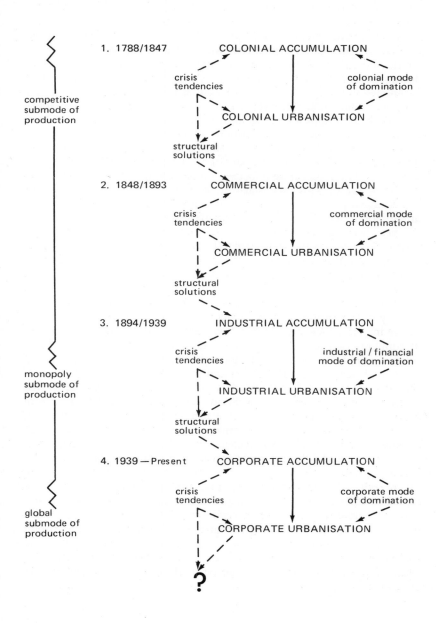

capitalism. The four stages of Australian accumulation are specified by the four long waves of expansion and decline in the capitalist centre. The pattern and pace of development in each stage is conditioned by structural constraints deriving from the particular manner in which Australia has been integrated into the world capitalist system, expressed through the particular or characteristic mode of domination defining Australia's place in that system. Crisis tendencies which strengthen at the centre, as development there changes from an expansionary phase to the long swing down, force structural 'solutions' or changes both within the centre economies and in their (dominance) relation to dependent societies of the periphery and semi-periphery. These structural changes re-establish favourable conditions for a new, long, upswing at the centre (or have done so in the past) and a 'new' pattern of dependent development (and underdevelopment) outside it; in this sense one can talk about the movement from one developmental stage to another, in both the centre and periphery. The problem here focuses on the way in which these processes unfold in space; with each stage of development one can identify the characteristic pattern of spatial organisation—or the characteristic mode of urbanisation—which expresses or contains it. Each mode of urbanisation at the periphery can also be seen as one element in the set of structural solutions at the centre which smooth the transition to a new stage of development, thereby recasting the structural constraints on peripheral developments including the spatial form in which such development unfolds.

Thus, in the first stage, the form and pace of colonial development was initially ordered through direct economic and political controls imposed by the imperial state. Development was severely constrained by shortages of supplies, capital and labour, and was spatially concentrated on the colonial administrative centres, notably Sydney. However, intensifying crisis tendencies within British capitalism during the declining phase of the first long wave, freed capital which was (partly) switched to the colonies, initiating pastoral expansion and the associated growth of commerce, encouraging, in turn, the further generalisation of capitalist relations of exchange and production. These changes in the nature of colonial accumulation were reflected, 'on the ground', in the creation of new port-cities and the extensive spread of pastoralism, as the colonies began to perfect their new role in the world economy and formed part of the overall 'solution' to the structural problems which beset British capitalism. Historically, these changes in economic and political relations between Britain and its colonies reinforced 'internal' changes in British forces of production, following the spread of mechanisation and rise of heavy industry sufficient to spark a long upswing in British capitalism and an explosive increase in international trade. These developments—in addition to the immediate and longer term effects of the mid-century gold discoveries—encouraged large inflows of capital and free labour to

Australia where development was constrained within limits imposed through international trading relations, managed by British merchant and financial capitalists and their colonial agents.

The consolidation of this second phase or stage of colonial accumulation entailed a degree of spatial reorganisation as the proliferation of small townships followed pastoral and mining expansion, and the capital port-cities grew and internally differentiated, reflecting the scale and concentration there of the commercial, financial and administrative functions tying the colonies into the capitalist world system. This pattern of international specialisation was further reinforced during the long swing down of British capitalism in the third quarter of the century. British capital was again switched to the colonies and tightly concentrated into the pastoral and public infrastructural sectors. Locally accumulated capital also fed through to the built environment, notably the housing sector; wider economic diversification was constrained by the competitive superiority and bulk of British exports, the priorities of British and colonial financial capital and the political and ideological controls tying Australia into the imperial system, all of which contributed to the making of the Australian ruling class. The physical construction of the built environment, in the context of hardening international specialisation, reflected and reinforced the spatial concentration and centralisation of capital and labour in the capital cities. Rapid suburbanisation—of an increasingly speculative nature—characterised growth in those cities during the 1870s and 1880s, as profitable alternatives for colonial accumulation disappeared in a (capitalist) world suffering a pronounced and general decline in average profit rates.

British investment in Australia was more than a short-term reaction to the build-up of idle capital at home. As Australia grew and prospered, markets expanded; Federation, by breaking down inter-colonial trading barriers, reinforced population growth, urban concentration, relatively high wages and improved communications. However, in reaction to increasingly severe competition from German and American industrial capital, the form of British investment in Australia began to change in the twentieth century in favour of direct investment in Australian industries. That is, with the demise of free trade internationally and the retreat to Empire of British capital, generally, from the late nineteenth century onwards, the latter increasingly maintained their dominance by setting up local branches or taking over Australian firms, in order to forestall or pre-empt the incursions of other foreign traders. In Castells' terms, dominance—dependence relations were increasingly constituted through the mode of industrial/financial rather than commercial, domination.

This is not to argue that one mode of domination totally replaced another—as a literal reading of Figure 1.1 would suggest. International trading relations continued to remain vital determining factors in Australian development, as they are today. Only a small proportion of

British capitalists trading with Australia relocated production there; lower British wages, preferential tariffs within the Empire, the indebtedness of Australian governments to British money lenders and the indirect coercive powers of the British state all limited the range and rate of economic diversification in Australia, especially in the manufacturing sector (Cochrane, 1980:43). Nevertheless, within these very real constraints, significant diversification and growth did occur, especially after the First World War, in mining, agriculture and manufacturing. The significant role of public infrastructural investment—for example, electrification for industrial and domestic uses—was increasingly directed towards supporting or facilitating Australian production in all sectors, but particularly in manufacturing, rather than (just) the flow of goods internationally. The fact that these developments were limited and uneven in effect is hardly surprising. Australia continued to remain dependent in crucial respects—for example, on high technology goods, foreign capital and the need to export traditional goods—though the particular form of dependence was changing in the manner suggested. Increasingly, foreign and local industrial capital (including the mining and agricultural sectors as well as manufacturing), rather than merchant capital, determined the directions of Australian development.

In the context of the third long downswing of capital accumulation in the capitalist centre, and within the constraints just noted, new manufacturing industries—notably, electrical goods, chemicals and automobiles—as well as established industries like steel and textiles, developed in Australia in the inter-war period, largely reflecting the interests and priorities of British capital. These industries were concentrated primarily in Sydney and Melbourne, close to markets, labour, government and transport, encouraging further development there and requiring the large-scale provision of urban infrastructure by the State governments. This was, in turn, largely financed by British loan capital. Conversely, heavy capital-intensive investment in the mining and agricultural sectors in order to maintain international competitiveness displaced rural labour, reinforcing the significant drift to the capital cities. Within those cities, industrial location tended to intensify pre-existing patterns of differentiation and segregation, while the rising use of cars and trucks facilitated continuing suburbanisation. This emerging pattern of industrialisation was sharply checked during the Great Depression as the effects of crisis at the centre were transmitted to Australia by plumetting international primary product prices and the halt in British loans, which, in turn, partly checked the rapid overall rate of metropolitan growth.

Economic recovery, culminating in the Second World War, signalled the final collapse of British hegemony in the world economy. Thereafter, Australian dependence on American (and later Japanese) trade and capital inflow rapidly intensified. Moreover, not only did the geographical source of dominance—dependence relations change—so, too, did their form. New

industries, in areas like chemicals and electronics, revolutionised
production methods, reduced production costs and increased average
profit rates; due to the huge capital and skill requirements necessary to
research and develop these high technology products and methods, they
were (quite literally) monopolised by capitalists in the central economies.
Consequently, other capitalists, especially those outside the centre, have
become increasingly dependent on them for access to the technologies
necessary to maintain competitiveness. In addition, foreign (direct)
investment has been increasingly directed towards securing *control* over,
rather than mere minority ownership of, key sectors of the Australian
economy.

This gradual transformation to what might be termed 'the corporate
stage of accumulation', has occurred in line with changes in the nature of
the capitalist mode of production itself. Gibson and Horvath (1980) have
introduced the term, 'submode of production', to capture these internal
transformations in both the dominant conditions of exploitation of labour
by capital and the form of competition between capitalists to appropriate
profits. The chronic tendency towards the concentration and centralisation
of capital had, by the 1930s, resulted in a significant though uneven degree
of monopolisation within the boundaries of national economies constituting the capitalist world. The decisions—including the location
decisions—of large capitalists were now significant factors in determining
the distribution of capital and labour over space, nationally and within
fairly clearly defined regional boundaries. Nevertheless, with monopolisation of significant areas of national economy, the seeds of breakdown
in this familar pattern of spatial organisation were sown. The internal
organisation of monopolistic capitalist enterprises, where the division of
labour is intense and hierarchically ordered, has led to the fragmentation of
production over space in the form of multi-plant operations, and the
separation and locational specialisation of the sales, financial and
managerial functions as well. Some urban scholars have seen in this
process the destruction of regions in the traditional sense. However, this
process has only fully developed with the internationalisation of capitalist
production in its current phase—that is, with the organisation of
production and redivision of labour on a global scale through the
institutional form of the transnational corporation. The spatial form
assumed by these current developments in Australia is most obvious in the
mining sector, where the so-called resources boom has involved the
channelling of hundreds of millions of dollars of foreign capital into
previously remote areas of the continent. The growth of new mining towns
has raised the phenomenon of the boom town, familiar elsewhere in the
world (Markusen, 1978). Foreign mining capital has also had an impact on
existing townships, as in the case of Sale in the Gippsland region of
Victoria, following the development of Bass Strait oil, and Portland in the
south-west of the State, in anticipation of the (now shelved) development

by Alcoa of an aluminium smelter. However, it is precisely in cases like
these, where skilled labour (especially managerial), technology and inputs
are often imported and profits are moved around the corporate group
globally in order to avoid taxation, that the traditional claims pointing to
the intra-regional growth effects of such activities are highly suspect.
Questions concerning the local distributional effects of resource
developments must also be faced, as the cost of and, therefore, access to
housing and other services threaten to favour newcomers associated with
the project over existing residents.

However, it is in a consideration of developments centred in the existing
metropolitan areas that the most far-reaching and serious implications of
the current stage of capital accumulation arise. The fragmentation and
global coordination of production have resulted in the real threat of
significant de-industrialisation in Australia. Increasingly mobile capital
moving out of the local manufacturing sector—previously concentrated in
the capital cities, especially Melbourne and Sydney—has raised the
prospect of deep-seated and rising structural unemployment, on the one
hand, and a reorganisation of the industry which does remain, in the
direction of an enforced national specialisation, further de-skilling,
increasing technological dependence and greater effective independence
from state regulation, on the other. Recent developments in the international automobile industry—including the much touted concept of 'the
world car'—illustrate this twin prospect. Continuing economic decline of
the capital cities is likely to be reinforced by the indirect effects of this
process on public policy. The Federal and—especially—State governments
are increasingly constrained to redirect expenditure to 'productive'
uses—that is, to activities and services which attract and facilitate foreign
investment under the new global conditions for the valorisation of capital.
Inevitably, this has led to a run-down of services elsewhere—to a decline in
policies favouring national capitalists and petty bourgeoisie and a savage
attack on 'the social wage', notably health, housing, education, and social
welfare. The other major destabilising effect of current global
developments on Australian urbanisation follows from the tendency for
foreign capital (and idle local capital) to switch into the built environment
for both production and consumption, and out of the sphere of production
into speculative real estate transactions, especially in response to falling
average profit rates in a period of intensifying crisis. This general tendency
lies behind the over-development of city centres, the gentrification of the
inner suburbs and the speculative property price spiral in the upper class
suburbs of the (mainland) capital cities, all visible during the 1970s.

It should be stressed, however, that these effects are not primarily the
result of conspiracies in the boardrooms of Detroit or the result of
collusion between foreign capitalists and Australian politicians. They are
the structurally located reactions of big and small capitalists and of
national and State governments, to the changing structural constraints of a

capitalist world system in deepening crisis. The outcome of intensifying crisis (in the declining phase of the fourth long wave) for the future form of capital accumulation—including the spatial form of organisation entailed—is uncertain, as is indicated at the bottom of Figure 1.1.

The theoretical project implied in Figure 1.1 and sketched above is an attempt to specify, from a Marxist perspective, the urban problematic in Australian history. The aim has been to avoid the tendency in traditional and recent Australian historiography to either ignore the spatial dimension of historical development or reify the concept by separating it from and opposing it to the very social forces constituting historical development. An attempt has been made to suggest a framework in which urbanisation in a capitalist world is analysed in terms of the forces or dynamic determining the movement of capital (and labour) over space and its (their) concentration and centralisation in space. As the dynamic driving, and structural constraints limiting, the process of capital accumulation change, so too does the form and outcome of this process in space. In this sense, the stages of capitalist urbanisation are theorised as the dominant elements of the spatial forms of the successive stages of capital accumulation on a global scale. More specifically, Figure 1.1 presents this framework from the perspective of the development of capitalism in Australia and in that sense—and that sense only—is spatially delimited or 'biased' in an arbitrary fashion.

Finally, it is worth stressing the methodological assumptions implicit in Figure 1.1. The stages of Australian capital accumulation and urbanisation are not offered as mutually exclusive categories for the mechanical production of historical analysis, but as a way of capturing the gradual and uneven transformations of the capitalist mode of production in space. The focus here has been on two structuring principles determining the broad contours of staged development: in the first place, the evolving effects of dominance–dependence relations constituting the penetration of capitalism from the centre out during four long waves of expansion and decline; in the second place, the internal transformations in the dominant or emergent form of capitalist competition and the capital–labour relation, unevenly articulated across space and between industries or sectors.

LEONIE SANDERCOCK

# 2. Educating planners: from physical determinism to economic crisis

In Australia, planners have always been slow to respond to social and economic changes. For most of this century, planning ideology, and planning as taught, derived from the simplistic British model of the late nineteenth century. The first and belated shift away from this tradition came in the early 1970s, the shift from physical to social emphasis. By the late 1970s, changes in the international economy—in the international division of labor and movements of capital and their differential impact on cities and regions, problems inherent in a slow-growth economy characterised by stagflation, and crises in the financing of urban services— suggested that a further shift in emphasis was essential. As yet, planners and planning education have not responded.

It was not only Australian political and social institutions and the process of capital formation and investment that were derived from overseas. So, too, was Australian thinking about its cities and their problems. The town planning movement which emerged around the turn of the century and was consolidated into Associations in each State by the end of the First World War was derivative of the key concepts of British thinking of the time. (This is evident in the importance of immigrants in the early movement, in the exodus to Britain between 1912 and 1915 of public servants from each State to study and report on British developments, and in the frequency with which British examples were cited in Australian discussions and reports.)

The development of town planning as a reform movement in Britain originated in the concern of some intellectuals and politicians about the social and economic consequences of the industrial revolution. The movement for sanitary reform (water, sewerage and drainage) was the result of an awareness of some of the alarming qualities of the new congested industrial districts. Other planning advocates were more concerned with the aesthetics and with the organisational complexities of urban development. Their concerns were health, convenience and amenity; order, efficiency and beauty. Their rhetoric often supported the aim of improving social conditions. They were concerned about social problems (like crime, violence, delinquency, overcrowding, ill-health) but their solution to these problems was to improve physical conditions, to provide parks, open space, playgrounds and to eradicate slums. This theory of social change, based on assumptions of environmental or physical 'determinism', was the conventional wisdom of the early town planning movement and was supported by some businessmen, property owners and their political and economic associates, bankers, councillors and the like (Gans, 1968, Sandercock, 1975).

The 'physical determinist' approach failed to come to terms with the real causes of the problems—the existence of low wages, poverty, the very nature of the economic system and its spatial expression. But most planning advocates believed that garden suburbs and garden cities were the answer to urban problems. They had adopted the physical planning component of Ebeneser Howard's garden city concept but had neglected the radical element of Howard's theory, that of municipal ownership of land. Notions of community and social integration were central to town planning ideology. So was the assumption that both could be achieved by *physical arrangements*. Such was the conventional wisdom of the first half of the twentieth century, and it was embodied in the first teaching of the subject of town planning by John Sulman, a British immigrant who became first President of the Town Planning Association of NSW in 1914, and a lecturer in town planning at the University of Sydney. In 1921 his lectures were published as the book, *Town Planning in Australia*, which was a basic text for thirty years.

In the aftermath of the Second World War there was sufficient hangover of post-war reconstruction enthusiasm in each State for governments to resolve to establish statutory planning authorities. Over the next twenty years this enabled those calling themselves planners to become entrenched in State bureaucracies and a cosy relationship developed between the professional institute, the handful of tertiary planning courses, and State and local governments. In this era the official/textbook view was that to plan was to express in a drawing the form of existing or proposed land uses and buildings, and that town planning was concerned with the arrangement of land uses and communication routes in the most satis- factory practicable form.

The favoured form was that derived from earlier British thinking, as it had evolved from public health reforms through the garden city movement and into the town planning texts as neighbourhood design, garden suburbs and metropolitan master plans and new town advocacy.

During this time, town planners were being educated in sedate town planning departments at the Universities of Melbourne, Sydney and Queensland and the South Australian Institute of Technology, by expatriate British planners, who taught courses dominated by pre-second World War planning ideas based on physical and design approaches. The town planners thus produced came from backgrounds in architecture, engineering and surveying, and were let loose on the urban fabric with no sociological, political or economic understanding.

The net effect of this core British tradition was that it was more successful in creating and conserving a finished product than in promoting or understanding more continuous processes of growth and change; more skilled in dealing with space than with time; stronger on architecture and design than economics; better equipped to make aesthetic judgments than to analyse how resources flow through the economy or how to enlarge or redirect those flows. This reflected a country which assumed that the motors of economic growth would keep turning, and no special steps were required to create and foster productive enterprise, jobs and earnings, or to link industrial development to the development of housing, transport, education and other sectors of an urban economy. Peace, full employment, Keynesian macro-economic management tools, and the welfare state were expected to solve the nation's main social and economic problems.

A profession dominated by aesthetic values was not well equipped to cope with strategic, big-city issues, unforeseen in the immediate aftermath of the Second World War, such as massive increases in wealth and population, the spread of the motor car and demand for urban freeways, decay of public transport, the move of manufacturing industry away from the inner city, the office building boom, and a revolution in engineering technology which transformed the whole scale of city buildings and cities. Despite its humane values and (rather amateurish) sociological concern for 'community', the whole style of planning was fundamentally élitist, as was so much of the liberal reform tradition from which it sprang.

But in the 1960s urban development entered a turbulent period which posed problems for all concerned with managing cities and their public services. As aspects of urban life that had been taken for granted began to be threatened by the single-minded growth process, residents began to react with whatever instruments lay to hand—Residents' Action Groups, green bans, squatting, local government politics, etc. Residents despaired that they had no way of making governments and their hired hands, the planners and engineers (the 'technical experts'), listen to them and appreciate their values.

What was, in fact, a basic conflict between the single-minded pursuit of economic growth, on the one hand (from which most city dwellers were benefiting), and its unpleasant urban consequences and social effects on the other (from which *some* were suffering), was wrongly perceived by many as a problem for which planners—as the hired hands of public and private developers—could be blamed: blamed for élitism, lack of responsiveness to the public, failure to consider values outside their own narrow world of technical and technocratic expertise.

Out of this conflict and those problems, emerged the first Federal Department of Urban and Regional Development (DURD), established by a government carried to power on 'urban promises'. This was a different kind of planning department, with explicitly redistributive purposes and social concerns and a structure that sought functionally to integrate economic and social and physical planning. The traditional planning schools were caught flat-footed and their graduates were not in great demand by DURD. (The pace and nature of urban development in capitalist society had proved the early planning courses not so much irrelevant as inadequate. Their planners did not have a broad enough range of skills to cope with changing economic forces, on the one hand, and changing social and environmental attitudes, on the other.) Their concentration on physical design and land use was too limited a view of urban dynamics. Their quantitative skills in forecasting (population growth, housing demand, employment location, etc.) were inadequate and their communication skills and sociological knowledge were deficient. Further more, they were identified with a planning process which was far too static and inflexible. For a time traditional planners were passed over in favour of politically committed young graduates with training in economics, law, sociology, geography, even history—committed to a more comprehensive, multi-disciplinary, democratic and redistributive approach to planning.

The intellectual underpinning for DURD came from a 'new breed' of urbanists (some even disliked the connotations of 'planner'), influenced by the work of Hugh Stretton on Adelaide and of the Urban Research Unit at the Australian National University. Ten years later, it seems no exaggeration to claim that Stretton's *Ideas for Australian Cities* (1970) was the turning point in our understanding of cities and city planning.

In contrast to the technical, apolitical, supposedly 'value-free' specialist and design-oriented planning courses, Stretton, a historian, had the temerity to argue that planners ought to be political (that is, honest and open about their political values and social theories), generalist, and oriented to social and community rather than design and technical issues. Moreover, they ought to recognise that, to date, planning had discriminated against women and children as users of the urban environment in favour of car-owning, employed, adult males. Stretton argued for town planning as a means of social reform and for planning authorities to embrace and employ generalist/humanist educated students like sociologists, historians, geographers. He also put the case for land-use planning's being integrated with central economic planning, and for the creation of an authority in which economic, social and physical planning were functionally integrated.

Stretton's ideas were complemented by the empirical work of researchers in the Urban Research Unit at the Australian National University, which had been established in 1966. They focused on the equity aspects of urban development and of policy formulation as much as on efficiency aspects, and because they were researching, rather than educating planners directly, they were free to move beyond the physical planning sphere of existing tertiary courses. Pat Troy, Max Neutze and Peter Harrison from the Unit became central in the establishment and policy orientation of the new DURD. It was indicative of DURD's different goals and focus that interviewees for jobs were questioned as to whether they had read Stretton's *Ideas for Australian Cities*, and what they made of it. (Or so the apocryphal story goes.)

So a new band of urbanists began to emerge, products of courses other than those offered by the orthodox planning schools and, some would say, more in tune with changing urban problems and needs. These men and women were politically committed, and from a variety of academic backgrounds—some urban economists, geographers, historians, sociologists, social workers, demographers, lawyers. They shared a multi-disciplinary view of and approach to the urban planning process.

Because of this new employment market with its different emphasis, and because city dwellers had grown suspicious of the town planners, architects and engineers—the so-called professional or technical experts—the traditional professional organisation, the Royal Australian Planning Institute (RAPI), was forced to reassess its role as the endorser or recogniser of professional qualifications in planning. The 1970s was a decade of questioning from without and agonising from within the 'profession' and saw the proliferation of 'paraplanning' courses in universities and CAEs seeking to address both the deficiencies in previous planning education and to provide graduates for the new urban market place that was opened up by DURD's existence in the first place, and followed by other government departments (like the NSW Department of Environment and Planning, the SA Department of Environment and Planning, and statutory authorities like Environmental Protection Authorities, Conservation Councils, Heritage Commissions, and so on). In some of these new agencies the employers are not concerned that prospective employees have a RAPI recognised qualification; some go so far as to argue that RAPI has become irrelevant. None of this is unique to Australia, of course, Attacks on the planning profession began in the early 1960s in the United Kingdom and USA (Jacobs 1961; Gans, 1968). Part of this attack took as its target the subject matter: the other part, the practitioners themselves.

Criticisms of the content of planning practice and planning education have emphasised that zoning controls have protected the interests of privileged property owners; that planning schemes have served as speculators' guides, encouraged graft and corruption, contributed to excessive prices for urban services and rising land prices (Stretton, 1970; Sandercock, 1975; Troy, 1978); that planning has not improved the lot of the poor, but has produced boring, monotonous suburbia (Jacobs, 1961; Sennett, 1970).

Attacks on planners themselves have been based mainly on the power they possess to influence the lives of others and their insufficient attention to the values and needs of their 'clients', the *users* or victims of town planning/housing/community facilities. Both Simmie (1974) and Goodman (1971) have argued that the only ends town planners serve are either their own or those of the existing power structure, and that their use of power is neither legitimate nor rational. Simmie pointed out that planners adopt restrictive practices to prevent entry to the profession, and that the élitism resulting from this discourages innovation and has led to the extreme conservatism, in practice, of British town planning. By the mid-1970s the emerging neo-Marxist critique stressed the facilitating role of planning in the process of capital accumulation and labelled planners as mere tools in this process, powerless to do anything but follow and assist the logic of capitalist development (Castells, 1977a; Ravallion, 1975, 1977).

Criticisms such as these, combined with the changing political and economic environment within which the profession had to practise, led both the Royal Town Planning Institute (Britain) and RAPI to begin to reassess their roles in the 1970s.

The growth of planning and 'paraplanning' courses in Australia has been discussed elsewhere (Sandercock, 1982). By 1976–77 the rapid increase in paraplanning or urban studies courses were making their presence felt, and to some extent threatening to undermine the closed shop or restrictive practices of the professional organisation (RAPI) and its recognised courses. The initial reaction of most of the established town planning schools was defensive, relying on arguments about 'excellence', 'specialism' and 'professional standards and skills'. By the early 1980s, however, some at least of these planning schools and the more progressive members of the RAPI had taken note of the earlier criticisms and were changing course content and education policy accordingly. In particular, there has been a recognition of the importance of social and environmental issues and values, of the multi-disciplinary character of planning, and its ever-widening field of activity. Some of the educational dilemmas inherent in this recognition include: whether to try to teach every student a significant amount of each of the potential activities of environmental planning, corporate planning, social and public administration, regional analysis, and so on; whether to emphasise detailed knowledge and technical skills, or problem-solving and an understanding of planning as process; and whether any of this can or should be done adequately at undergraduate level.

Sex and politics have also begun to assert their presence as significant issues in the education of planners. Both were introduced into public debate in Australia with the publication of Stretton's *Ideas for Australian Cities* in 1970. Following Louis Mumford and Jane Jacobs, Stretton noticed that women (and their children) seemed to come last in planners' deliberations and designs. He also observed that planners tended to hide dishonestly behind foliage of value-freedom and political neutrality instead of recognising the distributive effects of their work. Over the past decade some progress has been made on both these issues, but not enough.

Daines's (1978) survey of planning and paraplanning courses and staff qualifications showed that, like the profession itself, planning education is predominantly staffed by men. The male–female ratio among full-time staff is about 8:1, among part-time staff about 9:1 (Zehner, 1980:10). Not surprising then, is the absence from most course content of any specific consideration of that 51 per cent of the planned-for constituency who are female. That 51 per cent, because of the sexual division of labour in capitalist/industrial society, and because of distinctive features of Australian cities, such as their astonishingly low densities, their orientation to the private car user, and their low levels of community facility provision (especially in low income outer suburbs), create specific problems and hardships for women which deserve the urgent attention of planners. Stretton (1970) made the point, yet despite a burgeoning literature on the subject (see Spagnoletti, 1977; Wekerle, Peterson and Morley, 1980) there has been very little absorption of that literature into the recognised planning courses. Interestingly, the non-recognised 'urban studies' courses do far better in this respect. This is presumably because the recognised courses are staffed predominantly by those with planning qualifications (Zehner, 1980:10). In other words, having been educated in sexist schools themselves, they are proceeding to pass on this blindspot to the next generation. Furthermore, it is no accident that residents' action groups have been notable for the predominance of, and active role played by women. Since their needs have been ignored or simply not understood by male planners, and they have not had their own kind sufficiently represented in the profession, the only place where women's opinions and concerns can be aired is in the arena of protest: in front of bulldozers, in the streets, and increasingly, in local councils.

It does not *necessarily* follow (and has not) that 'improved access by women to the profession means that planning in practice is more responsive to women's needs. In fact, the recent rash of literature on the plight of women in suburbia, the neglect of women by planning authorities, and so on, suggests that, although a beginning has been made in recognising and identifying the problems, little action has followed (Signs, 1980; Markusen, 1980; Hayden, 1981; Rothblatt *et al.*, 1979). The explanation is not hard to find. Improving the lot of women in the city involves converting more than planners to their cause. It involves being able to change the *political* process of resource distribution at all levels of government, so that funds are made available for facilities (shelters, childcare, community health centres) as well as planners' being made aware of sexist designs/plans.

Inevitably then, planning education as well as the planning process must be openly politicised. And perhaps the most significant theme to emerge in the literature of the past decade concerns the *equity* effects of planning decisions (Stretton, 1970; Parker and Troy, 1972; Sandercock, 1975; Troy, 1978, 1981; Neutze, 1978). Crudely put, the argument is that planners ought to be asking the question 'Who wins and who loses in the distribution of goods, services and property values which are influenced by or the result of planning decisions?' And they ought to be making the answers clear to their political masters.

Planning education has begun to respond to its environment over the past decade. Has this adaptation been fast enough? What of the future? Is the profession again falling behind?

The environment of planning from the 1940s to the mid-1970s was one of population and economic growth. Consequently, it was felt that 'if the indicative development control system could be made more systematic in approach, more sensitive to change, more participatory in policy formulation and less influenced by personal profiteering, it would be able to operate effectively'. (Logan 1981:114) By the 1970s it was felt that planners would need to be educated in conservation questions, social and political inequalities, and more participatory methods of planning.

There has been a marked change in the understanding of the planning process. From a simplistic three-stage sequence of survey-analysis-plan (Geddes, 1915), the notion of continuous and cyclical planning has grown (McLoughlin, 1969; Chadwick, 1971). Not only is there a need to monitor changes in cities and regions in order to adjust the assumptions upon which a plan is based, but there also must be a continuing evaluation of the degree to which a plan's controls or incentives are having the intended effects. This increasing emphasis on rationality has more recently moved towards a restructuring of government agencies so that they act more as a corporate entity than as a set of autonomous divisions (Logan, 1980:112). All of these changes are being incorporated into planning education to a greater or lesser degree.

But what happens when the growth machine stops, or changes direction? Since the mid-1970s, Australia has been through a period of much slower growth and considerable structural economic change, that have pushed unemployment rates to their highest since the 1930s Depression. For the next few decades development thrusts appear to be bound up with minerals, and the country's energy advantages have attracted massive overseas investment. Yet the cities have once again become neglected areas of Federal policy. The entire DURD enterprise was dismantled between 1976 and 1978 by the Fraser Government in the new prevailing climate of conservative non-intervention, rationalised by the ideology of small government, low taxes, and emphasis on treating private investors with kid gloves. This has occurred while the economy itself has been undergoing a major restructuring, which some have called a de-industrialising, and which involves the decline of manufacturing industry and its urban-based employment, in favour of the mining and energy industries, which are both capital intensive and rural-based.

In its recent appraisal of possible urban strategies, the Australian Institute of Urban Studies (AIUS, 1980) warned that large foreign capital inflows for resource investment would require huge amounts of public funds to provide the infrastructure necessary to service the mining and smelting boom. The implications for cities are greatly reduced funds for urban facilities and programs, rising unemployment, and decreasing rates of home ownership as home loan funds compete on the capital market with loans for resource developments.

Urban problems remain as acute, indeed more so, as they were a decade ago, added to as they have been by steadily rising unemployment and its attendant social unease, disillusioned youth, increasing homelessness and so on. Clearly, Australia is in a period of economic transition that is of immense significance for the future well-being of different classes of people within its cities.

Chapter 11 discusses how the whole notion of a resources boom and its alleged 'trickle-down effects' seems to have evaporated, as of mid-1982. By January 1983, official unemployment had risen to 10.7 per cent and thousands of jobs were being lost each week.

How can urban and regional planners respond to this different environment? There may be fewer opportunities for planners to guide private development in existing cities simply because there will be less of it. Total resources for improving the cities, where most people will continue to live, will be fewer, but social problems will be more widespread (Logan, 1980). The traditional planning activities of preparing and revising land-use zoning schemes for some distant future will seem inconsequential in the face of more immediate problems. Can planning education adjust to these changes?

Outlined below are some of the most pressing issues now facing planners at the State and local level.

Firstly, there are the problems of new suburbs on the metropolitan fringe—specifically the crisis in the financing of services for these areas. Local government planners can see that there are major problems of lack of facilities in Sydney's outer west, for example, yet Section 94 of the new N.S.W. Environmental Planning & Assessment Act appears not to be the solution that everyone had hoped for. Developers, both private and public, are unhappy with the practice of developer contributions, and will either succeed in passing on the costs or in defeating the legislation through political channels. But the problem remains.

Secondly, there are similar problems for local government and planners in rapid resource development areas like the Hunter Valley, where the State appears willing to subsidise 'productive' infrastructure for private enterprise yet to neglect the need for social infrastructure for the community and labour force. The Greater Lithgow Council has just negotiated a reasonable infrastructure financing policy with the Bird's Rock Colliery, but the NSW Government so far seems content to allow this *ad hoc* approach in preference to drawing up State-wide guidelines which would both help local authorities in their considerations as to whether to approve a development proposal, and the companies putting forward these proposals to work out social infrastructure contributions at their feasibility study stage.

Thirdly, and related to the above, there is the failure at Federal and State government level to provide universal childcare rights and facilities. This failure creates crises for single mothers and low-income households which, in outer suburbia especially (where public transport is poor and jobs for women fewer), affect housing repayments (leading to the 'moonlight flit') and the ability of women to contribute to the paid workforce. A host of social and psychological traumas for which statistics are mostly lacking, are thereby also created. Yet local councils suffering budget cuts have less money available for social planning expenses at the very time when they are most needed, because of the macro-economic factors (like increasing interest rates and the declining social wage) making life more difficult for low and no-income earners.

Finally, there is the problem of ghost towns and boom towns. Yesterday's boom towns become today's ghost towns—like Whyalla, with its huge public sector investment in infrastructure and 40 per cent unemployment since BHP's disinvestment in the town (Aungles and Szelenyi, 1979). And today's boom-towns-in-the-making—Mudgee, Muswellbrook, Singleton, etc.—may well be the ghost towns of 2010. What provisions are being made to protect local populations on the one hand, and public investments on the other, from the increasing problem of late capitalism, capital flight and disinvestment (or, of increasing capital mobility compared with labour immobility)?

What do practising planners and planning schools have to say about these crises of the 1980s? The answer, to date, is, very little. While private consultants can readily shift their activities from metropolitan areas and central business district (CBD) stragegy plans to environmental plans for the Hunter or Latrobe Valleys etc., those planners on local and State government payrolls are increasingly bemused about what *they* can do. This returns us to the content of their education, as well as forward to questioning whether, as State employees, they are simply doomed or predetermined to performing roles as the agents of capital.

Corresponding to the struggle by planners to carve out a niche for themselves in the bureacratic power structure with the creation of separate planning departments in the public service, was the claim that planning was a distinctive operation based on unique knowledge and operational skills, and the move towards a fairly uniform content of planning education in the tertiary institutions. Entry qualifications to the professional institute (RAPI) were tightened, closed shop arrangements were negotiated with public sector employers, and the system of 'recognising' courses in the universities and CAEs was developed. In the more-or-less uniform course content, emphasis was on physical planning and regulation of land use and development. Little emphasis was given to substantive matters such as housing, transport, industry or commerce; to social issues such as urban poverty or regional inequality; or to more general matters of the operation of the land market, development process or planning system. The need to foster the notion of a distinctive skill led to excessive time spent on 'practical' work, which was usually very impractical but so time-consuming as to leave little room or motivation for research. Planning educators have usually come from a practical background rather than a research one, and have encouraged consultancy rather than academic research (McLoughlin, 1981). Planning schools have, therefore, lacked a research atmosphere and most of the research which has been of value to planning practice and which has shed light on Australian urban problems has come from somewhere else— departments such as geography, economics, sociology, political science, even history, and from 'specialised' centres like the Urban Research Unit.

The linkages which ought to exist between education, research and practice, have been almost minimal. Only some geographers (Daly, 1982; Cardew *et al.*, 1982) and political economists (Stilwell, 1980; Larcombe, 1981) have had anything to say about the effects of international economic forces on Australian cities and regions. Planners have poorly understood the workings of the property market, the housing market, or the whys of, and ways in which, resources are allocated in cities. Planning educators do little research on these issues.

Planners in practice and in academic life have been ignorant of, or unconcerned about the place of land ownership, land development and redevelopment in a market economy, and its effect on the planning process. They have not become engaged in debates about the nature of the public sector, the limits placed upon it, and the role of the state in capitalist society. They have not thought at all about their own class position and interest in the process of state intervention in the city.

At present, planners are bemused and paralysed by the apparent crisis in the financing of urban services; by the questionable effectiveness of different kinds of state intervention and planning policies; and by the enormous problems of regional unemployment and decline. Faced with these problems, morale in government departments among planners is at an all-time low.

In order to respond to the current crisis effectively, planners need far more understanding of and skills in public finance, labor market analysis and forecasting, industrial reorganisation and regional economics, economic development planning, and more generally, a grasp of political economy. Misconceived notions of professionalism that have existed since the early post-war period are in danger of rendering redundant those who call themselves planners and planning educators.

# Part Two  POLICY

LEONIE SANDERCOCK

# 3  Urban policy: from Whitlam to Fraser

In December 1972, for the first time in Australian political history, the cities became a Federal election issue. In his now legendary policy speech to 'the men and women of Australia', Gough Whitlam stressed that decades of neglect by conservative Federal governments had led to acute urban problems. There had been such an escalation in land prices over the previous five years that many young couples could no longer contemplate owning their own home. There were large parts of each metropolitan area still unsewered. There were housing estates in far-flung suburbs with few, if any, urban social services, and no environmental amenities at all. There were long journeys to work for people living in those suburbs, on congested roads, or on public transport services that were overcrowded in peak hour and ran too infrequently at other times of the day. There were few opportunities for employment for women in the outer suburbs, and no local facilities to relieve their domestic routines—no childcare centres, libraries, community centres.

Whitlam promised that a Labor government would tackle these problems and improve the urban environment or 'quality of life' of people living in the big cities, and particularly of those in the western suburbs of Sydney and Melbourne, the so-called 'deprived areas'. There is no doubt that these promises played an important part in the election of the Australian Labor Party (ALP) to Federal office in December 1972. How had the cities got into such a mess, and what did the voters in 1972 expect in the way of change? Did the Department of Urban and Regional Development meet these expectations? Could it have? How did the ALP understand and define the nature of urban inequalities? Were they—is any social democratic government—in a position to do anything about them?

People in the liberal democracies in the twentieth century have voted fairly consistently for a market society rather than a socialist society. Australia has been no exception. There has rarely been mass political support for reformers' views, let alone for those of revolutionary groups like the

Communist Party. Characteristic of the market society is the market city, the city oriented in its design and functioning to efficiency in production and to maximising opportunities for individual consumption. This sort of city has specific effects on people's lives, opportunities, environments, friends and politics.

Left to themselves, as Australian cities have been under long stretches of conservative *laissez-faire* rule, market cities have a changing but characteristic structure, central to which is property ownership—of land and its rising capital values, and of industrial investment and its location and the jobs available as a result. The political power which owners secure tends to reinforce this structure. The distribution of people across the market city takes predictable patterns, determined by income and class, age and household structure and other determinants of status. These patterns are inequitable in access to jobs, shops, professional and social services, in the quality of the environment (access to beaches, harbour, mountains, etc.) and in the density and layout of urban neighbourhoods. But government and public sector services can provide opportunities for changing this by providing open spaces, swimming pools and other public facilities, and by the very location of public services like hospitals, clinics, schools and transport. In other words, government intervention in the city, through the mechanisms of service provision and location, and town planning, could redress or compensate for some of the inequalities inherent in the functioning of the market city.

**Post-war reconstruction and after**

Historically, the Curtin and Chifley Labor Governments of 1942–49 were the first Federal Governments to take an interest in the fate of Australian cities. In 1942 the Curtin Government set up a Department of Post-War Reconstruction to produce a blueprint for a better world when the fighting ended. The plans for the post-war period involved the continuation of wartime controls and regulations, a planned economy and full employment, city planning and population planning, decentralisation, regional and participatory planning, and planning to ensure adequate housing for everyone, with special emphasis on slum clearance. City planning was seen for the first time as a national problem that demanded a national strategy. It was seen less in terms of visual appearance, health and amenity, than in social and economic terms. The problem of the allocation of land among various uses was seen as part of the general social policy problem of the allocation of scarce resources. Housing and city planning were among the more dramatic issues and promises of the reconstruction program because they raised all the general ideological issues of planning versus a free market. But once the war ended, so too did the truce between business and industrial interests and the Labor Government. With peace came a resumption of the attack by conservatives on state intervention in the economy.

This was a seminal period in Australian history, particularly for the future of the cities. The Labor Government was full of the best intentions for city planning in place of haphazard growth and for decentralisation by regional development. None of their ambitious plans, except those for housing, eventuated before the Government was defeated in the 1949 elections, and the plans were then forgotten for twenty-three years. What were the reasons for this?

Between 1945 and 1948 the banks, the oil companies, the medical profession, the States' Upper Houses, and the High Court resisted, with all the financial and institutional powers available to them, Labor's reconstruction program. The effects of this 'conspiracy' were reinforced, however, by the dominance of the ideas of the capitalist class. Labor leader Chifley claimed of the 1949 election that 'the real issue . . . . was a straight-out fight between the two great forces, socialism and capitalism' (Crisp, 1960:373). If most Australians saw the election in these terms—and it is likely that they did, given the context of the 'cold war' and the Berlin Wall, and because the three major parties presented it that way—then their choice was quite clear. They chose capitalism. After years of scarcity and rationing, the majority of people wanted to be able to have the choice of satisfying different economic and social needs. They wanted to be able to buy petrol, and other consumer goods. There is no doubt that much of what occurred was the result of capitalist manipulation [like the campaign waged by the banks and its employees (May, 1968)], but it would have been impossible for this to occur if the general political climate had been adverse to such happenings, if the majority of Australians had not wanted precisely the sorts of things they thought those capitalists could deliver. And much of what happened, and failed to happen, in urban planning and in the cities in the 1950s and 1960s can only be understood by keeping this in mind.

The reformist urban program of the post-war reconstruction government required some basic changes to existing structures of power. A redistributive approach to city planning required changes in the system of property rights and ownership; regional and participatory planning required redistributions of power as well as of resources. The government simply could not get the votes for such changes, as the 1949 election showed only too clearly. And the majority of Australians continued to vote for conservatism rather than reform for the next twenty-three years, with rather dire consequences for particular parts of the urban population. The Liberal-Country Party coalition which came to office in 1949 made it clear that Commonwealth assistance to the cities would not be extended beyond the agreement already made for funding State housing programs. The Prime Minister, R.G. Menzies, in December 1950, refused to assist the NSW Government with finance to implement the Cumberland County

Plan (drawn up in 1949 for the Sydney region) on the grounds that to
accept any direct responsibility would establish a precedent for Commonwealth assistance in urban affairs. Succeeding Liberal-Country Party
Governments maintained an aloof attitude, leaving the States to cope as
best they could with their escalating urban problems during the 1950s and
1960s.

There were differences, of course, in the nature and scale of the
problems that developed and intensified over these two decades in the
various cities. Some of these were due to different historical legacies,
others to the different rate and nature of economic growth. (Adelaide, for
example, had less of a sewerage problem than Sydney and Melbourne
because of legislation in 1920 and 1955 prohibiting approval of subdivisions unless they could be economically sewered.) But each city shared
to a greater or lesser extent the problems that flow from unregulated urban
growth and inadequate and unco-ordinated public service provisions. All
States in these decades were politically unwilling and financially unable to
act. Most States introduced some kind of statutory planning process
during the 1950s (South Australia did not do so until 1967) in an attempt to
regulate, through zoning and subdivision control, some of the worst
aspects of capitalist urbanisation. By and large these plans simply
reinforced the power and enhanced the profits that property owners
derived from their property. By indicating which areas of the city would be
open to urban development at what time, the metropolitan plans served as
speculators' guides, informing those investors in urban land where to buy
next in order to make quick profits. The statutory planning process, or
land-use planning, was in fact proving counter-productive. By restricting
the development potential of some land, it was creating an artificial
shortage, and contributing to the escalation of land prices that had become
a serious problem by the early 1970s. Furthermore, the whole process has
been wide open to possibilities of corruption associated with zoning
decisions (Sandercock, 1975:232–8).

Whenever they have deemed it necessary, then, property owners have
been able to use the political institutions of the state to prevent
encroachments on their property rights by planning-legislation or
regulations. Since 1945 they have been able to manipulate the planning
process itself to make gains from property ownership and to use the same
political institutions to support the national hobby of land speculation.
Such planning as was attempted by the States was, therefore, hampered at
every level by private property interests' exerting influence on public
authorities and by the corruption of some public officers and politicians
with foreknowledge of planning decisions. The land-use plans produced in
each city have been subject to constant pressure, as a result of the capital
gains in land value that can accrue to individuals from changes in the
plans. Government service authorities have also been subject to pressure to
change their programs to provide services that would increase the value of

particular areas of land. These problems could only be avoided if the land were in public ownership for a period prior to urban development. But no State was prepared, or able, to take that step.

By the early 1970s, the range of problems that had come to be labelled 'urban problems' were clearly, none of them, capable of solution through the statutory planning process or at State level. These problems were identified in Whitlam's 1972 policy speech: the rapid inflation of land and house prices, the rundown of urban public transport, the backlog in sewerage provision, the overdevelopment of central cities, the lack of community facilities in the outer suburbs, the over-centralisation of urban resources in city centres, the long journeys to work, and the need for new towns to relieve the pressures of Sydney and Melbourne. One thing was clear: urban policy, in 1972, had to amount to something more than support for statutory planning. Whitlam came to power with promises to reduce the price of land and housing, overcome the sewerage backlog, build new towns, pour money into urban transport (rather than freeways) and concentrate resources into the 'deprived areas' of the big cities, specifically to the western suburbs of Sydney and Melbourne. The Department of Urban and Regional Development (DURD) was created in December 1972, and programs were mounted in each of the promised areas.

**The rationale for DURD**

In his 1972 policy speech Whitlam argued that 'in modern Australia social inequality is fixed upon families by the place in which they are forced to live even more than by what they are able to earn'. During the campaign he indicated that he believed that the main causes of inequality in Australia were not those arising out of ownership of wealth and property, but regional disparities in the costs of land and housing and the provision of urban and social services, education, health and other community facilities.

Catley and McFarlane have argued that this approach to urban problems involves a 'retreat from equality' or a redefining of the concept of inequality (Catley and McFarlane, 1975:276), which is no longer understood as a function of the ownership of the means of production but is simply a function of location—where people live and how accessible to them the city's jobs, goods and services are. Is this a fair critique, or does it involve unreasonable assumptions? What was the ideological basis of the DURD philosophy?

In the build-up to the formulation of the Labor Party's urban policy before 1972 ideas were sought from a wide variety of individuals and institutions. But perhaps the single most influential source was the work coming out of the Urban Research Unit at the Australian National

University. One of the reasons for this influence was the close personal link between one of the researchers in the Unit, Patrick Troy, and the man who became the Minister for Urban and Regional Development, Tom Uren. Troy was seconded to DURD from 1972 to 1975 as consultant and played a major role in shaping the new department and giving it ideological drive. The head of the Unit, Max Neutze, was an important influence in the formulation of land policy, and both he and another member of the Unit, Peter Harrison, were later to be actively involved in the Victorian and NSW Land Commissions.

But the link was not just personal. The research work of the Unit at that time, although strongly empirical, was informed by a concern with questions of equality and social justice in the city and was, therefore, always oriented to the key urban policy debates—housing, transport, provision of urban infrastructure like sewerage, and so on. This made the work of the Unit unique at a time when the town planning departments in the old universities were still preoccupied with neighbourhood design and the techniques of statutory planning. The Unit was concerned with questions of *distribution* in the city and, therefore, with urban politics. Which people got most out of the city and why? What was the pattern of distribution of urban resources—which areas were best- and which worst-served in terms of access to educational, health and community facilities, sewerage, open space and so on? Why did patterns of distribution demonstrate such sharp inequalities between different parts of the metropolitan area, and what could be done about it?

In other words, this research was concerned to demonstrate *locational inequalities* in Australian cities and to suggest policies that a reformist government might adopt to overcome, or at least compensate for, these inequalities. The concern with locational inequality became central to the DURD philosophy, unifying its many programs with an explicitly redistributive objective. DURD was concerned with the equity effects of urban development, and with improving the lot of that 20 per cent of the national population at the bottom of the heap. (This view was presented by DURD spokesmen at a Royal Australian Planning Institute Conference at Terrigal in September 1973. See also Troy, 1973.)

The argument was that urban growth has significant effects on income distribution, whether deliberate or accidental. If 'real income' is defined as command over resources, it is clear that real income is a function of locational accessibility—how close you live to employment opportunities, schools, beaches, welfare services. Access to these can only be obtained at a cost—the cost of overcoming distance, using time, or of buying housing in accessible locations. Poorer households have a very limited choice of locations. As the spatial form of a city is changed (by developing or relocating housing, transport routes, employment, sources of pollution), so also is the cost of access to different things for a household at a given location, and hence both the distribution of real income and property values in different locations are affected. Some services are located by public action (educational and health services, and open space, for example), others by private enterprise. Obviously then, the redistributive aspects of general government functions are far from trivial, and increase with city size. The very act of locational choice has distributional significance, and much of what happens in a city, particularly in the political arena, can be interpreted as an attempt to influence the locational choices of public and private organisations in order to gain income and wealth advantages. City planning, or more broadly, urban policy, could be used to influence the redistribution of income by changing the location of jobs and housing, the value of property rights, the price of goods and services to the consumer. This, precisely, was DURD's intention.

To say, as Catley and McFarlane have done, that the Whitlam Government, through DURD in particular, had redefined the problem of inequality may be true, but it is not particularly useful since it merely states the obvious—that the Australian Labor Party is not a socialist party but a social democratic one, and as such, chooses to tackle the consequences of the capitalist economy (like locational inequality) rather than to dismantle that economy. This policy, furthermore, is in response to the preferences of the majority of Australian workers who want more say in, and more of, the benefits of the present system rather than its replacement by any socialist state. The ALP in 1972 was not without its memory of 1949.

How successful, then, was DURD in practice within the terms of its own philosophy?


**DURD in action**

There were some half-dozen key programs established by DURD in 1973. Earliest underway were the growth centre programs and the sewerage program. It was generally believed that urban inequalities increased with city size, and that it was important to develop new towns to take the pressure off the two biggest cities, Sydney and Melbourne. Agreement was reached early with the NSW and Victorian Governments regarding the establishment of a new town at Albury–Wodonga, and later, money was also provided for Bathurst–Orange in NSW and Monarto in SA. Funds for tackling the backlog in urban sewerage services had been part of the election promises, and were made available immediately. Other programs took longer to establish and some, the Land Commission program for example, never got off the ground in those States where the State government philosophy was in conflict with that of the Whitlam Government. The purpose of the Land Commission program was to establish public land development agencies in each State which would 'establish a presence in the market sufficient to influence the general level of land prices and the rate of development of particular areas' (Budget Paper No. 9, 1975:28). The Area Improvement Program (AIP) and the Land Commission program were perhaps the most radical of DURD's initiatives. The AIPs were established 'as a way of involving people and organizations in identifying regional problems, working out regional development strategies, and devising appropriate means of implementation' and were mainly directed towards supporting projects and studies 'in areas where urban infrastructure and community services have not kept pace with rapid growth in the immediate past, or where there is marked relative deficiency, or which have strategic significance for future development' (Budget Paper No. 9, 1975:71). The programs began in 1973–74 with pilot schemes in the western parts of Sydney and Melbourne, and were extended in 1974–75 to cover thirteen regions.

The AIPs were administered mainly through the existing local government structures in the different regions, and the aim was to encourage local participation in cataloguing the deficiencies of the region, in formulating regional development strategies for major functions (such as recreation, employment, drainage), and in examining the planning intentions of all levels of government. Obviously the AIPs were an important expression of DURD's redistributive objective, and also of the objective of encouraging public participation in planning and decision-making. Grants to local government, under the *Grants Commission Act 1973–1975*, were another important expression of redistributive goals. The Grants Commission's recommendations on financial assistance to a State for local government purposes were to enable local governing bodies in one region to function 'at a standard not appreciably below the standards of the local governing bodies in other regions' (Budget Paper No. 9, 1975:69) and to even up differences between one local government and another within the same region. In 1975 the Federal Government accepted the recommendation of the Commission that grants totalling $79.9m be paid to the States for disbursement to 885 councils. Projects that were supported under the Grants Commission and AIP schemes included design and documentation of community facilities; improvements to the physical environment by municipal drainage and local flood mitigation projects; and improvements to waterways and their environs, especially where these made recreational resources available. Other projects included the acquisition of parkland and open space; landscape design and construction; the planning, construction and management of solid waste systems; provision of information resources and services; public education activities on urban issues; and support for administrative services to the regional organisation of local councils. One of the more talked-about projects under the AIP scheme was the building of an artificial hill in the flat, western Sydney suburb of Auburn.

Another aspect of the attack on locational inequality was the development of a policy for location of Australian government activities.

By 1975 the Minister for Urban and Regional Development had acquired the responsibility for administering the *Land Acquisition Act* and other related functions previously undertaken by the Department of Services and Property. In assuming responsibility for property acquisition, leasing and disposal, DURD had the opportunity to harmonise the government's property requirements and the location of government activities with the government's urban and regional objectives. In the past, government offices had been concentrated in the city centres of Melbourne and Sydney, and in Canberra. The centralisation of government employment, complementing the tendency for large private offices to locate in city centres, contributed to no small extent to the overgrowth of central business areas and all the undesirable consequences that follow—lack of employment opportunities in other parts of the metropolitan area, impossible strain on peak hour public transport, crowding of roads into and out of the city, hence demands for urban freeways, and so on. In an effort to stem this over-centralisation DURD decided to give priority to locating appropriate activities in the designated growth centres (Albury–Wodonga, Bathurst–Orange, and Geelong in particular) and in selected sub-metropolitan centres within the major cities. It was hoped that this move would not only provide a better distribution of employment opportunities throughout the major cities but that it would also have a positive effect on private sector investment decisions, and generate corresponding moves by State governments in a co-operative approach to urban development.

One of DURD's more publicised programs was its involvement in urban renewal schemes in Melbourne and Sydney. The Federal Government's participation in this activity was designed specifically 'to preserve scarce accommodation in the inner areas for lower income households, to achieve and maintain a broad socio-economic mix of population, to preserve and enhance the historic landscape qualities of old neighbourhoods, and to encourage residents to become involved in the planning, development, and management of their neighbourhoods' (Budget Paper No. 9, 1975:36). The Government's involvement in projects at Woolloomooloo and Glebe in Sydney and Emerald Hill in Melbourne provided, above all, the opportunity to demonstrate its concern for the specific problems of the inner areas and to demonstrate a co-ordinated approach to the planning process involved. Overall, some $35m was committed to the initial outlay for projects.

Perhaps the best indication of the degree of commitment of the Government to urban problems is in the Budget allocations of 1973–74, 1974–75 and 1975–76, especially the last, since the deteriorating economic situation led to considerable pressure on the Government to cut back on its more expensive social reform programs. The 1973–74 Budget provided $136m for the cities, raised the allocation for the States' public housing programs by 25 per cent and provided $32m of a proposed $700m program of improvements to urban public transport systems. There was $30m for the States to begin to tackle the backlog in urban sewerage services, and special grants for local councils in the 'deprived west' of Sydney ($5m) and Melbourne ($3m) to improve their services and amenities. Evidence of wider ambitions in influencing patterns of urban development was the provision of $33m for growth centres and $30m for Land Commissions.

In 1974, Budget expenditure in all these fields was increased: Land Commission allocations to $57m, growth centre funds to $52m, sewerage to $105m, area improvement programs to $14m. Altogether the total outlay on DURD programs in the 1974–75 Budget was $433m, an increase of $266m on the first year's allocation to the department, and a firm indication of the Government's commitment to this area of social policy.

Despite economic differences by the time of formulation of the 1975–76 Budget, levels of spending for most of the established programs were maintained: growth centre and Land Commission funds amounted to $124m; sewerage to $133m; welfare housing to $356m (a drop of $20m from 1974–75) and area improvement funds rose to $18m (Budget Paper No. 9, 1975:97–8).

**Obstacles to urban reform**

Budget allocations, however, do not tell the whole DURD story. On paper, it looked as though DURD had become an established spending department by 1975, with important policy initiatives and a powerful minister. But DURD's birth had not been an easy one, and had left scars, and some unhealable wounds. There were four particularly sharp problems that held back the implementation of the DURD philosophy, at least in the short term (1972–75), and several others that are perhaps more in the nature of long-term contradictions for any social democratic government.

For those on the left concerned with urban policy, it seemed essential that the creation of any urban affairs ministry under a Federal Labor government should bring together, under the one portfolio, those policy areas with crucial significance for the pattern of urban inequalities—in particular, housing, transport and environment, and conservation. Only by controlling the location of investment of these areas of high public-sector capital expenditure, it was argued, could an urban affairs ministry have any impact on the problem of urban inequality. But this was not to be. The Labor caucus elected twenty-seven men to the ministerial benches, and there had to be enough ministries to go round. Housing, transport and environment were not fused into a single urban super-department. They remained separate empires, and as such, more or less rivals to the fledgling

DURD. Despite a minister with a strong position and power base in Cabinet in Tom Uren, DURD was always struggling to persuade these departments to share its vision of the nature of urban inequality and its program of urban reform.

As a new department DURD drew many of its recruits from young people outside the public service who had previously been involved in 'grass roots urban action'—that is, people who had been working to bring about change by organising community action or working through the education system, and who felt more or less optimistic in December 1972 about the prospects for change under a Labor government. These people did not sit easily in inter-departmental committee meetings with the more conventional career public servants from the established departments. DURD gained a reputation, not only among other Federal departments but also with those State departments involved in negotiating programs with DURD, as the abrasive department. Missionary zeal, moral outrage, and shorts and thongs were not styles of negotiation that got far in the dour, pseudo-neutral, quiet-suited world of the Canberra bureaucracy.

The DURD 'house style' was one, but not the most important, reason for a third group of problems, concerning the relationship of the department with Treasury. There were two acute sources of conflict in the relationship. The first centred around different economic philosophies. The neo-classical economists in Treasury confronted the radical interventionist economists in DURD and neither would, nor could, give an inch, without taking the proverbial mile. In general, the neo-classical economists affirm the virtues of the competitive private-enterprise economy and condemn the Keynesian and post-Keynesian interventionism of modern reformers and the welfare measures that contemporary governments have adopted. This conflict became acute as the problem of inflation increased in 1974. DURD's radical interventionist economists wanted to maintain and increase levels of public spending on reform programs; Treasury neo-classicists wanted public-sector cutbacks. The second source of conflict was over more familiar 'territorial' rivalry. Since DURD had not been able to subsume the functions of Housing, Transport and Environment (not to mention Education, Health, Tourism and Recreation, or Services and Property, all of which made decisions with vital consequences for equity in urban areas) then the next best alternative was to try to exercise some overriding influence on the resource allocation of these departments, particularly on its geographical distribution. (For example, if the Department of Transport wanted to build a railway line, DURD wanted to influence where that line went.) Treasury, however, had other ideas. Traditionally it had been the only department with the ability to 'interfere' with other departments, and it resented this new competitor for influence. Treasury was more powerful, its permanent head more formidable and experienced than DURD's permanent head. Treasury won most of the battles.

A fourth set of problems arose out of the need to secure the co-operation of the State Governments before certain programs could be implemented. The land commission program is an example. The purpose of the proposed Land Commissions was to purchase land in, or near, major urban areas which would be developed and sold at low capital cost. This was designed to bring about, through competition with the private sector, a stabilisation and eventual reduction in average land prices in the metropolitan areas. Spin-offs from this procedure would include effective planning and servicing of the areas involved, and the retention for the community of some of the equity in the developed land. While the prospective role of the commissions was accepted readily enough by the Labor governments in South Australia and Western Australia (until Tonkin's defeat in 1974), the conservative governments of Victoria, NSW and Queensland were much more reluctant to co-operate. While quietly welcoming the extra money for sewerage, they resented the conditions attaching to funds for Land Commissions, growth centres, local government and urban transport. The Victorian Government eventually established an Urban Land Council which, in the words of the Victorian Minister for Local Government, would 'advise on and promote growth *outside* the metropolitan area'. He went on to say that 'the prime objectives of government activity are *to aid private enterprise* to effect comprehensive and well planned development and to provide primary and sullage sewerage, and services, *rather than acting as a developer in competition with the private sector*' (*Age*, 8 May 1974). The Federal Government's aim in establishing Land Commissions, however, was precisely to compete with the private sector and thereby reduce the price of land.

This kind of situation was one of the central dilemmas for DURD. Some of its programs could be achieved through direct Federal Government action (for example, purchasing inner-city housing for renewal and renting to low-income earners; locating some government offices in outer suburbs; growth centres) but most of DURD's new initiatives (especially the role proposed for the Land Commissions, and the aim to update urban public transport and scrap freeway programs) required the exercise of State powers and, therefore, the close co-operation of the States. Frequently, that co-operation was not forthcoming. It is as unrealistic to expect a State Liberal government to abolish land speculation as it would be to expect a State Labor government to abolish welfare housing, just because a Federal government (of opposite political complexion) says it must. Although in these situations the conflict is usually about political economy (who is getting what out of the urban economy and why) it always tends to be disguised as a conflict about 'the erosion of State sovereignty'. Therein lies an ongoing problem for any future urban affairs ministry with reformist intentions.

All these problems put severe restraints on the DURD achievement and weaken the optimism of urban reformers everywhere. In any conceivable future urban affairs ministry under a Federal Labor government these problems will recur. It is hard to imagine—given what we know about the nature of the ALP and the nature of the bureaucracy—that any Federal caucus would be so bold as to create an urban super-ministry subsuming such departments as housing and transport; that Treasury would ever tolerate such a rival for its supremacy; or that any conservative State government would agree to implement the more radical plans emanating from a Federal Labor government.

And there are other problems, longer term contradictions perhaps in the DURD philosophy, that must be confronted in any analysis of the DURD achievement before future strategies are planned. Whether they were misguided or ill-conceived, it does seem in retrospect that some of the DURD programs might have been quite counter-productive in the longer term—had there been a longer term—as for instance, the Glebe, Woolloomooloo and Emerald Hill urban renewal projects. The effect of renovating properties in those parts of the inner suburbs is to raise property values in adjacent parts, thereby forcing up rents and purchase prices and forcing *out* more low-income earners. Yet the main objective of that program was to preserve inner suburban accommodation for low-income earners. Another example is the Land Commission program. Too little research has been done on this issue for certain evaluation, but it may be that a more comprehensive public ownership scheme than that proposed under the Land Commission program (where land is only held in public ownership for a certain period prior to development, and only land needed for development is acquired) will be necessary if development is to be determined by social rather than market values. It may be that not only development land, but all land and buildings would have to revert to the state, in order that planners might have an adequate choice of locations for all forms of development. Planning authorities cannot effect desirable changes until they can initiate development without reference to the economic imperatives of the market. It may be that they cannot even prevent undesirable changes unless they own all buildings. It is likely that only in this way can they prevent the takeover of cheaper districts by professional and entrepreneurial classes, and the loss of shops, industries and community facilities to more profitable locations.

The question ought to be asked whether it was in fact within DURD's power to solve any of the urban problems it identified—city size, length of journeys to work, lack of community facilities, land prices and poor public transport services. To solve these problems implies an overall economic control of the private sector, a co-ordination of all public-sector activities influencing urban growth, and an increase in public-sector expenditure such as has never happened before in Australia and is perhaps beyond the realms of possibility for a social democratic government operating under all the constraints of a mixed economy. This can be considered as two problems—the problem with the public sector and the problem with the private sector.

DURD wanted to offer a more diverse choice of location of jobs to people living in the big cities. Admittedly it could relocate government offices and employment centres. But the private sector still provides most of the jobs, and DURD never had any control over the investment patterns and location decisions of private capital. It had no way of controlling the speculative boom in central-city office space that was occurring and that would determine future job locations for some time to come. Without control over these kinds of private-sector decisions, DURD had no control of the big issues like city size, growth centre strategy, and journey to work—all issues that featured in the 1972 election promises.

DURD also wanted to reduce land prices, upgrade public transport, catch up with the sewerage backlog, build more public housing for rental, provide better community facilities, more public open space, renovate inner city housing and allocate it to low-income earners, and so on. *All* these programs demanded massive capital expenditure. By the 1975–76 Budget it was clear that the expansionary spending of 1973–74 and 1974–75 was no longer possible under deteriorating economic circumstances, particularly the rapid rate of inflation. Whether this was a short-term problem or part of the long-term fiscal crisis of the capitalist state cannot be argued here. Suffice it to say, one powerful school of thought argues the latter—that is, social democratic governments in the future will not be able to go on increasing public expenditure without disastrous consequences for the rate of profit of the private sector. Since it is not expected that the capitalist class will sit back and tolerate a falling rate of profit, the prospect, in the short term at least, is for a decline in public-sector spending and a deterioration of urban public services. Exponents of this school of thought cite the fiscal problems of New York and the public service cuts in Britain to support their thesis (O'Connor, 1973; Alcaly and Mermelstein, 1977).

### Return to *laissez-faire*

Whether this is a short-term or long-term problem, it has certainly shown no signs of improving since 1975. While public expenditure on urban programs at least stayed stationary (and therefore in real terms decreased, because of the rate of inflation) under the last Labor Budget, under the Fraser Government the public-sector cutbacks began immediately. In comparison with the $408m provided by the last Labor Budget for the departments of Urban and Regional Development and the Environment, the first Fraser Government provided $251m, a 37 per cent cutback since 1975–76. The Land Commission's allocation was cut back from $60m in 1975–76 to $24m; sewerage from $113m to $50m; growth centres from $64m to $19m. And there were even greater cuts in the 1977–78 Budget. From the $251m allocated to urban and regional development in 1976–77, there was a further drastic cutback to $153m, a 39 per cent decrease on the previous year. The Budget paper was forthright: 'The levelling off in this expenditure reflects reductions in staff members and administrative expenditure generally, consistent with the Commonwealth's policy of reducing its involvement in the area of urban and regional development' (Budget Paper No. 1, 1978–79). The 1978–79 Budget contained a further cutback, from $153m to $108m; only three departments (Finance, Northern Territory, and Industry and Commerce) had smaller budgets than the Department of Environment, Housing and Community Development (Budget Paper No. 1, 1978–79).

What had occurred was a retreat to the Menzies era of non-involvement in urban affairs, a *laissez-faire* philosophy which believed in leaving the fate of the cities to the free play of market forces and argued the less government intervention the better, especially in the housing and property markets. By the time of the 1978–79 Budget the Land Commission's allocation was down to a mere $15m (from $26m in 1977–78), and the funds for welfare housing had been seriously cut back in accordance with the self-help philosophy of the Fraser Government. After the Labor defeat in December 1975, DURD was superseded by a new and, ironically, more comprehensive Department of Environment, Housing and Community Development—ironically because, while Labor had grand co-ordinating aims, it had failed to establish a co-ordinated urban affairs ministry, while the Liberal-National Country Party coalition had set up a comprehensive ministry, but solely for the purpose of simplifying and reducing expenditure on urban programs.

Cuts in welfare housing have caused alarm, especially as rising land prices and rents in the private rental market are increasing the numbers of people on housing authority waiting lists. Welfare housing has in fact suffered cuts since the last Labor Budget. Labor's 1974–75 Budget provided a 42 per cent increase (in real terms) in gross welfare housing advances to the States, but a 2 per cent decrease followed in the 1975–76 Budget (in money terms a drop from $386m to $365m). The first Fraser Budget provided $375m, a 10.5 per cent decrease in real terms, and the 1977–78 Budget allocation of $390m was a further cut of 8 per cent in real terms. The cuts in Aboriginal housing were the most drastic of all. After an 18 per cent decrease in funds in 1976–77 there was a further drop of 23.5 per cent in real terms in 1977–78. The only explanation for this ruthless approach, put forward by the Treasurer, was that this 'reflects a thorough reassessment of the programme leading to cost-effectiveness' (*Shelter*, 5 November 1977).

In contrast to the harsh treatment of welfare and Aboriginal housing, home owners received significantly increased benefits from the 1977–78 Budget. Against the reduction in welfare housing advances, these gains can in fact be seen as a further redistribution of resources through the tax system from the poor to the wealthy. For instance, the most significant *increase* in housing expenditure was the $27m increase for home savings grants to an allocation of $35m. This represented a dramatic increase in real terms in a scheme which favours the more affluent home seekers. (Unfortunately the Budget does not provide other information on the level of support given through tax rebates on rate and mortgage interest deductions.) Overall, then, the 1977–78 Budget allowed the continued redistribution of housing resources from those on low incomes to the more affluent members of the community. Thus the 1978–79 allocation of $316m for welfare housing, a $74m cutback from the previous year, came as a disappointment but not as a surprise. The Liberal-NCP Government had allowed the key redistribution programs of the Whitlam urban policy to run down and was intent on reversing the trend of increased public-sector spending established under Labor.

The preceding story may seem (in terms of pages allocated to each) like an unbalanced account of urban policy under Whitlam and Fraser. But in fact it simply reflects the unbalanced reality. For twenty-three years after 1949, urban policy was neglected by successive Liberal-Country Party governments. For three years the ALP in government worked to develop a wide-ranging urban policy. Over the first three years of conservative rule, most of that policy has been dismantled as part of the overall cutbacks in public-sector spending. These cuts reflect a callous lack of concern, both for that 20 per cent of the population 'at the bottom of the heap', and for the quality of life of the majority of city dwellers.

## Postscript

This chapter is based on an essay written in early 1978. On a reappraisal of it in 1982 the unanswered questions are conspicuous. The question was raised as to how successful DURD was within the terms of its own philosophy, and whether there should ever be another DURD. Those questions were neither answered in the essay nor, during the past four years, have they been addressed by any one else.

Such was the strength of commitment of most urbanists to the DURD concept that critical appraisal has not been forthcoming. The dismantlers of DURD were instinctively seen to be the enemy, or else the bureaucracy at the time, for providing so many obstacles to the implementation of the programs. The most detailed account of the fate of DURD, Lloyd and Troy's *Innovation and Reaction* (1981), especially focuses on the 'bureaucratic obstacles and obstinacy' theme. Others, including the author, were so impressed with the degree of commitment to urban problems evident in the size of each successive Budget allocation that they never asked whether that money was well spent on well-conceived programs, or not.

However, Jones (1979) and Painter (1979) in reviews of Australian urban policy and its literature, are highly critical of many aspects of the DURD experiment: 'A rapidly expanding public sector in the early seventies provided the atmosphere of growth that protected many of the mistakes made by DURD' (Jones, 1979:298). Among these mistakes he included the new town policy, area improvement program, and more generally, DURD's 'very ambitious goals' and naive faith in an enlightened bureaucracy as the main agent of social change.

The new town movement in Australia had had a gestation period of about eight years prior to 1972. But by 1974–75 it had become clear through the Borrie Report on national population, that demographic trends were making the movement obsolete. A rapid decline in the birth rate and a sharp reduction in the rate of immigration weakened the case for new towns, despite South Australian Premier Don Dunstan's attempt to argue that they were intended just as much to provide an alternative life style as they were to syphon off excess growth from the existing capital cities. Jones (1979:297) argued that the new town movement in Australia 'showed the inherent fallacy of much of urban planning that relies on 'crisis' theories to prompt dramatic action'.

Social segregation, long a theme of sociologists and geographers, was brought into the urban policy debate by Stretton (1970). DURD's response to the social segregating function of cities was its Area Improvement Program, channelling special assistance to so-called 'deprived areas'. Jones used the Henderson poverty inquiry and Ian Manning's (1976) data to challenge the deprived area theory. Many of the reports of the Henderson poverty inquiry showed that many people living outside the large cities were more deprived than those living in capital cities. Manning's research showed 'an amazing lack of concentration of social deprivation'. Thus Jones concluded that Australia does not have areas of concentrated deprivation similar to other countries, and that 'the urban policy thrust of the Labor government can be seen as an attempt to apply the pork barrel politics, made infamous by the Australian Country Party, to the capital cities' (Jones 1979:299).

More generally, the point was made that DURD's ambitious aims (for comprehensive planning and co-ordination of all public investment in cities with redistributive as well as efficiency intentions) were 'impossible'. Jones seems to advance three grounds for this impossibility: first, the innate conservatism of town planners; secondly, the inadequacy of federal government powers in all of the areas necessary to influence urban planning and development; and thirdly, the inadequacy of the state of the art itself—the lack of understanding of the complexities and dynamism of cities, and of the unintended and unforeseen consequences of many government programs.

Australian urban programs from 1972 to 1975 were rushed and organisationally inexperienced. They did not have time to develop the relatively systematic allocation mechanisms used in Federal road and education programs. And it is probably fair comment to add that DURD's attempt to develop an urban and regional budget was an aim 'far in excess of the state of the art in economic and social theory and Australian statistics. Measuring the output of the public sector and unmet needs is an extremely difficult task' (Jones, 1979:301).

In one sense, the urban programs of the Whitlam years were very conservative. They assumed the continuation of economic growth and intended to finance their reforms from that source. In fact, the era of low growth and industrial decline set in during these years, and it was only possible to finance the social and urban reforms because of the rapidly expanding government revenue which was due to the impact of rapid inflation on unadjusted progressive income tax scales:

> This enabled DURD to achieve apparent success in its planning and co-ordinating efforts. But this was largely an illusion because the States were often quite keen to enter into agreements for extra resources. The real planning and co-ordination problems involve existing resources. There is little evidence that this was achieved during this period. (Jones, 1979:300)

Painter's analysis is even more searching. Essentially he agrees with Jones that the mega-co-ordinating role that national urban policy attempted was and is impossible:

> DURD was trying something more ambitious. It was seeking to impose a consistent urban and regional perspective on governmental activities. Urban policy in this sense is not a conventional compartmentable function of government. Unlike most functions, it does not simplify but complicates. It is essentially pretentious, making claims on grounds of mere policy to have a co-ordinating role. Urban policy goes against the dominant logic of functional specialisation. There are inherent limits to its success given this functional context of governmental activities. (Painter, 1979:344)

He advocates simpler, more direct approaches to dealing with 'urban problems'—for instance, policies aimed at 'direct redistribution of income'. But this advice ignores the fact that it was precisely the political/electoral difficulty of straight income redistribution measures which set reformers thinking about the more indirect or social wage solutions during the late 1960s.

There is much to argue with in these provocative critiques. But it is true that DURD became identified with some dubious spending programs and has thus come to be seen as representing the type of wasteful government spending that helped create the anti-government movement in the late 1970s. Insofar as taking a more comprehensive view of urban problems creates insoluble administrative difficulties, 'such an approach is self-defeating. It deflects attention and resources from other public activities and it raises unrealisable expectations which produce disillusionment with government' (Painter, 1979:346). It is regrettable that the major work on DURD by 'insiders' (Lloyd and Troy, 1981) did not address itself to these challenges.

With three exceptions (Wilson, 1978; Painter, 1979; Jones, 1979) the existing literature on the DURD experiment has been written by those who had been ideologically and emotionally involved. The definitive study of the performance of Labor urban policy has yet to be written. A start has been made, in a doctoral thesis, by Lionel Orchard of Macquarie University, but flesh has yet to be given to his fresh insights (Orchard, 1982).

LEONIE SANDERCOCK

# 4 A socialist city in a capitalist society?

## Property ownership and urban reform in Australia

This chapter deals with two interrelated themes: property as power, and the problem of the nature and limits of state intervention in the city.

In the dominant (that is, social democratic) debate about urban problems in Australia there has always been the implicit, confused and never-thought-through notion of a socialist city within a capitalist society—that is, the assumption that there is a solution to urban problems that is separate from any solution of the broader problem of the capitalist society that contains them. Central to this assumption has been the idea that if only land policy could be reformed, most of the other desirable urban reforms would follow. The consequences of state intervention in the urban land market would be the stabilisation of land prices, the opportunity for coherent and comprehensive urban planning, a reduction in the costs of public provision of urban infrastructure, a more open, democratic, participatory planning process, and so on (Troy, 1978:14–24). But would it? Is there not a contradiction in this whole notion? To follow through this riddle of a socialist city in a capitalist society attention is focused on two issues: the philosophy and achievements of the Department of Urban and Regional Development (DURD) from 1972 to 1975, particularly in the area of land reform; and the importance of property investment to finance capital, particularly insurance companies. Such a focus ought to throw some light on the possibilities and limits of urban reform in capitalist Australia.

In his policy speech in November 1972 Gough Whitlam identified various problems that were prominent *in* the cities, and called them urban problems—rising land prices, declining public transport services, sewerage backlogs, inadequate community facilities, overdeveloped central business areas, and so on. To this catalogue he added an important statement: that 'in modern Australia social inequality is fixed upon families by the place in which they are forced to live even more than by what they are able to earn'.

66

During the campaign he indicated that he believed that the main causes of inequality in Australia were not those arising out of ownership of wealth and property, but regional disparities in the costs of land and housing and the provision of urban and social services—education, health and other community facilities.

It should be pointed out that this philosophy of locational inequality, this concern with questions of *distribution* in the city, with the equity *effects* of urban development, was very much a description of symptoms, rather than an analysis of the causes of urban problems. But the city is, in the first place, a pool of labour—a relatively self-contained area where a whole community enters into common production and consumption processes on a daily basis. Production is the first key process in the development of urban areas. The second, the competition for space and location, the competition in the land market, is a reflection of the competition between firms and other agencies in the economy with limited resources. Channelling these forces of competition and coping with their effects is the essence of the urban planning problem.

Whitlam and the Australian Labor Party, through DURD, chose to ignore the causes of urban problems, which lay in the sphere of production, and to try to ameliorate some of the more blatant social and economic effects of the capitalist mode of production. In doing so, they were behaving as social democratic parties characteristically do—tackling the consequences of the capitalist economy rather than trying to dismantle it. The question of DURD's success needs, therefore, to be settled, and the question posed as to whether there would be any point in creating another DURD under some future Labor Government. Or was DURD just an unrealistic, misguided or contradictory exercise from the beginning?

There were some half dozen key programs established by DURD during 1973—programs for growth centres, land commissions, area improvement, sewerage, urban renewal and for the updating of urban public transport. These were ambitious programs, and the Government's real concern with their solution was evident in the urban and regional budget allocation, which rose from zero to $135 million in the first year and $436 million in the second year of DURD's existence. But was that enough? Solutions to any of these problems had three basic requirements: co-ordination of all public sector activities affecting urban development; a huge expansion of government spending; and some overall control of private sector investment and location decisions. It is necessary to establish whether or not any of these requirements were met or are ever likely to be, under a social democratic regime.

In the years leading up to the Whitlam victory, the Australian Labor Party's urban advisers, and numerous other more 'neutral' urban commentators, had argued that any effort by a Federal government to intervene in the nation's urban problems must be done through the agency of an urban 'super-ministry'. That is, a new department should be created to encompass all aspects of urban development—housing, transport, environment and conservation, and so on. The impossibility of achieving such a ministry in an Australian Labor Party government, and the problems DURD faced as a result, were discussed in Chapter 3. Another problem, that of Federal/State co-operation and co-ordination, was also described in that chapter. While these problems of public sector co-ordination were not solved by DURD, it does not necessarily follow that they are insoluble for all time.

The other two sets of problems (the need for increased public spending and for some control over private sector investment and location decisions) look more intractable, and would perhaps be better described as long-term contradictions.

To solve the problems of rising land prices, rundown urban public transport, sewerage backlogs, inadequate community facilities and the twin process of decay and gentrification of the inner suburbs, would obviously require an enormous increase in public expenditure. Within two years of its creation DURD commanded a budget of $433 million. In the following and final year of the Labor government, in a budget which reduced overall levels of government spending, DURD was cut back to $408 million. By that time the Whitlam Government was faced with what the capitalist press insisted on calling an economic crisis of mismanagement. By this, the press meant that the levels of inflation and unemployment that existed in Australia had nothing to do with a broader international crisis (with complicated origins including how the US financed the war in Vietnam in the 1960s and 1970s, the oil price rise in the early 1970s, and the emergence since the 1940s of powerful multinational corporations) but was caused by the Labor Government's economic policies, in particular, their extravagant public spending.

This line of conservative criticism became a significant part of the 1975 election campaign, but its importance here goes beyond that level of opportunism into perhaps the most difficult debate of this decade, concerning what some writers have called 'the fiscal crisis of the state' (O'Connor, 1973). O'Connor and others postulate that the capitalist state must provide the infrastructure and subsidies which will ensure the profits of monopoly capital. It must subsidise and protect the accumulation process, while continuing to permit the private appropriation of profits. At the same time, the state must absorb the popular discontent generated by the social costs of the accumulation process, much of which is expressed through or as urban problems. This theory of the state argues that the fiscal crisis is the result of the increasing demands on government arising from these dualistic functions. The state's absorption of the social and private costs of accumulation, combined with the continued private appropriation of the social surplus, produces an inherent tendency towards fiscal crisis. If profits are to be maintained, there is a constant tendency to let the costs and taxes of state spending fall more on the workforce and less on industry. In the long run this results in a 'Catch-22' dilemma for the state. Both industry and the population continually require more state intervention, each on their own ultimately contradictory terms—the one to maintain profits and reduce costs and the other to improve living standards and hence increase private sector costs. The overriding constraint is that the state should not encroach on the operation of the private sector by making too many goods and services available 'free' (education, health and so on) or by competing with the private sector in productive activities (manufacturing cars, or steel, or housing, for example). Rising inflation and rising unemployment are recent manifestations of the Catch-22 situation. It seems that in the advanced capitalist economies there is a limit or barrier to the growth of the state, if the market economy is to be preserved in its present form (Broadbent, 1977).

The Whitlam Government came to power with a social and welfare program whose implementation was based on the assumption of an expanding economy. When the economy contracted, the Labor Party found itself in an ideological vacuum. It had always assumed that its public spending programs could be paid for out of the expanding growth rate. When that was no longer possible the Labor Government floundered and failed to develop alternative ways of financing its programs. This could have been done, in theory, by either increasing taxation or increasing public ownership of productive enterprises. The latter solution has been advocated by Catley (1978:57) who argues that a meaningful alternative to Fraserism:

> must centre around the expansion of democratic public ownership of the means of production in the face of the opposition of its present domestic and foreign owners . . . The lesson of 1972–5 was not that Labor cannot run a capitalist society: nor that it moved too fast; nor that revolution is the logical alternative. It was that welfarism depends on production, which follows it own laws while left almost exclusively in private hands.

The problem with this argument is that it begs the whole question of the political problems posed by the fiscal crisis of the state. Would the private sector ever be prepared to tolerate the falling rate of profit that would follow either from increased taxation or from public sector involvement in productive enterprises?

DURD wanted to offer a more diverse choice of location of jobs to people living in the big cities. It could relocate government offices and employment centres, but the private sector still provides most of the jobs. DURD never had any way of controlling the investment patterns and location decisions of private capital. It had no way of controlling the speculative boom in central city office space which was occurring and which could determine future job locations for some time to come. Except in South Australia, it had no way of controlling the speculation in land for urban development that had doubled residential land prices in most States between 1972 and 1974. Without control over these kinds of private sector decisions, DURD had no control over the big issues like city size, land prices, growth centre strategy and the journey to work—all issues featured in the 1972 election promises. The reason for this lack of control lay in the power of finance capital in Australian economic life. Therefore, the limits imposed on urban reform by the private ownership of land and the power of finance capital must be considered in any discussion of the feasibility of the socialist city in a capitalist society.

When the Whitlam Government made public in early 1973 its intention to establish Land Commissions in each State to try to stabilise and lower the price of residential land, the Victorian Government was quicker than most conservative State governments in its response. At a Cabinet meeting on 16 July 1973, it detailed the Victorian Housing Commission to become an instant land banking authority to spend $8 million as quickly as possible on broad acres in an effort *to be seen to be* pre-empting the DURD idea. But the VHC paid urban prices for rural land (some of it unsuitable for urban development) and, according to a subsequent public inquiry, wasted $4.5 million of public money (Sandercock, 1979). In the process it bolstered the land boom and protected the interests of property speculators. This was precisely the opposite of what DURD intended to achieve through the establishment of a Land Commission. The Victorian Liberal Government, however, was acting in accordance with its long tradition of support for and defence of property interests. What was at stake for those property interests? How important is finance capital (or property capital as part of it) in the urban development process through its property investment activities, and what limits does this place on urban reform, particularly reform of the land question?

Some recent work on capitalist land ownership in the United Kingdom analyses the effects of the private ownership of land on the operation of the capitalist mode of production and on the wider structure of production and circulation (Massey and Catalano, 1978). This research breaks down ownership of land by capital into three different categories. The first, 'former landed property', refers to a number of groups of agents, including the landed aristocracy, the landed gentry, the Church of England, and the Crown Estates. This group owns nearly 40 per cent of the total land area of the UK but, in acreage terms, most of this is rural land. (The Church and the Crown Estates do, however, have important urban estates.) This type of land ownership resulted from the specific nature of the transition from feudalism to capitalism in the UK and is not, therefore, what one might call 'purely capitalist'. Land for this group is not just one sector for investment like any other, chosen simply on the basis of its potential economic return. Rather, it is an integral part of a wider social role in which considerations other than 'return on capital invested' are of real importance. And this wider role influences the nature of the economic relation to land ownership.

The second type, 'industrial land ownership', is not really land ownership as such:

> For this group, the ownership of land is neither the result of selecting sectors for investment nor the basis of a separate economic or other function. Land in this case is owned because it is a condition of production. The economic relation to land ownership is consequently dominated by considerations of the relevance of particular characteristics of land to the process of production. For this type, conflict with landowners as such can be as important as its own benefit from land ownership (Massey, 1977:417)

The third type, 'financial land ownership', is, like the second, more directly a product of the capitalist mode of production but, unlike industrial land ownership, this is land ownership 'as such'. For finance capital (that is, property companies, pension funds, insurance companies), land and property ownership is just another sector to invest in. The ideological context for these groups is related to their present economic function and does not (as in the case of 'former landed property') place constraints on that function. This division of bourgeois land ownership into three structurally distinct groups indicates, according to Massey, 'that no one catch-all category of landed capital—that is, no single coherent fraction of capital based on the ownership of land—can be said to exist' (Massey, 1977:418). This obviously has important political consequences for the possibilities of land reform. A more detailed analysis of financial land ownership is first necessary, however, since this type is clearly the most central to political issues of land ownership.

In the cities, although the absolute amount of land owned by the groups composing this type is small, it nevertheless dominates the shape of the land market precisely because it is financial land ownership and *as such*, is solely concerned with the maximisation of return on land. And, significantly, it is precisely where the financial form of land ownership is dominant that the most explicit political struggles are found: 'The dynamic created through this form of land ownership has been partly responsible for the spatial problems of urban areas, and specifically for those aspects of the problems to which the Community Land Act was supposedly a response' (Massey, 1977:421).

Some political economists claim that finance capital dominates Australian economic life (Rivers and Hyde, 1975; Massey, 1977:421; Cochrane, 1976). Over the past twenty years property investment in the central city by insurance and finance companies has become increasingly important. But why? What are the functions of finance capital? What kind of surplus value is produced by property investment? Is it essential to the functions of finance capital? And what limits does this place on land policy reform, in theory and in practice?

If the basic proposition that labour is the source of all value is accepted, then it follows that only industrial capital produces surplus—that is, capital is only productive in the sphere of production. But it is only through circulation that the capitalist converts his capital into productive capital and extracts, with the sale of commodities, the surplus value created in production. Circulation thus prepares the way for and completes the extraction of surplus value. Taken in itself, circulation does not add any value to the commodity or *create* surplus value. But in order to speed up the process of capital accumulation it is important to speed up the circulation process. Hence, the division of labour among the different sectors of capital is to the advantage of the capitalist class. Hence, the specialised functions of three types of capital have developed, with industrial capital controlling the process of production and of surplus value, commercial capital controlling the circulation of commodity capital, and financial capital controlling the circulation of money capital. Commercial and financial capital provide a service to industrial capital and in return share in the surplus created in that sphere. Insofar as finance capital is involved in the land and property market then it is extracting a profit that is created in the sphere of production. Property capital (that is, that part of finance capital involved in the land and property market) creates no surplus. It simply buys in order to sell at a higher price. Or, as Vieille put it, the landowner 'speculates on urban dynamism and the provision of facilities by the community, and takes today the value expected tomorrow' (Lamarche, 1976:106). But in so doing, and forcing up land prices, finance capital is forcing up the costs of production of industrial capital and producing conflict within the process of accumulation. Clearly then, the interest of finance capital in land ownership is not necessarily compatible with the interest of industrial capital in accumulation.

There have been several studies of the role of finance capital in property investment in the UK (Ambrose and Colenutt, 1975; Marriot, 1967; Massey and Catalano, 1978; Amery and Cruickshank, 1975) some more systematic than others, but nothing comparable has been done for Australia. Ray Archer (1967) provided some interesting data on insurance and property development companies, but that information is now ten years out of date. If Archer's figures for 1956–65 and those of the author for 1965–81 are put together, and abbreviated, Table 4.1 results.

The total property assets of all life insurance companies in Australia and the proportion of this total invested in New South Wales and Victoria is indicated in Table 4.2.

In 1976 AMP invested a total of $510 million, $98 million of which went into property (AMP Society, 1976). In 1977, $80 million of National Mutual's $200 million total investment was in property (National Mutual, 1977). All these figures indicate the increasing importance over the past twenty years of property investment for finance capital. For the seven largest companies (which comprise 90–95 per cent of the total statutory funds of all insurance companies) the investment has risen, on an average, from between 2–5 per cent in 1956 to 8–12 per cent in 1965, and 20–26 per cent in 1976. A breakdown into types of investment for National

**Table 4.1  Property assets of the seven largest life insurance companies as a total $m, and as percentage of total assets**

| | 1956 | | 1965 | | | 1970 | | | 1973 | | | 1976 | | | 1981 | | |
|---|---|---|---|---|---|---|---|---|---|---|---|---|---|---|---|---|---|
| | Prop-erty assets $m | % | Prop-erty assets $m | Total assets $m | % | Prop-erty assets $m | Total assets $m | % | Prop-erty assets $m | Total assets $m | % | Prop-erty assets $m | Total assets $m | % | Prop-erty assets $m | Total assets $m | % |
| AMP | 22.4 | 3.2% | 175.7 | | 11.0% | 358.7 | 2477.3 | 14.48% | 616.8 | 3348.9 | 18.4% | 957.2 | 4380.3 | 21.8% | 1.9 | 7.6 | 25.4 |
| Colonial Mutual | 12.8 | 5.4% | 55.4 | | 8.5% | 101.1 | 952.0 | 10.6% | 176.7 | 1139.4 | 15.5% | 262.3 | 1412.7 | 18.5% | 505.9 | 2281 | 22.2 |
| National Mutual | 8.9 | 3.6% | 59.8 | | 9.3% | 136.4 | 988.0 | 13.8% | 255.8 | 1345.8 | 19% | 428.1 | 1730.1 | 24.7% | 889.0 | 3519.7 | 25.2 |
| T & G | 8.6 | 3.8% | 26.7 | | 5.7% | 68.3 | 646.4 | 10.6 | 134.0 | 823.2 | 16.2% | 254.8 | 942.3 | 27% | 365.9 | 1264.9 | 28.9 |
| City Mutual | 2.0 | 2.8% | 5.2 | | 3.0% | 17.6 | 271.8 | 6.4% | 31.4 | 344.1 | 9.1% | 51.0 | 413.4 | 12.3 | 112.0 | 580.3 | 19.3 |
| Prudential | 1.9 | 4.5% | 26.7 | | 18.3% | 69.6 | 708.7 | 9.8% | 99.0 | 337.6 | 29.3% | | | | 152.4 | 583.7 | 26.1% |
| MLC | 14.8 | 5.7% | 45.2 | 581.4 | 7.78% | 69.6 | | | 128.9 | 913.2 | 14.1% | 226.2 | 1109.8 | 20.3% | 379.3 | 1640.6 | 23.1% |

*Source*:  Annual reports of insurance companies.

*Urban political economy*

Table 4.2   Property assets held by all life insurance companies in Australia

|      | Total       | New South Wales | Victoria |
|------|-------------|-----------------|----------|
| 1956 | $    60.6m  | $ 34m           | $   9m   |
| 1965 | 312.6m      | 143m            | 93m      |
| 1970 | 751.2m      | 324m            | 227m     |
| 1973 | 1,402.6m    | 593m            | 453m     |
| 1975 | 1,969.2m    | 758m            | 613m     |
| 1978 | 2,695.2m    | NA              | NA       |
| 1981 | 3,686.6m    | NA              | NA       |

*Source*:   *Life Insurance*, Australian Bureau of Statistics.


Table 4.3   Forms of property investment, National Mutual Life (%)

|                                         | 1977 |       | 1981  |
|-----------------------------------------|------|-------|-------|
| Offices                                 | 43   |       | 40.6  |
| Industry, factories, warehouses         | 22   |       | 15.84 |
| Retail shopping centres                 | 15   |       | 35.48 |
| Residential units                       | 6    |       | —     |
| Sub. division of land                   | 2    |       | —     |
| Land and buildings for redevelopment    | 4    | Hotel | 2.85  |
| Other (motels, car parks, etc.)         | 8    | Other | 5.23  |

*Source*:   *Australian Property Investor* July 1977.


Mutual in 1977 indicates the predominance of offices in the overall
investment pattern (Table 4.3).

   Although more information is needed, these preliminary figures indicate
both the scope and intensity of 'financial land ownership'. Not only are
these companies playing a crucial role in the overdevelopment of the
central city (Archer found that five of the twenty largest property
developments in the Sydney CBD from 1956–65 were owned by AMP);
their investments now extend into retail shopping centres, hotels, motels,
etc., and acquisition of previously undeveloped land (broad acres) for
subdivision and urban development. For example, T. & G. Insurance were
developing a large residential estate at Mill Park in Melbourne and
acquired 2632.5 hectares at Mt Ridley for the same purpose. The Mt
Ridley land was not zoned for urban development, but the company
succeeded in 1976 in persuading State Cabinet to override this zoning, a
procedure which the Cabinet then dubbed 'negotiated planning'
(Sandercock, 1979:27–31). Clearly financial land ownership is having a
significant impact on metropolitan form. Lamarche (1976) goes on from
this to argue that 'the problems experienced by workers in their homes in
the large cities depend to a major extent on land speculation and in
particular on property capitalism'. Broadbent (1977:124–8) notes the:

large blocks of financial capital seeking to undertake large-scale developments as a source of rental income and increasing asset values...These large-scale redevelopment schemes are a concrete manifestation of the growth of financial capital and the financial sector....This capital circulates in the economy and must find a profitable outlet; competition in the land market generates rents and values and thereby provides this outlet. One of the incipient contradictions in this situation lies in the fact that competition for land is a local, urban-scale phenomenon whereas the capital propelling this local competition is circulating through the national economy—through national organisations.

This has profound implications for urban planners who are constantly faced with problems caused by such activity of finance capital, yet have no means of tackling those causes. A second contradiction in this situation is that ultimately the cost of the rising rents and values caused by the activities of finance capital is passed back to the sector where surplus is created, to industrial capital, whose rate of accumulation is impeded by these rising costs. It follows then that it may be in the interests of industrial capital to do something to curb the property activities of finance capital.

What then follows from this, in terms of political action and change? If one pauses here to look at some attempts at land reform in the UK and some compatible situations in Australia, one can see these two contradictions being played out. Indeed, one possible interpretation of the recent *Community Land Act* in the UK (1975) is to see it as 'just one more victory for industrial capital, in this case against the moribund remains of something called "landed property"' (Massey, 1977:404–5). The history of various attempts to take land into public ownership provides some support for the 'barrier theory' of the encroachment of the public sector on to the private sector outlined by Broadbent (1977)—the theory that there are limits to the growth of the public sector which are determined by the extent to which such growth would interfere with the profitability of the private sector. Applying this argument to the case of urban land, it would mean that the growth of public ownership or taxation could proceed only so far before it undermined the private market, at which point it would be abolished.

Successive efforts at land reform since 1947 by British Labor governments floundered in these dilemmas. In 1947 a 100 per cent development tax was imposed which, it was argued, recouped for the community the rise in land values which were created by the community. But the effect of the development tax was to dry up the private land market and (in the absence of any public sector-initiated development to replace the private sector activity) to create shortages and make it easy for the subsequent Conservative government to abolish the tax. Yet subsequent efforts by Labor governments to encourage public sector land development have also floundered, from the Land Commission to the *Community Land Act*. The case of the UK Land Commission shows the sheer logistical, legal and operational difficulties of trying to nationalise land by stealth, that is, by piecemeal intervention in the land market. In the five years or so of its existence it acquired and assembled very little land—a tiny fraction of the thousands of hectares developed each year—yet the process of buying land laboriously in the market year by year meant employing thousands of planners, surveyors and valuers and increasing public sector expenditure. The fact that the UK Land Commission lasted only five years and that the DURD Land Commission program had such trouble getting off the ground (and was never accepted in some States) indicates the incipient contradiction in a policy of public sector intervention in the land market. Either the political resistance will be sufficient to prevent the policy in the making, or shortly after; or the policy will be sufficiently restricted in its execution so that only small quantities of land will be acquired, at the margin of existing development, ensuring that the land market as a whole continues to function. Thus, the Land Commission approach has no impact at all on the profitability of property ownership for finance capital. And by providing a basic resource cheaply and thereby reducing pro- duction costs for the private sector, such land reform may well be to the advantage of industrial capital. In other words, one can see how this operation of a Land Commission or a *Community Land Act* could easily become the traditional public sector-run monopoly or basic service— providing a basic resource cheaply.

Clearly what *needs* to be done is something far more drastic—a once-and- for-all change in the rights of all landowners over their land at one stroke and a fundamental leap from a market-based and market-led economy to a public sector-led economy. But is there not a Catch-22 here? On the one hand, the conflict of interest between industrial capital and finance capital with respect to land ownership suggests that there is room for reformist manoeuvre within the capitalist structure. The state can intervene in the land market. And yet, when it has tried to do so, the form the intervention has taken has been such as to have no detrimental effect on the main property interests of finance capital and has possibly even benefited industrial capital. The history of the South Australian Housing Trust's operations in the Adelaide land market supports these points. Not only was cheap land provided for industrialists, but the fact that housing land was also cheap for the productive workers meant that labour costs could be kept down, thus further benefiting industrial capital (Sandercock, 1975: 52–4). Yet there seems to be some barrier preventing something like a Land Commission from being fully effective (in terms of its aim to have a significant effect on the overall land market and to recoup the increase in land values due to community growth for the community). That barrier, in political terms, is the power of finance or property capital to halt reforms at the point at which (if not before) they begin to threaten or undermine the private market. One example of this under the Whitlam Government in Australia was the success of the campaign mounted by insurance companies to prevent the establishment of an Australian Government

Insurance Corporation (Rivers and Hyde, 1975), a campaign similar in many respects to that waged by the banks against the previous Labor Government's attempt to nationalise them in 1947 (May, 1968).

It would appear, then, that the concept of a socialist city in a capitalist society—that is, of significant urban reform within the capitalist structure—will be most difficult to realise. Insofar as land reform is central to urban reform it has, in the past, only progressed a little way before it has been challenged and abolished. Insofar as contradictions exist between the activities of finance capital and the needs of industrial capital, there does seem to be room for manoeuvre even if not in the short term. In the medium term though, it may be that the likelihood of land reform will be determined by the political struggle between these two sectors of capital. Really significant long-term change may only be possible when this contradiction reaches a point of undermining the capital accumulation process. Private ownership of land is not a logical necessity for the continued existence of capitalism. (I disagree with Harvey (1973) on this issue, but the argument is outside the ambit of this chapter.) It is a result of the specific historical conditions of the establishment of capitalism in this country that the general form of land ownership is private. But different forms of land ownership are *possible* under capitalism, the most obvious alternative to private ownership being ownership by the state.

Therefore, whether or not land is ever 'socialised' within the capitalist mode of production will depend not so much on efforts at land reform by departments like DURD, but rather on the ongoing effects of the contradictions of private ownership—particularly in respect of its tendency to increase the costs of production of industrial capital and thereby to impede capital accumulation.

LEONIE SANDERCOCK

# 5 Who gets what out of public participation?

The demand for public participation in planning has become the great populist red herring of the 1970s in Australia. Evidence of both overseas and Australian practice has shown that participation is *not* a substitute for planning or for regular government: it often leads to non-planning and semi-anarchic government. It is *not* an effective means of radical social change: it often has the opposite effect. And it is *not* an effective way of involving the 'have-nots' in decision-making: all the procedures of participation so far tried are biased towards involving the middle class.

But there are other ends participation may serve.

In some circumstances the process may be more important than the product. People want to be informed. They want to know that they have a ready opportunity to complain. An open planning process, providing easy access to both information and to the planners, can reassure people that they are being thought of. Participatory mechanisms, even those involving no devolution of power, may make public authorities more honest, more humane, more considerate of the people they are serving than they would otherwise be: more thoughtful of broader issues than their single purpose functions, more sensitive in performing their duties. In addition, participation at local level may elicit informed and useful responses on questions of local detail, on issues that may not seem important to planners (who are, therefore, unlikely to think of them) but are usually of great importance in the lives of those suggesting them. So at this level, participation may produce a better result for residents, without threatening what planners regard as their expertise, and without bogging down the planning process irretrievably.

But the bigger issues of housing and land, transport and metropolitan growth, are issues of public policy with which participatory mechanisms cannot deal successfully. In other words, in the context of the debate about the role of the Commonwealth in the cities, notions of participation are, at best, marginal and at worst, irrelevant.

## The ends of participation

Over the past ten years, the 'voice of the people'—all sorts of people—has grown in protest against the claims of authority, as the issue of democratic rights broadened from voting every three years to demanding a voice in urban renewal and local planning, protection of consumers, constitutional rights in welfare, the legitimacy of university government and the conduct of the Vietnam war. How did this come about?

One way of understanding community action, or the push for public participation, is to see it as an attempt to redress the balance of power between citizens and government. As planning (national economic, social or urban) becomes more comprehensive in scope, more 'expert' and far-reaching, the processes of official decision-making seem more and more remote from the influence of any individual voter. The more sophisticated the industrial economy, the more serious this problem becomes. As resources and people are released from older constraints, people become more mobile, and as the economy becomes more complex and inter-dependent, the autonomy of functions and regions breaks down.

This promotes increasing centralisation of government—integration only occurs at the apex of political and administrative power. So people become increasingly remote from the policy-makers they are supposed to influence and, simultaneously, must compete with new procedures for resolving issues of policy. To collate information at the centre, the executive has to devise methods capable of reducing the interrelationship between millions of facts to a manageable calculation. Overloaded with data, it cannot readily assimilate and so turns to technically sophisticated systems of analysis whose simplifying assumptions tend to pre-empt questions of political choice.

Since people's wishes are diverse, conflicting, and often ambiguous, and thus difficult to feed into such an analysis, electoral issues are directed towards indeterminate images and slogans which represent but do not define goals. So the political debate becomes divorced from the analysis of data and both become meaningless because they are no longer related. People are overloaded with information they do not trust and cannot respond to. There seem to be two processes of government: one formal and democratic (where the people are represented), but increasingly empty; the other obscure, technical and decisive, where expertise colludes with political self-interest (highway engineers with car and oil companies, planners with property owners, etc.). It becomes increasingly clear that, quite apart from these two processes, there are other spheres of power beyond the control not only of the people, but also of popularly elected governments. This is now part of the assimilated popular meaning of Kerr's dismissal of Whitlam.

So, over-centralisation, lack of communication between public authorities, their indifference to the effectiveness of their work and their unresponsive attitude to the people they serve—in other words oppression by the public sector at least as intolerable as that by the capitalist class—are the problems from which community action has emerged. Such action has been expressed as the demand for some say in decisions, particularly those decisions which affect the immediate environment.

Examples are the London Squatters Association's taking the problem of homelessness out of the hands of authority, and housing families in defiance of the law; neighbourhoods organising against redevelopment plans in the inner cities; radical building workers preventing demolition of old buildings and communities which would have been replaced by socially or ecologically undesirable projects, and so on. And there is the emergence of a new conventional wisdom which holds that all this strife could have been avoided if only public policy-makers had incorporated the public in their policy-making. This new conventional wisdom belongs not just to radical community activists but has increasingly been asimilated into the (public relations) vocabulary of public authorities and politicians.

But what is most striking, after the initial shock of the new rhetoric, is the extreme diversity of motives behind such declarations and the utter confusion which develops when the attempt is made to put the new ideas into practice. These two problems deserve closer attention.

It cannot be taken as self-evident that public participation is a 'good thing'. People with different social and political values have advanced quite different reasons for supporting the notion, and too little thought has been given to the tougher problems associated with putting it into practice. In short, participation can mean most things to most people, according to their preconceived values.

Participation presupposes some program of community organisation. But in practice it proves difficult to establish and sustain an unambiguous purpose for community organisation. It can mean the polite formality of block committees or the clamour of protest marches or green bans. In the USA, community action programs were intended, by some, to redistribute power—to extend to people some measure of control over projects which served them. But since people were not organised to assume such power, control remained with planners as a responsibility to foster whatever organisation seemed appropriate. As the devolution of authority was postponed, more paternalistic aims intruded: to promote self-help and social control through social cohesion, to facilitate the assimilation of middle class values, to disseminate understanding of planners' policies.

Clearly, community organisation can be interpreted with very different emphasis according to the standpoint of the organiser. It can be used to encourage the residents of a neighbourhood to come to terms with the demands of a wider society, or conversely to force the institutions of that society to adapt more sympathetically to the special needs of a neighbourhood. It can be seen as a form of therapy to treat apathy and social disintegration. It can be a way of persuading the people of an area to accept redevelopment programs. It can mean an education in the conventions of democratic participation as practised by middle class society, more for its own sake than for any particular (radical) purpose. Or, it might mean a new source of power with which to reinforce reformers' pressures for social and institutional change.

## Models of participation

Before any further analysis can be presented, the various models of participation must be examined and the political and social values implicit in them clarified, as well as the different methods associated with their implementation. Five possible models will be considered: participation as market research, as decision-making, as the dissolution of organised opposition, as social therapy, and as grass-roots radicalism (Dennis, 1972).

The concept of participation as market research emphasises the responsibility and power of the bureaucracy, and the participant is seen as a consumer or customer. Participation as market research is seen by those responsible for planning and for delivery of social services as a matter of securing reliable feedback from 'clients' in the form of useful advice and suggestions, usually about questions of detail rather than questions of policy. This view of participation is prevalent in most Australian public authorities, and is based on a rationale of bureaucratic efficiency.

By contrast, the view of participation as decision-making sees the citizen not as the beneficiary (or victim) of 'welfare colonialism' but as a policy-maker, a voting member of a governing board, or part of a team of planners. This belief in the worth and possibility of rational participation in policy-making by citizens is very much an enlightenment view. Underlying it are certain fundamental conceptions about people and societies—the reasonableness of individuals and the natural harmony of their interests, an optimistic view of human nature that rejects the conservative proposition that people always act out of self-interest.

Direct participation is advocated by some democratic theorists not only for its desirable practical consequences, but also because of the intrinsic worth of such activity in the development of human personality. There are some obvious objections to this line of argument. Participation may be good for people—but so are gardening, football and various other activities. There already exist numerous opportunities for people to participate—in political parties, trade unions, voluntary organisations. Mostly they do not. Doubtless new opportunities for active participation would appeal to some (probably those active already), but the evidence that this would be a means of self-fulfilment for vast new armies of formerly apathetic citizens is somewhat lacking. The problem with this view is that it bears little relation to existing evidence as to how people actually behave.

From the point of view of planning authorities, another way of viewing participation is to see it as a means of dissolving opposition. While some authorities committed to initiating participation have been disappointed by apathetic community responses, others have felt themselves in a state of seige by dissatisfied 'victims' of their 'services'. Various strategies of 'dissolutionary participation' have been used to cope with this troublesome opposition which makes bureaucratic lives uncomfortable. For instance, authorities may emphasise the forms of participation while channelling action into administrative functions and preserving decisions in their own hands. They may co-opt leaders of opposition groups into the decision-making process in a way that divorces them from their supporters and channels them into unproductive activity.

Some authorities use the rhetoric of participation to inhibit the emergence of opposition groups by dealing with each resident separately and not making public statements about whole areas, or 'unfairly favouring' a special section of the population by dealing with particular structured groups. This technique prevents the 'personal troubles of the milieu' from being turned into 'the public issues of social structure', to use C. Wright Mills's language. As a way of paying lip service to participation while using it to block genuine movements to affect the decisions of those in power, authorities may also add to each statement about participation the practical strategy of going forward at a snail's pace and hoping the opposition will tire before they do. This approach fits closely with bureaucratic and professional notions of technical expertise, with the belief in the infallibility of the technostructure, and with the belief that decisions are primarily technical rather than political questions and should, therefore, be left to those with the appropriate technical skills.

Participation as social therapy—that is, participation as a way of citizens' being encouraged to swell the labour force available to carry out public projects—is more characteristic of social welfare programs than urban ones, but not necessarily limited to them. The Skeffington Report (Skeffington, 1968) described ways citizens could carry out unpaid tasks in their contribution to participation in planning. On the boundary of participation as decision-making, and participation as employment on modest chores, are schemes in which local authorities offer residents the chance to examine and itemise problems like tree-planting, rubbish collection, parked lorries; to cost possible improvements; and then to choose between them for action up to the value of a certain sum with which the authority is prepared to part. This approach, cautiously and pragmatically experimental and adaptable to political changes, seeks to find smoother ways of adapting people to change.

Participation as paid employment or voluntary work under the guidance and control of a planning agency represents the citizen at his most co-operative. Participation as grass-roots radicalism represents the citizen at his most conflict-oriented. He participates by using against the authority all available and tactically appropriate sanctions—rent strikes, squatting, green bans, and other overt and preferably disruptive forms of protest. Such participation seeks to induce conflict. Basic to it is a belief that what is wanted is a challenge by the poor on behalf of their own interests to bureaucratic domination and abuse of political power. This approach fits with either social democratic or Marxist politics, depending on whether the intention behind organising the poor is short term and self-sufficient (for example, winning a specific struggle to stop a road or redevelopment project) or oriented towards a longer-term 'consciousness-raising' through specific issues. The Builders Labourers' Federation's green bans were an interesting combination of both those intentions. The Alinsky approach in the United States is the most widely known implementation of this model. Alinsky argued that the problem of the poor was lack of power, lack of any means of threatening the status quo. His 'formula' for organising the unorganised was to 'rub raw the sores of discontent' and to create 'hate objects' on which the poor could focus anger and frustration and turn it into productive protest.

The trouble with this theory is its naive assumption that there is a reservoir of popular enthusiasm waiting to be tapped. Now it is true that an eight-lane freeway pointed in its direction can arouse the most apathetic and conservative neighbourhood into direct action, but in general it is difficult to persuade people to serve on committees, form opinions on local issues, and hold their elected representatives responsible for the conditions of urban life. Most cases of participation in planning have been motivated by self-interest and have been conservative in aim rather than constructive. Wanting to prevent certain changes is not necessarily bad, but it can often create as many problems as it solves if simple prevention is the aim rather than the offering of constructive alternatives. For example, blocking a freeway proposal serves no purpose if its effect is to channel more traffic through residential streets.

Furthermore, such local activity rarely lasts long. It is not difficult to get people involved in campaigns to secure amenities, but much more difficult to administer them once they are secured. Residents' action competes for attention with all the other demands on people. And deprivation itself inhibits the social action of the deprived. As Cobbett pointed out 150 years ago, one cannot agitate a man on an empty stomach.

**Who benefits?**

These then, are some of the different reasons advanced in support of public participation. Each rationale has its own set of methods which reflect its values and purposes. If one supports the market research approach, then one concentrates on leaflets and public meetings, surveys and opinion polls. If one believes participation means decision-making, then one appoints citizens to policy-making boards or committees. If one

wants to nullify troublesome opposition, then the rhetoric of participation
can be a useful guide for co-opting radical leaders and diminishing their
stature in their supporters' eyes by giving them no real say. If one sees
participation as social therapy, then one involves people not so much in
deciding what should be provided, but rather in the actual provision of the
service itself. And if one thinks participation is the ultimate expression of
grass-roots radicalism, then one organises 'the poor' to fight 'the power
structure' with whatever weapons seem appropriate to the circumstances.

In practice, however, there are some intractable problems, whatever the
theory. If information is a precondition for successful participation, can
the public be informed without information control by public authorities?
At what levels of administration and policy can people actively participate?
Who participates? Who convenes and controls meetings? Who writes the
agenda? At what stage of the planning process? How? Questionnaires?
Surveys—of facts, or opinions? Who designs and executes them? Who
chooses the choices? Above all, what is participation expected to achieve,
and how is its effectiveness to be assessed. What happens when greater
openness about planning proposals multiplies objections and effectively
prevents any decisions from being taken? What forms of community
organisation best represent the underprivileged? If the most important
purpose of participation is to give 'ordinary' or 'poor' people more say in
decisions affecting their urban environment and daily lives, how does one
guard against the possibility that those who now win in the economic
market place will also win in the political market place created by
participatory procedures; or that the new procedures will be any more
'democratic' than existing ones; or that, by giving priority to the principle
of participation, one might, in the process, have to sacrifice other
principles, like equality (if a neighbourhood decides to use its power to
exclude blacks or Jews or public housing or homes for the mentally
retarded or whites . . .)?

One of the two great dangers of indiscriminate advocacy of 'power to the
people' is that it might result in a weakening of government capacity to
achieve many of the objectives the advocates themselves want attained,
while placing power in the hands, not of 'the people', but of a gaggle of
small groups of committed activists. The second great danger is that *more*
power is placed at the disposal of the best organisers, the middle class.
Thus, one is back at the point where it all started. 'Peoples' democracy
usually has nothing to do with democracy and little to do with 'the people'.
It is no answer to the problem of making government responsive to make it
more vulnerable to the pressure of those who merely shout the loudest or
are the best organisers.

### 'Maximum feasible participation' for whom?

The demands for participation and community action emerged in the

1960s in response to (among other things) over-centralisation of government, the indifference and unresponsiveness of public authorities, perceptions of the state as an arm of business interests, and so on. Radicals claimed that there could be no real social change until the disadvantaged groups in the community were involved in decision-making.

In the United States, community action programs were committed by legislation to a democratic ideal of participation, but left with little guidance as to the form participation should take or even its essential purpose (Marris and Rein, 1973). Those programs floundered in the transition from principle to practice. Who truly represented the people of the neighbourhood to be served by a program? Anyone who enjoyed an identifiable status was already, for that reason, partly assimilated into middle class American society. Anyone who could hold his or her own in a committee of public officials, business leaders and politicians was unlikely to be poor and uneducated. The formal organisation through which the projects authorised their decision-making inevitably precluded the effective participation of unsophisticated people.

How is a community to initiate its own projects and articulate its needs without challenging the authority of local government? And who, then, represents the community? Participation implied a devolution of power. Could the government concede that devolution without sacrificing the integrity of its own planning? The dilemmas were endless. In practice, each project was forced to choose between its institutional alliances and its sponsorship of redistribution of power within the city.

The use of the neighbourhood as the focus of community organisation brought people together not because they were poor, members of an ethnic minority, interested in a particular issue or service, or committed to a specific ideology, but because they lived in a target area. Consequently the issues chosen for action were not always or even usually those most salient to the poor. The search for issues on which everyone could agree usually resulted in taking action on the lowest common denominator. Neighbourhood groups also had difficulty maintaining class and ethnic mix. Middle class members tended to drive out the poor, and one ethnic minority usually took over a group. The costs to the programs in the amount of time required to maintain community groups were considerable, given that attendances fluctuated according to the presence of issues, that there was continuous turnover of members, and that many of the groups did not persist beyond a few months, especially when staff support was reduced. On the other hand, some groups stirred up so much local conflict that mayors began complaining to the Federal government about the programs.

No consensus ever emerged on what it meant to secure 'maximum feasible participation' of the poor. Did it imply an advisory relationship in which the poor were to be consulted as consumers whose opinions should be taken into account along with those of other interest groups? Or should the poor have a more substantial part in planning programs and policy-

making? Did it imply administrative control of programs by residents?
And who could speak for or represent the residents? These dilemmas
reflected a basic confusion over the meaning and intent of participation
programs which was never satisfactorily resolved.

Precisely the same dilemmas remain unresolved in the United Kingdom
in the efforts to implement the Skeffington Report's recommendations on
participation. Nowhere did this Report clarify the aims of participation,
and it made one very large and unsupported assumption—that participation is a pilgrims' progress leading from ignorance and apathy to
understanding, consensus and constructive action. One group of British
researchers found the results of participation programs to be meagre (in
contrast with the magnitude of the expectations surrounding their
introduction) because planners, untrained in the skills of mass communication, have relied on traditional methods (exhibitions, public meetings,
questionnaires) which have not been successful in involving the community. Another group of researchers put the argument more forcefully.
They concluded that opportunities have increased 'for a small, well-
educated, articulate group to have its say and make its influence felt. But
for the great majority of the public there has been no noticeable change.'
They pondered, therefore, that 'if participation is simply likely to give the
elite yet another means of manipulating the system in its favour, is there
not a strong case for abandoning the whole notion' (Hoinville and Jowell,
1972).

Another interesting case study of a proposed 'model community' at Fort
Lincoln in Washington highlights the difficulty of achieving anything
positive (as distinct from 'stopping things') and the important conflicts of
interest that participation programs can arouse. At Fort Lincoln a
proposed model community, economically and racially mixed and
involving substantial public housing for the poor and the blacks, was
opposed and stopped by the participation of neighbouring residents,
themselves lower middle class blacks who had just left the inner city ghetto
(Dorthick, 1970). The problem is that the participatory process provides
no way of weighting the interests of different groups among the
participants and adjudicating them in cases of conflict.

Clearly, then, overseas experiments in participation have not resolved
certain dilemmas inherent in the concept. And the most ambitious theory
or model of participation, that of improving the lot of the poor by getting
them into the act, has proved the most disappointing. In both the USA and
UK, participation has attracted well-educated and articulate groups and
continued to exclude the poor, ill-educated and apathetic while the new
procedures have delayed the planning process and frustrated planners and
politicians. Finally, the Fort Lincoln situation illustrates how giving the
principle of participation top priority may mean sacrificing other
principles that the government is also meant to stand for, like equality of
opportunity. How do innovators in social policy overcome fears and

prejudices and selfish local preoccupations with status and property values?

What then, can be concluded about the nature and desirability of participation programs from these and other, Australian experiments? Most obviously, there is no evidence to support the optimistic rhetoric of the past few years which asserted that participation is the solution to urban planning problems. In some cases it has helped solve conflicts, in others it has created new conflicts and solved nothing. In some cases participation has produced real innovations in planning, environmental and welfare goals, in others it has retarded such goals and deprived some sections of the community of their rights. In some cases participants acted in a completely self-interested way, in others they showed a sophisticated understanding of the metropolitan implications of most planning policies. On some occasions 'good planning' and a reasonable political decision system have been thwarted by 'bad participation', on others 'good participation' has corrected bad planning choices and improved the functioning of the political decision system. In almost all cases the poor, migrants, the young and the old have been excluded.

There seem to have been two levels at which people have wanted to participate. The first has been 'protest participation': trying to stop something, usually something that is part of a very large question of metropolitan policy, that is, a macro-planning issue—like the anti-freeway and anti-high rise public housing redevelopments. The second level could be called 'backdoor' or micro-planning issues: complaints about garbage, suggestions about pedestrian overpasses, local playgrounds, tree planting, improvements to public housing project designs, and so on. At the latter level, participation can usually produce a better result for the residents without threatening the 'professional integrity' of the planners or bogging the planning process down irretrievably. But the bigger issues—of housing, public transport, metropolitan growth—are issues of public policy that participatory mechanisms cannot deal with adequately, partly because participation is not fully representative and has none of the checks and balances of old-fashioned government.

## The relevance of participation

So the simple conclusion about, and the greatest charge against, the participation case is that it is irrelevant at the level of major policy issues. Participation is *not* a substitute for planning or for regular government. It is not an effective means of changing important policies. So why should participation be advocated, especially for the poor? The poor want better housing, better jobs, better schools. They want results. If participation can achieve these for them, then it is valuable. So far, it has not. If governments provide those things, as they should, the poor do not need participation. And if governments do not provide those things, then participatory mechanisms are unlikely to improve the situation of the poor. They are better off conducting their struggle at the point of production.

In other words, the issue of participation is irrelevant to the struggle of the poor for fairer shares of land and houses and jobs and services in this society, and therefore irrelevant to the main role of the Commonwealth in the cities, which is to improve those shares. It is arguable, though, that the Commonwealth has an important secondary interest in creating local community organisations which would generate a more radical understanding in the community of the nature of urban inequalities, thereby creating a climate for acceptance of more radical programs to deal with those inequalities. An essential requirement of such a program would be provision by the Commonwealth of information to local communities. More articulate involvement by the community is unrealistic without access to information. The provision of information should apply to issues involving Commonwealth responsibility, as well as to those for which it is not directly responsible.

Does that leave any reason for supporting participation at all? At the 'backdoor' level, yes. Participation may keep public authorities more honest and humane, more thoughtful and concerned about their functions and more considerate of the people they are serving than they might otherwise be. A more open planning process can reassure people by keeping them informed and consulting them. Such a process can usually elicit informed responses on questions of local detail—on issues that may not seem important to planners but are usually very important in the lives of those suggesting them.

Above all, if it can sometimes pressure or persuade public authorities to perform their duties more sensitively, public participation is worth a certain amount of expense and delay. In this respect the Commonwealth may find it useful to deal with representatives of different interest groups on issues for which it is directly responsible—for example, trade unions, representatives of the building industry, etc. While these are not in any way trivial achievements and concerns, they may seem to be so when compared with the magnitude of the expectations that have surrounded the debate and rhetoric about participation. It is time those expectations were given a quiet burial, as Barrington Moore has done: 'Though it does contribute to human dignity and is not something to be despised, sharing in decisions is no panacea, no general cure for the evils of injustice and arbitrary power' (Moore, 1972).

# Part Three  HOUSING AND LAND

MICHAEL BERRY

# 6 Posing the housing question in Australia: elements of a theoretical framework for a Marxist analysis of housing

Housing analysis in Australia is in its infancy. There is no shortage of answers—in government, academic or business circles—but the questions remain unclear. With the partial exception of the contributions of Stretton and Kemeny, the debate is cast along narrow economic lines, fixated on market processes and consequences. Housing as a social fact is isolated or abstracted from social reality and is treated as just another durable consumer good. There is, in general, no conception of how the production and allocation of housing is related to and conditioned by macro social processes, still less how the production, distribution and consumption of housing contribute to the reproduction of the Australian social formation as a whole.

What is needed most at this stage is a coherent theoretical framework which enables one to situate housing within a wider analysis of Australian society and to see housing as both a basic object of use or use-value and as a complex set of social relationships. A Marxist approach offers most hope for significant progress in this direction and the basic elements of such a framework are, therefore, sketched out here. Little attempt has been made to fill out the analysis. Many of the assertions are speculative, designed to illustrate general points, raise new questions, make new connections or direct research in new directions. It is hoped these will indicate the richness and promise of housing as a field for serious social analysis and provide, at this early stage, a programmatic statement of suggested directions for future research.

**Posing the question**

Housing in capitalist societies can best be analysed from three different but interrelated viewpoints (Berry, 1979). At the most visible level, housing in countries like Australia is a commodity, primarily produced and distributed through the agency of labour-employing, profit-seeking capitalists. At a second level, housing is a necessary element in the social reproduction of labour power, and hence in the reproduction of capitalism itself; workers need houses to live in and capitalists need live workers to exploit. Finally, at a third level, all housing requires land and, therefore, 'competes' with other possible land uses in the spatial patterning of the urban system. All three levels or dimensions to the housing question raise problems for analysis—some of these are addressed in the remainder of this chapter.

As a commodity, housing is extremely costly to produce—that is, it embodies a relatively large amount of human labour-time in production. This technological and social fact poses problems for the house-building capitalist who, in order to cover his capital outlay and reap an average profit must sell his house at a price several times higher than the average annual wage of workers. Housing, unlike many other consumer goods, can rarely be sold to final consumers, the workers, in a direct, once-over transaction. Consequently, surplus value extracted in the production of housing remains unrealised unless and until specific institutional arrangements arise to link the capacity of workers to pay to the high cost of housing production. This functional requirement creates the scope for the intervention of myriad non-productive capitals in the housing sector. Thus, the operations of mortgage lenders, financial institutions extending credit to builders and property firms investing in real estate, as well as the mediating roles played by estate agents, solicitors and other 'exchange professionals', all serve to encourage the realisation of housing and its final consumption by workers. The resulting profits actually realised by the productive, financial and commercial capitals advanced in the housing sector depend on the factors determining the conditions of exploitation in the building industry and the success with which financial and commerical capital reduce the time building capital is frozen in unsold houses. They also depend on the general conditions of exploitation and the competitive clash of individual capitals in the society at large. Of course, there are no built-in mechanisms which ensure that this basically anarchical process will satisfy either the real housing needs of all or even most workers, or the long-term interests of the capitalist class in general.

The link between housing and the reproduction of labour power is also complex. For capitalism to survive, certain pre-conditions for the capitalist mode of production must be routinely reproduced. The reproduction of the capital–labour relation entails, among other things, reproduction of the labour force—of labour power in its commodity form. 'The reproduction of labour power means not just the presence of a labour force (a demographic or physiological question, ie. 'simple' reproduction) but of a labour force which is adequately housed, fed, clothed, cared for, etc., to provide the work capacity (and acceptance of existing relations of production) required to perpetuate the productive system' (Pickvance, 1976:19).

There are, thus, two functional prerequisities—one material, the other ideological—underpinning the reproduction of labour power in a form necessary for the perpetuation of the system as a whole. The labour force must be suitably skill-differentiated and productive to fuel the process of capital accumulation. This requirement is embedded in the very dynamic of capitalist development. Individual capitalists are constrained by the logic of their position to accumulate or perish. Increasingly this has become dependent on raising labour productivity through the application of science to industry, the introduction of machines, etc., which, in turn, is dependent on the continuing intensification and polarisation of the division of labour. Modern industry increasingly needs a workforce differentiated into highly skilled and semi-skilled white collar workers, on the one hand, and increasingly deskilled blue collar workers, on the other (although 'deskilling' is now eating heavily into the lower rungs of the white collar workforce as well).

The workforce itself must be suitably acquiescent and disciplined to the requirements of modern industry. The mass of workers must be at least passively resigned to the necessity if not desirability of routinely submitting themselves to the capitalist labour process in whichever form the latter takes.

In order to satisfy these dual requirements, it is claimed, workers *en masse* must consume an 'appropriate' mix of key wage goods—in particular, in the areas of education, housing and health, or what one sociologist, Castells (1977a, 1978), has termed 'the collective means of consumption' (or 'collective consumption' for short). What this functional imperative means in the context of, say, Australian housing developments, can only be established by concrete analysis.

To date housing has been considered from the perspective of its production and consumption, as any commodity might be considered. But housing is not like any commodity, or even like other basic wage goods. It is a spatially fixed asset in consumption. The use-value of housing depends crucially on its location with respect to other urban activities, services and resources.

The land and housing questions are intertwined and, therefore, require an understanding of the nature of urban ground rent and its influence on the price and distribution of housing or, more accurately, of the house-land package.

There have been several recent attempts to extend Marx's analysis of agricultural rent to account for urban land use: the area is highly controversial (for example, see Harvey, 1973, 1974; Breugal, 1975; Edel, 1976; Berry, 1979). However, two major points clearly emerge. It is generally agreed that the effects of location are explicable in terms of a theory of differential rent. At any point in time, land at different urban locations offers different levels of profit in alternative industrial, commercial and residential uses. Capitalists (including house builders and landlords) compete with and amongst themselves, bidding land prices up until land at each location is turned to its most profitable use. The landowner reaps a windfall gain without any effort, simply by holding legal title to a particular 'portion of the globe'. The more advantageously located the land, the larger the gain. The periodic payment, real or implicit, from land user to landowner represents a ground rent and when that payment rises, due to increasing locational advantage, it is capitalised into rising land prices, the major source of so-called 'capital gains'.

This would appear to imply that capitalists compete for land in a free market. This, of course, is not so. Certain monopoly elements structure the land market. Large property developers exert an independent influence over the 'naturally' emerging pattern of differential locational advantage by clustering certain developments (Lamarche, 1976). Similarly, large land developers stagger or stage the release of new residential, commercial or industrial land, and by restricting supply, increase its rental and capital value. On the demand side, large financial institutions and conventional lending policies segregate 'final consumers' of land into separate submarkets tied to different sectors of the city, with implications for the forced extraction of rental payments over and above considerations of locational advantage. Finally, and most importantly, various state agencies impose arbitrary restrictions on land development use, particularly through zoning, building regulations and subdivision controls, as well as by controlling or influencing transport networks. The rental returns to landowners analytically attributable to these factors are explicable in terms of the categories, absolute rent and monopoly rent. The former exists whenever there are effective barriers to the flow of investment to particular land uses—that is, whenever there is a shortage of land for particular uses, due to government restriction or the monopolistic control of landowners. The latter exists whenever particular use-values supported by particular land uses are chronically undersupplied with respect to effective demand and those land uses are undersupplied due to government restriction or monopolistic control by landowners.

Consideration of the commodification and land use aspects of housing allows several of the elements discussed above to be included in an attempt to understand the real factors conditioning social exchange in the housing market. The current price or market value of a house—the everyday level at which the housing question is experienced can now be seen to reflect the following factors: firstly, the historic *price of production*, determined by the labour embodied and average profit rate ruling during construction; and secondly, *ground rent*—differential, monopoly and absolute. Two interacting points arise here. How is one to account for the observable fact that the prices of existing houses rise as the prices of production (that is, construction costs and/or the average rate of profit) of new houses rise? This phenomenon could be considered as a form of differential rent, not on the land, but on the house itself. By analogy with differential rent in agriculture based on the differential fertility of the soil, existing house owners reap a windfall gain due to the greater 'fertility' or lower value of labour power historically embodied in the construction of their houses. Alternatively, it could be seen as a form of temporary monopoly rent based on the inherent difficulty of significantly increasing the total supply of houses in the short period. For example, if governments arbitrarily increase the servicing requirements of new residential land or increase building standards, the cost of new housing will rise and the rate of increase in supply fall. Whenever the rate of increase in the demand for housing rises above this level, say because of the ready availability of mortgage finance or an increase in the net rate of household formation, the price of all housing will tend to rise. Existing house owners, therefore, enjoy the benefits of a temporary monopoly position.

How can one explain the fact, that house prices in equally accessible or well-located areas with respect to the central business district (CBD), nevertheless display vast differences? Of course, differences in the size and standard of houses are important, but not exclusively so, since similar differences exist between vacant residential land prices in such areas. Abstracting from other locational factors and the historically recent phenomenon of 'gentrification' provides several possible explanations. Ignoring the 'trade-off' models of orthodox economics (for example, Alonso, 1964), one might consider such differences as the result of differential rent based not on physical location, but on 'social location'. Higher income earners will pay more for a location in an homogenous high-income residential area than in a mixed area; consequently, the landowner reaps a 'snob rent' to the extent that the effective demand of 'snobs' is reflected in rising property prices which ration socially scarce locations. Alternatively, one could note that state intervention by local government and other planning authorities effectively structures residential space, creating new, or at least reinforcing and intensifying existing pockets of social exclusivity. In this case, landowners in such areas do not reap a differential rent but an absolute rent based on the restriction of capital inflow to particular areas. Landowners in exclusive areas will be well aware of the benefits of continued exclusivity and may use their political influence to 'protect local property values' as far as possible.

Another factor that is involved is *inflation*. Land and housing serve as a speculative hedge against inflation in capitalist societies. Thus, part of the rise in nominal house prices is explicable in terms of the fall in value of money and part in terms of excess demand due to speculation. *Revalorisation* is yet another factor. The useful life of a house can be extended through periodic maintenance, renovation and building extension, which partly accounts for price rises among established houses. Finally, there are *other market fluctuations*. Temporary and longer-term supply–demand distortions may be brought about by 'natural' factors, for example, the effects on new household formation of so called 'baby booms'—or state intervention. In the latter context, a vigorous public housing program may permanently influence house prices in the private sector; in particular, public rent policy and allocation procedures will influence the rent levels which can be charged by private landlords.

The three-dimensional approach to housing analysis, outlined above, can be extended by consideration of three areas of substantive theoretical (and political) concern: the significance of housing tenure; the relationship of housing to class structure and struggle; and the impact of state intervention in the housing sphere. While consideration of the two latter topics ties housing analysis into the central concerns of recent Marxist debate, some justification might seem to be required for the proposed focus on housing tenure.

Much conventional housing analysis focuses *only* on questions of tenure. Tenure appears as the basic analytical category with which all research and policy questions are approached and understood (see, for example, Murie, Niner and Watson, 1976). This one-sided and highly misleading emphasis stems from an over-concentration on the sphere of distribution and, in particular, on the form and consequences of market processes. Although not all-important, tenure is relevant to an understanding of the functional division of housing activities among individual capitalists engaged in the productive, commercial and financial sectors and the institutional means through which surplus value is realised and distributed. A concern for (more) owner-occupation dominates public political debate. The ideology of home ownership is very real, especially in Australia. For all these reasons it is vital to situate tenure within a wider analysis which integrates the economic, political and ideological elements of housing in a non-reductionist and non-functionalist manner. State housing policies cannot be routinely reduced to the functional requirements of capital accumulation, and dominant housing ideologies, like those surrounding owner-occupation, are not natural or eternal givens but real manifestations of real social processes to be understood as such before being transcended in theory and practice.

**Housing and tenure form**

Housing in Australia is primarily produced for profit and its realisation entails the intervention of firms advancing industrial (that is, building), commercial and financial capital. In this context, the different tenures have evolved as the legally sanctioned exchange mechanisms through which housing is allocated to final consumers and social surplus value distributed to individual capitals advanced. At this highly abstract and, therefore, crude level of analysis (for example, prior to any consideration of state intervention) the rise of owner-occupation and private tenancy as the dominant tenure forms *appears* as the natural result of the competition of individual capitals, each attempting to maximise profits and hence, the chances of economic survival. Housing will be produced and allocated to owner-occupiers and tenants only to the extent that capitals advanced at all stages in this process reap profits comparable to levels achievable elsewhere in the economy. In the age of classical capitalism, prior to massive state intervention, housing was not a profitable investment sector, or at least was only profitable at the human cost of overcrowding and appalling living conditions for the overwhelming mass of the population. However, with rising real wages and increasing state intervention, housing, especially in its owner-occupied form, has become more profitable as a field for capital investment. This is the case not just for firms advancing financial capital but for builders, exchange professionals and property developers as well—though not necessarily in a form which satisfies the functional imperatives of capital accumulation, still less the real needs of the population at large.

The actual patterns of tenure which emerge, the extent to which and the manner in which individual capitalists and the state intervene, and the ideologies which reflect and legitimate these outcomes, are conditioned by concrete historical circumstances and depend for their elucidation on concrete historical research. They can hardly be established in advance by theoretical fiat. Real differences exist between, say Australia, Britain and Sweden and should stimulate interesting work.

One under-researched area has been the role and impact of property capitalists in engineering significant local changes in the tenure structure of the existing housing stock. Little is known about the institutional form of capital engaged in the residential landlord function in Australia—in particular, the mix of corporate and petty landlordism. Limited overseas evidence suggests that large institutional investors typically face different constraints on and opportunities for profit-making, in comparison to small-scale landlords, differences which show up in practices relating to selection of tenants, investment in maintenance of properties, the importance of personal rather than market relations between landlord and tenant, vacancy rates, and so on (Harloe, Issacharoff and Minns, 1975).

There have been no successful large-scale attempts to survey private landlords in Australia; however, several small-scale, locality-based studies have been carried out. For example, the Centre for Urban Research and Action (1979) has recently completed a study of lodging and boarding houses in St Kilda, an inner suburb of Melbourne. The study focuses on the local economic and political forces which are contributing to the steady decline in the supply of cheap rooming accommodation close to the city centre. It raises interesting questions about the role of corporate investors and their links with members of the local council, which has pursued planning policies highly favourable to the renovation, even wholsesale redevelopment, of the aged residential housing stock in St Kilda. Renovation and redevelopment in inner suburban areas like St Kilda have generally resulted in a change of land use, as in the case of commercial development or the resumption of land for large public projects, or a movement of houses out of private renting and lodging into owner-occupation. An earlier study (Centre for Urban Research and Action, 1976) described the latter process in another inner Melbourne suburb, Fitzroy, where the prices and average turnover rates of properties rose sharply during the first half of the 1970s. Consequently, many poorer Fitzroy residents have been displaced, forced to move elsewhere, most often still in the inner suburbs, thereby adding to the demand for a dwindling stock of low-income housing in those areas. Private tenants have been especially hard hit during this process but, as the study shows, many of the original owner-occupiers have also fared badly. By selling out early in a period of rapidly escalating prices, they have left the lion's share of the capital gains to the wealthier, incoming owner-occupiers and the professional speculators, especially those investors and real estate agents whose names constantly have reappeared in the sales records of individual properties which changed hands several times in a single year. The impact of direct state intervention was dramatically demonstrated in Sydney by the completion of the Eastern Suburbs Railway, which resulted in the demolition of hundreds of workers' houses in Woolloomooloo and Kings Cross in order to provide a fast public transport link from the wealthy suburbs beyond, to and from the city centre. At the same time, on the other side of the city, the NSW Liberal Government had legislated a statutory authority to redevelop the historic, low-income housing area, the Rocks, to a high-cost commercial and residential enclave. Throughout the 1960s and early 1970s, the freeway building programs in most of the capital cities were sacrificing working class housing to the mobility needs of the well-off and the evidence, such as it is, strongly suggests that poorer tenants and lodgers have suffered most (Mullins, 1973).

Thus, at the level of commodity production, tenure appears as a central category for an understanding of the pattern of capitals advanced in the production of housing, the realisation of value in exchange and the distribution of housing costs and benefits in consumption.

It is clear, moreover, that housing is a basic element in the reproduction of labour power at the level of sheer physical survival. However, of far more interest and practical import today is the extent to which housing could, and in fact does contribute to the *extended* reproduction of labour power—that is, the extent to which the production and distribution of housing helps meet the functional requirements of a suitably skill-differentiated and increasingly productive workforce, on the one hand, and reinforces the ideological subordination of workers to the labour process, on the other hand.

It is far easier to see links between education and productivity, say, than between housing (especially in the context of different tenure forms) and productivity. Similarly, the ideological 'content' of mass education is more visible than in the case of housing. In fact, little more than theoretical speculation has been offered to date on the question of any link between housing consumption and productivity. The following brief comments should be seen as suggestions rather than substitutes for further work in this area.

Rising basic housing standards may be seen as related to rising health and education levels, which, in turn, are related to rising productivity. The links between housing standards and health are obvious and have all but monopolised the attentions of housing reformers for the past hundred years. In the case of education, King (1973) has suggested a link between the availability of private housing space to individual family members and school performance of children. It can be noted here that 'school performance' relates not just to the prospects for individual advancement and success at school, but also to the efficiency with which the whole school system entrenches capital-oriented skills and attitudes (Bowles and Gintis, 1976).

In a capitalist society owner-occupied housing is inherently more secure, from the resident's point of view, than rental housing. This follows from a basic difference in the nature of the social relationship between resident and capitalist in each case. Mortgage credit is long-term credit. The owner-occupier paying off a mortgage, protected by the general laws of contract, has considerable security of tenure in so far as he continues to meet the periodic repayments. The mortgagor does not invest his capital in the house as such, but in the capacity of the mortgagee to repay. The former, therefore, has no access to the use or disposal of the house except in so far as it impinges on his right to be repaid. In practice this means that the mortgagor will not evict, harass, or otherwise interfere with the owner-occupier's use of the house for the mutually agreed term of the loan, provided only that repayments are met. Once the mortage is discharged the owner-occupier becomes his own landlord and his security of tenure is total. For Stretton (1974), a house is a bundle of domestic means of production. An owner-occupier has total control of the uses to which these means are put (within constraints imposed by government regulation) and a strong economic incentive to accumulate further means.

The landlord, on the other hand, invests his capital directly in the house (and land). The law, both common and statute, defines and protects his rights to use and dispose of his property almost at will. If more profitable investments present themselves elsewhere, he will move his capital by selling the house and land underneath to someone else who will not necessarily want to keep it in its current rental use. In order to facilitate capital mobility the tenant must be expendable; short-term, even weekly, tenancies therefore characterise the private rental sector in Australia. In practice this means that the tenant lives with the ever-present threat of eviction, harassment and interference from landlords, especially in Australia where state intervention to protect tenant rights lags far behind

British, Scandanavian and Canadian experience (Bradbrook, 1975; Community Committee on Tenancy Law Reform, 1978). On closer examination it may turn out that housing security is related to such factors as health, school performance, 'positive' work attitudes and labour turnover. There appears to be no work done in this area, apart from general descriptive studies of geographical mobility and labour turnover, but clearly, useful work could be carried out.

Widespread owner-occupation encourages the spread of economistic orientations among workers and functions as a mechanism of social control. A long-term mortgage ties the material interests of the owner-occupier to conditions favourable for the steady receipt of wage-income, since secure employment and a secure, preferably rising, income are primary conditions for access to mortgage finance. The historical creation of a class of debt-encumbered owner-occupiers has encouraged the institutional separation of the economic and political spheres, a separation which Giddens (1973), among others, sees as the primary basis for the perpetuation of capitalism. In Australia, rising owner-occupation has almost certainly reinforced the arbitration system in directing workers' attention to narrow economic concerns—award levels, margins, relativity, penalty and overtime rates, etc.—and confining working class action, by and large, to disputes over the same issues. Future research could also profitably be directed at uncovering the links between rising owner-occupation and the prevalence of private, home-centred, consumption-oriented life styles, which provide opportunities for the expansion of capital accumulation.

At the ideological level, widespread owner-occupation has been instrumental in diffusing values and attitudes favourable to private ownership, in general, and private ownership of land, in particular. Little work has been done to gauge the real effectiveness of owner-occupation in this context but the rhetoric has certainly figured prominently in the legislative evolution of housing policy in Australia and Britain, especially on the conservative side.

Although housing and, in particular, tenure relations linking production and consumption imply certain functional imperatives for the reproduction of labour power, there is no structural logic in capitalist society which necessarily satisfies those imperatives. There is no automatic social mechanism or 'hidden hand' which matches the quantity, quality and tenure mix (as well as location) of housing to the needs of the system. In capitalist society, social wealth and productive power are allocated as a consequence of the unrelated decisions of competing, profit-seeking capitalists who will invest in housing only to the extent that adequate profits can be made there. Not only does capitalism not guarantee an appropriate housing outcome, there are strong reasons for believing that the outcome will be dysfunctional for the system as a whole. This follows from a consideration of the structure of the capitalist labour market which necessarily reproduces permanent and pronounced economic inequality.

This fact limits not only the spread of owner-occupation, but also the degree to which private landlordism flourishes. Historically this has meant that prior to state intervention, in countries like Australia and Britain, working class housing was almost entirely supplied by private landlords, who could make adequate profits only by overcrowding workers into poorly maintained, poorly serviced, often unhealthy dwellings. In the absence of state intervention or private philanthropy on a grand scale, the capitalist housing outcome threatened capitalism itself by threatening the routine supply of adequately housed, healthy and acquiescent workers. Further, the spatial logic concentrating large numbers of workers together in the industrialising cities was creating the geographical basis for militant workers' movements.

In other words, there is an inherent contradiction between two basic preconditions for the survival of capitalism (Stone, 1978). On the one hand, economic inequality must be reproduced through the labour market; on the other, workers must be adequately housed. It is this functional gap which creates the space for or functional necessity of state intervention in housing, although the success with which the state intervenes, and has intervened in concrete historical situations, is highly problematic.

It has already been suggested that the existence of ground rent as a social fact significantly influences the price, quantity, quality, location and distribution of housing. These effects are complex, both because of the differing tenure arrangements and the fact that housing can no longer be considered in isolation from other urban land uses. In Australia, the owner-occupier is not only the resident, the consumer of the house-land package, but also the land-owner and, therefore, the recipient of (implicit) ground rent and the capitalised value of accumulating capital gains. In the case of rental housing, however, tenants do not own the land on which 'their' house sits and they must pay a total 'rent' or hiring charge for access to shelter. In this latter instance, ground rent and capital gains accrue to someone else with clear implications for the real housing costs facing tenants, as opposed to owner-occupiers.

One of the most important effects of the flexibility of urban land in use and its scarcity in exchange is that the price of housing is higher overall than it would be where land was publicly owned and allocated on non-market principles, especially where absolute or monopoly rents are extracted. This, in turn, implies a higher-than-otherwise cost of reproducing labour power and an excessive drain on social surplus value. Private ownership of land encourages speculation in its future market value and deliberate attempts—through the market and through the state apparatuses—to manipulate space in order to maximise future rental gains. These factors all reinforce high housing costs to workers and are definitely not functional for the reproduction of capitalism as a whole. In Australia, the Victorian Housing Commission land deals' scandals are perhaps the most dramatic examples of the link between state-sponsored private speculation and inflated housing costs (Sandercock, 1978).

Contradictory effects exist here once the existence of tenure-related differences in real housing costs is related to the fragmented class structure of modern capitalism. It is not really possible to grasp the essentially residual status of private renting (and tenants) in Australia without considering the impact of land ownership and speculation. In general, land and the buildings on it will only be turned to rental accommodation when and where they cannot be used for other, more profitable purposes—that is, where and when credit (including mortgage) availability, general economic conditions or government regulation preclude the latter. In the case of petty landlords, dependent for short-term economic survival on the rents paid by their tenants, these background factors are closely determining. They have little room for manoeuvre; high vacancy rates, in particular, can be disastrous. Larger landlords, on the other hand, have more latitude. It will often pay them to evict sitting tenants and leave properties vacant—for example, where dereliction can be engineered in order to convince planning authorities and historic building enthusiasts of the necessity, even inevitability, of redevelopment. In particularly large redevelopment projects the rental incomes from current use are insignificant compared to prospective returns and the holding costs of subsequent delays in construction. In such cases there is a strong incentive to get sitting tenants out as early as possible. These considerations were, for example, clearly uppermost in the minds of large private developers who were invited by Sydney planning authorities to buy into the redevelopment of Woolloomooloo, a working class residential district on the edge of the CBD, during the office building boom of the late 1960s.

Large landowners and developers are also more likely to be able to bend the constraints hampering the operations of small landlords—for example, by exerting direct or indirect influence on the policies of local governments and other planning authorities, and through having greater access to finance and credit. Many finance and insurance companies have themselves invested heavily in land holdings and development in Australian cities in the post-war period (see chapter 4), a fact most visible in the occasional spectacular failure of such firms as Associated Securities Limited. It is worth noting, too, that the 'deliberate dereliction' redevelopment strategy is not a private monopoly. Public housing and road building authorities have also been criticised for these self-fulfilling practices (Hargreaves, 1975) although their rationale has, of course, been politically, bureaucratically or ideologically inspired rather than directly profit-related.

## Housing and class relations

*Housing classes*

Conventional economic analyses which treat housing like any durable consumer item—as a commodity essentially expressing a subjective relationship of utility between an object and the individual consumer, and an exchange relationship between objects or things—obscure the social relationships which structure the sphere of exchange and the individual process of consumption. The reality of class structure is denied by an approach which focuses on the spheres of exchange and consumption in isolation from the sphere of production. In such a problematic, questions of class mobilisation and fragmentation are not raised.

Recently, however, some urban sociologists, building on the original work of Rex and Moore (1967), have attempted to reintegrate housing and class analysis through a consideration of 'housing classes'. As originally conceived, housing classes were presented as analytically distinct from classes forged in production and were held to form an independent base for urban conflict; housing interests could cross-cut class interest leading to new and complex patterns of intra-class conflict, organised around the consumption of housing in the city, the latter conceived by analogy with the capitalist firm as an independent social entity.

The theoretical weaknesses inherent in this essentially Weberian approach have been stressed by Pahl (1975), Bell (1977, 1978) and Lambert *et al.* (1978), among others. In particular, the tendency to ignore the class determinants and consequences of relative access to housing renders any extreme notion of housing class arbitrary and misleading. At this level, housing class analysis fits within the general Weberian project of establishing separate and cross-cutting dimensions of social inequality, an approach which Marxists have long criticised as ideological, serving to direct attention away from the underlying structural reality of class division and conflict based in the reproduction of material life. There are, however, two redeeming features to this line of analysis. It does at least raise the right question, namely, the relationship of housing access to structured inequality, and contains an important grain of truth. Housing-related issues form a seemingly independent axis of social conflict in advanced capitalist societies, since groups can be observed actually mobilising around such concerns. However, this fact should not encourage the juxtaposition of housing and class analyses in opposition to each other, but should lead to the reinterpretation of housing struggles within a suitably developed class analysis. A major move in this direction can be made by explicitly relating housing access to processes of class fragmentation.

Furthermore, the earlier, crude analysis of housing classes has been overtaken by more promising developments, both Marxist and non-Marxist. Saunders (1978, 1980) has argued plausibly for the class-like behaviour of owner-occupiers as a group in Britain, especially at the local level. Castells (for example, 1977a, 1978) has consistently sought to locate the source of class-based conflict in advanced capitalism in the sphere of consumption rather than the sphere of production. For Castells, however, this stress on the politicisation of urban life and the problematic of collective consumption is not tantamount to dropping class analysis from the agenda, but follows from his attempt to uncover the structural transformation in class relations and crisis tendencies, which characterise the latest phase of capital accumulation.

Castells' work has been highly controversial in Marxist circles and has provoked a large critical response, as well as some very interesting concrete analyses. Mullins's (1977) reworking of his earlier Brisbane freeway study was probably the first attempt to use this approach in Australia. The conflicts which erupted around the Woolloomooloo redevelopment scheme in Sydney (mentioned above) might also be interpreted as a (failed?) urban social movement. The stake for existing residents was the maintenance of low-cost, well-located housing and neighbourhood facilities supporting traditional and mutually valued activities. This was clearly at odds with the interests of private developers whose profits depended on national, even international economic conditions and entailed the radical transformation of existing land uses in Woolloomooloo. Mobilisation against these attempted changes drew on the last remaining tenants in a particular street, an increasing number of incoming squatters and a few long-term owner-occupiers who had rejected the relatively high prices offered by developers to get them out. The organisational link with the trade union movement proved crucial. In particular, the green bans placed on demolition and construction in the area by the Builders Labourers' Federation (NSW Branch) sufficiently interrupted and challenged the routine operations of the property market and planning system to enable effective mobilisation on the political and ideological fronts. The contradictory nature of the requirements and consequences of capital accumulation to which Castells points is clearly apparent in this case: minimally adequate housing for inner city workers, the reproduction of a hermetically sealed but subordinate local working class community, the maintenance of relatively congestion-free mobility and the continuing depoliticisation of exchange relations were all threatened by the need of, and opportunity for, capital to remake space in the light of new profit imperatives associated with the minerals boom and the increasing penetration of foreign capital.

*Housing and class fragmentation*

It was noted earlier that capitalism has historically evolved a highly differentiated or segmented labour market. Collins (1978) has argued persuasively that labour market segmentation lies at the base of working class fragmentation in countries like Australia. Segmentation, he suggests, arises through the interrelated processes of 'primary' and 'secondary' differentiation of job types (described though not adequately explained by variants of the 'dual labour market' thesis); differentiation of primary jobs into 'subordinate' and 'independent' categories; racism; and sexism.

Underlying and driving these processes are historically specific developments in the capitalist mode of production, namely, changes in the forces of production and in the social relations of production 'internal' to the capitalist firm, on the one hand, and the evolving role of the 'industrial reserve army' of the unemployed, on the other. In the former case, the technological imperative of continuing capital accumulation and the need to reimpose tighter social control over the labour process have led to an increasingly polarised, skill-differentiated and hierarchically co-ordinated workforce. These developments encouraged and were reinforced by new and differentiated wage payment schemes and incentives, new promotion policies and differentiated 'career paths', the marginal intervention of capitalists into the provision of welfare services (paling into insignificance in countries like Australia when compared to the exploding welfare role of the state) and the development of 'scientific' techniques of management of which 'Taylorism' became the most notorious. Historical changes have also characterised the composition of the Industrial Reserve Army, so that women and certain socially subordinate ethnic or racial groupings have come to predominate in this area.

Intensifying labour market segmentation has entrenched income and status differentials within the working class which, in turn, have largely determined the relative access of workers to housing—in terms of quantity, quality, location and tenure. For example, owner-occupation has bitten deep into but not clean through the Australian working class. Mortgage finance has been monopolised by capitalists and workers in primary jobs, leaving secondary workers to compete for shelter in the private rental and chronically undersupplied and socially stigmatised public rental sectors. Since owner-occupation entails significantly lower lifetime real housing costs than private renting (Apps, 1973), the fragmenting and divisive effects of labour market segmentation are thereby extended and intensified. The immediate interests of workers are further divided, lessening the scope for unified working class action which the proletarianising effects of early capitalism promised, and increasing the scope for a more efficient overall exploitation of workers. These divisive effects continue past retirement. Below poverty-line age pensions increase the incidence of 'after housing cost' poverty for non-home owners in Australia. This has two main effects. It reduces the drain on surplus value posed by the support of the non-productive population; and it punishes non-home-owning pensioners for not having encumbered themselves with a house mortgage during their working lives, and intensifies the lifetime differencies in material and symbolic rewards of those locked in different segments of the labour market. Consequently, the individual benefits of owner-occupation encourage acceptance of the existing institutional structure of the workplace among 'higher' workers, and renders 'lower' workers dependent on relatively high-cost rental housing and hence, doubly dependent on or desperate for jobs no matter how poorly paid, dangerous, dirty and insecure. In Chapter 10 attention is drawn to the link between housing tenure and poverty in Australia; tenants as a group are significantly more likely to fall below or near the poverty line than owner-occupiers. Thus, by expressing and reinforcing the processes of class fragmentation, housing production and distribution arrangements in Australia are functional for the reproduction of capitalist relations in general, an outcome at odds with the dysfunctional effects of high housing costs noted above.

In a similar fashion, the promise of owner-occupation has encouraged the growth of two-income families and the willingness of women, in particular, to accept the worst jobs. The housing situation has intensified the exploitative capacity of capital, both through the lure of owner-occupation and the sanction of the rental alternative. This is most dramatically evident in the plight of non-English-speaking migrant women who work in declining manufacturing industries (Centre for Urban Research and Action, 1976), especially those hidden from view in today's cottage industry—the outworkers (Cusack and Dodd, 1979).

Since the individual benefits of owner-occupation and house–land ownership in general depend critically on the existence of accumulating capital gains, and since the latter depend significantly on rising ground rent levels, the fragmenting effects of housing production and distribution are intimately related to the land question. Where differential rent is the dominant form of ground rent the effects on class structure and conflict are internal to the working class. Landowners are merely the passive beneficiaries of capitalist exploitation and the real or fundamental interests of a fragmented and internally divided working class are still unambiguously opposed to the interests of the capitalist class. The situation changes, however, when other ground rent forms are significant.

In the case of widespread absolute rent, the effective monopoly of landowners imposes higher land and housing costs on both workers and capitalists, acting as both a cause of deteriorating housing standards and a further drain on social surplus value. Capitalists and workers here have a partial common interest in opposing landowners, at least to the extent of breaking the basis for their monopoly power.

The case of monopoly rents is less clear-cut: the extent to which class conflicts generated cut across or remain within class lines depends largely on the nature of the monopoly concerned. For example, in the case of 'gentrification', the chronic undersupply of appropriate housing types and locations supports rapidly accumulating capital gains and further working class fragmentation. A similar effect follows from the related phenomenon of 'ghetto-isation', where a chronic undersupply of housing available for low income and poor people (caused by factors such as the displacement effects of gentrification elsewhere in the city, the exclusive or 'redlining' policies of financial institutions, and the disincentive effects of government taxation policies) results in 'unnaturally' high housing costs for trapped minorities. However, where the basis for monopoly is widespread, universally high housing (and other land use) costs may express a general opposition of the interests of workers and capitalists in general, to the interest of the landowners and particular capitalists benefiting from resulting monopoly rents. This situation could arise, for example, immediately after a war when arbitrary general shortages of building supplies, labour and serviced residential land face a rapid increase in housing demand. The consequential redrawing of the conventional lines of class conflict would tend to be temporary, however, due to the eventual breakdown of the monopoly situation as capital flows into an excessively profitable area and the state intervenes directly to encourage such developments.

### Housing, class and sexual inequality

Housing is more than a durable consumer good; it is also a producer good, a bundle of domestic means of production which supports a thriving domestic economy (Stretton, 1974). Sex-structured nuclear families supported in detached suburban housing form an 'urban peasantry'. The peasant mode of production is characterised by small-scale production, unpaid labour and production for immediate consumption. These features clearly characterise housework, childcare and (privatised) leisure or recreation activities and relate centrally to the role of women in the family.

However, care should be taken not to push this analysis too far. The domestic economy is subordinated to the dominant capitalist mode of production in countries like Australia. Access to housing—and hence, the material supports of the domestic economy—are critically dependent on the (usually male) breadwinner's place in the capitalist labour market. Similarly, the capitalist economy has massively penetrated the domestic economy through the mass 'consumption' of recreational goods like television sets, swimming pools and backyard barbecues, the commercialisation of gardening, hobbies and house repairs, and, of course, the predominance of 'labour-saving' devices for housework. Household members are bound just as tightly to the hire-purchase company and mortgage lender as traditional agricultural peasants have been to the ubiquitous money lender. The nature and consequences of these relations defining and confining the urban peasantry could be usefully researched.

The 'new' urban sociology is centrally concerned with the social processes conditioning the reproduction of labour power. And yet, as Cass (1978a), Rose (1978) and Gamarnikow (1978) aptly comment, this concern has been developed seemingly in ignorance of the large body of work by feminists and other contributors to women's studies who are vitally concerned with the same reproduction processes. Women rather than men are the central agents for the reproduction of labour power. As Cass (1978b) argues elsewhere, the forced monopoly of childcare responsibilities by women is the basis of their association with unpaid domestic labour (and their material dependence), with obvious consequences for the reproduction of future labour power. Furthermore, women's domestic labour contributes substantially to the current reproduction of labour power, by way of routinely delivering up their men to the point of capitalist production, duly fed, clothed and sexually satisfied, *without* these expenses being born by capitalists in the form of higher money wages and the resulting drain on social surplus value which this would entail. In this sense 'women's unpaid domestic labour supports, like an infrastructure, the wage structures and profits of the industrial-capitalist economy' (Cass, 1978b:28).

Sexual inequality is a large and complex question and is concerned with far more than housing-related issues. However, to the extent that the provision, management and consumption of housing impinge on the subjection of women through domestic labour, a clearer overall picture of the social processes reproducing labour power can be gained by considering both aspects together. The following two cases illustrate this and point to directions for further research.

High rental housing costs and the lure of owner-occupation it has been suggested, have encouraged an increasing participation of women in the lower reaches of the capitalist labour market. However, this has not led to a corresponding redefinition of domestic economic roles. The symmetrical family has not arrived. Instead, wage-earning women are forced to bear the main burden of domestic labour in addition to their paid jobs. The housing situation has intensified the exploitation of women, helping to add a proletarian status in the capitalist labour market to their continuing proletarian status in the home.

Moreover, the more limited access of single women, especially those with children, to housing reinforces existing patriachal family structures. Women are less likely to gain mortgage finance in their own right and more likely to be discriminated against by landlords and agents (Women's Liberation Halfway House Collective, 1977; Faulkner and Berry, 1976; Women's Electoral Lobby, 1975). Women are thus tied more securely to the structure of the nuclear family, at least to the extent that they care to sleep with a roof over their heads.

The predominance of detached, owner-occupied suburban housing, reflecting the highly fragmented and individualised reward structure of modern capitalism, has expressed and reinforced a prevailing privatisation of social life, focused on the basic unit of the family. This is a picture of an urban peasantry minus one important element normally associated with peasant life, namely, widespread communal ties based on kinship and locality. To this extent married women are confined further to the institutional structure of the nuclear family, increasingly dependent economically on their husbands' position in the capitalist labour market.

A cautionary note should be sounded here: by the outlining of certain functional interrelations and prerequisites for the reproduction of labour power, it is *not* intended to imply that capitalism is routinely reproduced. Quite the reverse; a Marxist perspective should sensitise us to the likely existence of contradictions unfolding at all levels of the system. Housing struggles and the contradictory elements of the women's movement itself would be inexplicable without such a view; one consequence of the women's movement has been to increase the efficiency with which labour power is reproduced by encouraging women to demand their right to be exploited in paid as well as unpaid work.

Finally, in the spatial form of the capitalist city, the main configurations are determined by the competitive clash of individual capitals and the consequences of state intervention or urban planning. As a result, the outcome reflects the requirements of capital rather than the needs of people in general or women in particular, though not without unintended and contradictory effects for capital accumulation and social reproduction (Lojkine, 1976). Capital conquers space in an attempt to reduce circulation costs. Women's domestic labour has no direct value for individual capitals (though it has significant indirect value for capital in general) and in this sense is irrelevant or incidental to the latter's unco-ordinated attempts to structure space.

However, evolving spatial form may not be neutral or innocent with respect to the reproduction of patriachal social relations. The case of urban transportation nicely illustrate this point:

> The structure of transportation systems reproduces this devaluation of female labour by simply ignoring the spatial requirements of domestic labour and by immobilising women in the home (haven, community, neighbourhood). Thus, transport is organised to reduce, not the time spent shopping with babies and small children, but time spent travelling to work within the capitalist wage sector. Zoning policies have implications for transport systems and both interrelate to limit women's access to the city. (Gamarnikow, 1978)

This whole area is profoundly under-researched. Stretton (1970) has offered tantalising insights in his critique of male-dominated planning practices in Australian cities. Cass (1978a) has echoed these thoughts and extends the critique to the very manner in which urban social scientists conceptualise the processes of urban development and planning; for example, the term 'dormitory suburb' is coined to reflect (reinforce) the 'fact' that commuting men sleep there at night, not that women work there in the day. However, little progress has been made in reconceptualising and explaining spatial form from the viewpoint, not of capital, but of the reproduction of existing patriachal social relations; in short, how and why are women trapped *in* space through the contradictory processes which both confine them to the house home and insert them in the lower reaches of the capitalist labour market? Fodor (1978) and Coutras and Fagnani (1978) offer interesting analyses in this vein which should stimulate further work.

**Housing and the theory of the capitalist state**

It has not been possible to discuss housing in the contexts of tenure forms
and class without implicitly raising the problematic of state intervention.
This is hardly surprising since, together with the massive global
concentration and centralisation of capital, the massive scope, scale and
penetration of the state in social life is the major historical development distinguishing late from early capitalism. However, the piecemeal
invocation of the state during the progress of a particular theoretical
project—in this instance, the housing question—prevents a fuller understanding of both. At some stage, housing analysts must face up to the
pervasive presence of the state and to certain unresolved theoretical
problems in the contemporary Marxist debate over the nature, form,
functions and consequences of state intervention in late capitalism.

In spite of their wide differences, the common aim of recent contributors
to the debate on Marxist theories of the state has been to develop a theory
of the capitalist state which neither reduces politics to economics nor
assumes that state intervention will necessarily realise the class interests of
capital. Three common concerns have arisen: to relate state invervention to
the functional requirements of capitalism, namely to those pre-conditions
necessary for continuing capital accumulation and mass legitimation of the
capital-labour relation; to theorise the state as the 'arena for', 'expression
of' or 'determinant of' evolving class structure and struggle; and, to
uncover the form and consequences of developing structural or systemic
contradictions and hence, to cast light on the systemactic *limits* to state
intervention.

These concerns come together in the attempt to give meaning to the
notion of 'the relative autonomy of the political'. At the level of
commodity production, state intervention falls into three broad categories.
*Market-supporting* policies provide the institutional framework within
which commodity production and exchange occur: the most notable
examples here relate to legislative and executive actions which define and
enforce general property rights and the laws of contract. In the case of
housing, for example, the state has initiated policies and procedures which
regularise and facilitate land transfers. The introduction of the Torrens
title in Australia last century, together with the institutional forms
necessary to implement it, greatly simplified and encouraged the market
exchange of housing and other real property.

*Market-supplementing* policies, on the other hand, alter some of the
external parameters to which competing capitalists, wage labourers and
consumers react but leave these actors free to interact in the (changed)
market situation: subsidies to private builders, subdivision controls,
uniform building regulations, rent control, mortgage interest, tax
deductibility, interest rate policies, and the like all change the terms on
which buyers and sellers face each other in the housing market and alter

the production, pricing and distribution of housing away from a pure market outcome. In the US and the UK, for example, a combination of monetary restraints on interest rates, government mortgage guarantees and tax deductibility for mortgage interest paid has resulted in a significant diversion of finance into mortgage debt and lower real housing costs for the larger section of the population now able to afford owner-occupation. Much the same has occurred in Australia with the exception that interest rate tax deductibility has (until the 1982 Budget) played a much smaller role and the diversion of financial capital into mortgages has been largely engineered through direct controls over savings bank interest and investment policies. Similarly, the implementation of rent control in the UK, Sweden, and, to a much lesser extent, in Australia has kept private rents below market levels, or more accurately, below levels which would have ruled in rental sub-markets in the absence of government controls.

Market-supplementing policies may also reinforce existing patterns of sexual inequality and working class fragmentation. The Australian government's decision not to grant 'the dole' to married women reinforces their economic dependency, while the Federal Home Savings Grant scheme, granted on the familiar basis that to him who hath shall be given, further intensifies reward differentials embedded in the labour process.

Conversely, *market-replacing* policies suspend or exclude market criteria in favour of administratively determined criteria and significantly modify or complicate the operations of the dominant 'principle of organisation'— in this case, the capital–labour relation. Public enterprise most clearly expresses this sphere of state activity. Public enterprise may be oriented towards revenue-raising functions; the prevention of private monopolies and their dysfunctional effects for capital accumulation and legitimation; or the provision of use-values which are unprofitable to and therefore alien activities for private capital. Perhaps Telecom (the Australian Telecommunications Commission) offers the clearest Australian example of public enterprise oriented towards revenue-raising. State-controlled water and power services have prevented the development of restrictive private monopolies in these crucial sectors. Finally, public housing, mass education, public hospitals and road construction have arisen partly to fill the gap left by the desertion of private capital.

In the case of public housing, the state has chosen directly to involve itself in the management and allocation of (part of) the housing stock, which represents a *socialisation* of the landlord function. Thus, public housing is cheaper than (non-controlled) private rental housing, even where, as in Europe but not Australia, the state depends on the direct participation of financial capital. Moreover, Australian public housing is 'welfare housing', which reinforces the existing determinants of class fragmentation. Welfare housing is aimed at those too poor to gain access to owner-occupation or appropriate rental accommodation but sufficiently 'deserving' to be able to afford and willing to pay ruling public rents and to meet the conventional behavioural norms of the State housing authorities. The recent introduction of market-related rents and rent rebates by the last conservative government is an attempt to re-emphasise this policy. Public housing, to the extent that it enshrines prevailing prejudices in favour of the nuclear family, simply reflects existing patriachal relations in society. This tendency is apparent in a positive sense in the allocation procedures of housing commissions which favour family over single applicants, and in a negative sense, in the virtual absence of activity by public housing authorities in the provision of emergency (half-way house type) housing. It is true that some State housing authorities have granted 'priority' to 'fatherless families', especially in relation to high-rise flats which are difficult to let to anyone else. However, given the closely determined relationship of rebated public rents to below poverty line single-parent pensions, a husbandless wife-mother moving into public housing is largely exchanging one form of paternalistic economic dependence for another. At present, Australian public housing does not offer a reasonable alternative to women trapped within the family home; it is oriented (to a limited degree) to the needs of the deserted not deserting wife.

State intervention, through market-supplementing and market-replacing policies, alters the price and distribution of housing and (partly or completely) devalorises capital advanced in the housing sector. In the case of market-replacing activities, private capital is totally displaced—housing is 'decommodified'—and the proportion of social wealth turned to the production of use-values rather than production for profit is increased (see Berry, 1978).

The state clearly has a large impact at the level of reproducing labour power. Since the general effect of state intervention is to reduce the price of housing to (some) workers below prices which would have ruled in a free market situation, it is tempting to arrive at a functionalist analysis of housing policy: government policy necessarily lowers the price of a basic wage-good, housing, which reduces the value of labour-power and hence wages, thereby increasing profits in the interest of capital in general. However, this crude functionalist position is difficult to defend even on its own grounds. On the one hand, one could argue that the price of housing could be much lower than it is if government socialised not only the landlord function but also the financing and construction functions. If the state actually built all houses and financed them through general taxation, the price of housing could be lower than now, at least to the extent of cutting out the profits of dispossessed financial and building industry capital. In theory, the price of housing could fall to zero as in the case of compulsory 'free' education. On the other hand, by concentrating on the price of housing one is ignoring the other functions of housing tenure, especially those relating to the impact of owner-occupation, not to mention the functions of housing which have nothing to do with tenure, *per se*.

The poverty of a functionalist approach is especially obvious if the conflicting functional requirements of the housing and labour markets, stressed by Stone (1978), are considered. If the state relies on the housing market to provide adequate housing to workers it would have to remove a significant proportion of lower paid workers from exclusive economic dependence on the labour market—that is, on the sale of their labour power. This could conceivably be achieved through an extensive guaranteed minimum income scheme which allowed the mass of workers to compete for and stimulate the further supply of adequate housing. However, with the removal of the threat and reality of unemployment, of job competition among workers and insecurity and desperation, the class power of capitalists would totter, both because workers would not feel the same compulsion to deliver themselves up to the capitalist labour process and because the basis of and impetus for labour market segmentation have disappeared. Alternatively, if the state left the labour market intact and subverted the housing market, the latter would collapse, bringing with it most of the financial sector, since the total mortgage debt has grown in countries like Australia and the United States to a significant proportion of the total debt outstanding nationally. The state is, therefore, confronted by contradictory steering imperatives which prevent the routine management of the system in the interest of capital in general.

The relative size of the total mortgage debt raises further problems for the state in its attempts to steer the economy. When monetary policy results in rising interest rates which feed through into the mortgage market, potential owner-occupiers are priced out of the market and existing owner-occupiers suffer rising housing costs. In order to steer the economy in this manner the state must threaten both the functional requirements met by a thriving owner-occupied sector and the basis of its mass support. In this latter instance, an output crisis in the political system is transformed into an input crisis—that is, into a withdrawal of legitimation.

These criticisms are reinforced by a consideration of the complex inter- and intra-class conflicts which condition the emergence of housing policy in the real world, and by the existence of a further basic contradiction between the necessary intervention of the state in the management of collective consumption and the general tendency of the rate of profit to fall. In the case of housing policies, this latter contradiction implies that, where state intervention effectively reduces housing prices and restricts the degree to which the surplus value extracted in the act of producing houses can be realised as profit, the rate of profit will (tend to) fall, thereby exacerbating crisis tendencies in the economy which, in turn, threaten the prospects for continuing capital accumulation and the legitimation of the system as a whole (Berry, 1978).

The existence of conflicting interests and contradictory steering imperatives which result in profoundly incoherent and ineffective state intervention were clearly present in the Woolloomooloo case and in several other housing struggles in Australian cities during the 1970s. In

Woolloomooloo, these contradictions surfaced at the level of inter-governmental opposition. The Federal, State and local governments concerned faced different structural constraints and were committed to conflicting ideological positions on inner-city redevelopment. The Sydney City Council initially sponsored large-scale redevelopment in the area but subsequently baulked at the unforseen congestion consequences of massive and unco-ordinated high-rise office developments which threatened to impose high costs on and insuperable planning problems for the Council. The New South Wales Liberal Government, notoriously pro-developer, initially maintained a low profile on Woolloomooloo, but finally unleashed the repressive police apparatus to evict the squatters of Victoria Street and clear the way for redevelopments there. At about the same time, the Builders Labourers' Federation (NSW Branch) was taken over by the Federal 'organisation and the green bans progressively removed. Redevelopment, albeit on a much more limited scale, finally got underway in the mid-1970s, several years behind schedule and oriented towards luxury residential rather than office uses, as originally intended. The Federal Labor Government, notoriously anti-developer, then negotiated an agreement with the NSW Government, through the agency of the State Housing Commission, to fund spot purchases and renovation of existing houses elsewhere in Woolloomooloo for public tenants. In an amazing scene at the Sydney Town Hall, representatives of all three governmental levels signed an agreement which effectively reversed the earlier commitment to high-rise, non-residential redevelopment. In the euphoria of the moment the bitter lament of a bankrupt Woolloomooloo developer—to the effect that 'developers in Australia will never trust governments again'—went unheard. Clearly, the actions of residents and the unions influenced the outcome in Woolloomooloo. However, this occurred only in a situation conditioned by deeper structural forces associated with the internal organisational differentiation of the state itself, and its relation to more general social developments—in this case, the collapse of the office building boom, the slow-down in the building and construction industry, the emerging economic recession, the tightening fiscal constraints on state expenditures and, to follow Harvey (1978), the rhythm of capital accumulation as it oscillated between the primary circuit and the built environment.

Finally, the functional necessity for urban spatial planning arises from the contradiction between the increasingly necessary co-ordination of production and consumption activities over space and the fragmented (anarchic) nature of individual land ownership (Lojkine, 1976). However, the actual form which this contradiction takes, and the obstacles to successful state intervention implied will depend on the actual form which land-ownership takes, and hence, to the particular forms which ground rent assumes. Thus, where landed property has been significantly penetrated by industrial capital, the obstacles posed for capital accumulation will tend to be smaller than where land is monopolised by the remnants of a feudal aristocracy or the speculative operations of financial institutions. Little serious research has been carried out in this area, although a useful start has been made by Topalov (1973, 1974) in France and Massey and Catalano (1978) in England. In Australia, Sandercock (1978, 1979) has raised and begun to answer similar questions, particularly with respect to the growth and impact of financial land-ownership and the related limits to effective state land policy in capitalist society.

The main problem with these studies is that they do not go very far. In a review of Massey and Catalano's book, Edel (1979) points out that these authors' main contribution lies in the methodological approach which they adopt rather than any substantive analyses which they offer. In particular, he argues, their description of changing land-ownership patterns in the UK does not allow for an adequate explanation of the emerging political debate over land policy. Sandercock's recent work can be criticised in a similar vein, since when she moves from description to explanation her analysis threatens a fairly crude reductionism—a competing fractions' theory of the state which reduces politics to economics in an unproblematic and mechanical way. This dimension of the housing question offers the clearest case of useful analysis held up by the absence of an acceptable theory of the capitalist state.

I am only too well aware of the tentative nature of many of the arguments and comments advanced in this chapter. However, it seemed worthwhile at this stage to attempt to locate housing analysis within a wider framework related to the key concerns of recent radical political economy. Traditional analyses of housing in Australia have concentrated on market processes— on interest rate movements, new building starts, the level of mortgage debt, bottlenecks and excess capacity in the building supplies industry, general property price movements, mobility and vacancy rates and the details of particular public policies. It has been argued that these and other secondary elements are explicable only in relation to the basic structures of Australian society and a Marxist approach to this problematic has been outlined. Of course, the proof of the pudding is in the eating, not the recipe, and concrete research along the lines charted by this approach is the only measure of the latter's usefulness.

# 7 Reforming land policy

There was no land, they used to tell,
Old Miller couldn't trade or sell;
A clever man! I wonder how
He'll turn the lot he's stuck with now!
          Ernest Moll 'At the Grave of a
Land Shark' in *Cut from Mulga*, 1940.

While Edward Heath was Conservative Prime Minister of Great Britain during the early 1970s that country experienced a boom in property and land speculation of such proportions that it provoked a spate of critical literature. Books with such titles as *The Property Boom*, *The Rape of Britain*, and *The Property Machine* appeared, expressing concern at the social and economic consequences of this speculative boom. Their argument was that the large amounts of both foreign and domestic capital that were being invested in land and property speculation could have been much more usefully invested in productive enterprises that would increase national output and help solve balance-of-payments problems and un-employment. Further, it was argued that the property redevelopment boom that was transforming the face of central cities all over the country was causing massive urban and social problems.

When the British Labour Party won office in 1974 it attempted to reform the system of land development through the *Community Land Act*. A similar recognition of the harmful economic and social effects of land speculation in Australian cities and regions led the Whitlam Labor Government into a similar effort at reform through the Land Commission program under the Department of Urban and Regional Development (DURD).

How successful have these measures been? Is there further scope for reform?

The characteristics of problems caused by land speculation in Australian cities have been discussed elsewhere, with emphasis on the harmful consequences for the quality of urban life (Sandercock, 1979). A hundred years ago the great land reformer of the nineteenth century, Henry George, argued in his famous book *Progress and Poverty* (1879) that the wealth accruing to individuals from the private ownership of land was the root of society's ills. The continued existence of poverty at the end of a century of dramatic economic progress was, he argued, directly attributable to the inequities that followed from a system of unequally distributed private land ownership. The problem was compounded morally for George because he believed that the increase in the value of land that enriched its owners came about through no virtue or productive activity of theirs, but simply because increasing population and economic growth created more competition for the scarce resource that land is, thereby forcing up its market value.

While one might share George's moral outrage, his remedies are not convincing. He advocated that all existing taxes be abolished and replaced by a single tax on land. Taxing land at different rates according to the different uses to which it was being put would, he argued, produce a much more efficient pattern of land use. It would no longer be economical for owners to hold large areas of land, putting it to no productive use, and simply waiting for its value to increase. Such speculative owners would be forced to sell to those who were prepared to use the land for some productive purpose, and a more equal and productive property-owning society would result.

That much-too-neat solution was utopian in its nineteenth-century context. It bears little relevance to the nature of today's land issue, which has less to do with whether it is being productively used and more to do with its unequal distribution and with the inequalities that that distribution then produces, particularly in large cities.

In Australia most land is privately owned and is distributed unequally between rich and poor. People tend to think of wealth and well-being in terms of people's earned incomes. But in fact, those who *earn* most also own more land and reinforce their wealth through the *unearned increment* in land value; that is, through the increase in the value of their land which comes about because of overall levels of population and economic growth. And those who earn least are reinforced in their relative poverty by their non-ownership or their small land-holding for personal shelter, and by the limited location and quality of land available to them on their low incomes. So, particularly in urban areas where there is an ever-expanding demand for land, those wealthy individuals and companies who acquire large holdings on the city fringes or choice sites in inner and central areas are able to hold the rest of the community to ransom, in more ways than one, simply by sitting back and waiting for values to increase.

The land racket ruins planning, adds exorbitant land prices to the cost of public services, makes for reactionary distributions of wealth and provides a basic inflationary pressure. As long as the situation exists whereby the decisions of planning and servicing authorities enhance the value of one lot of land rather than another, the planning process must be secretive. Yet, during the 1970's, most of the criticisms of the operations of planning, housing and transport authorities have focused on their lack of understanding of and responsiveness to the people for whom they are planning; this, it is argued, is because there has been too much secrecy and not enough participation by or consultation with the public. Usually there is, at some stage in the process of preparing town plans, some form of public exhibition of the proposals to elicit public reaction. But by this stage all the other options have been considered and eliminated by the authority, and the public is never advised what the alternatives were and why they were eliminated.

This restrictive, closed planning process is the inevitable product of an attempt to plan cities without having any financial control over their basic resource, the land. A more positive, active, and open planning and development process with the widest possible involvement of the community at the earliest stages of the process could only begin to happen if land passed through public ownership during the conversion from rural to urban use, and if all non-residential land was held in public ownership.

It would seem reasonable, therefore, to conclude that land policy reform is an essential pre-condition to the success of most other urban problems. It is difficult to see how there can be a solution to the problems of city size, suburban sprawl, overdevelopment of the central city, inadequate provision of community facilities, excessively bureaucratic and techno-cratic planning, and so on, without first finding a solution to the land question. In his own way Henry George would have agreed with this conclusion. But no government has ever or is ever likely to attempt his solution—the imposition of a single tax on land which would abolish all other taxes (income tax, company tax, and indirect tax). However, some capitalist countries have tried in different ways to overcome the problem of unearned increment and inequalities in land distribution.

The country with the most thorough history of examination of the problem is undoubtedly the UK but Sweden has been far more successful in actually doing something about it. Between 1972 and 1975 the Federal Labor Government in Australia tried to establish a new land development policy but ran into many (predictable) obstacles. In one State (South Australia), however, there has been a successful policy in operation since 1973 (Sandercock, 1979). But overall, in Australia the private market has largely determined the way the cities have grown and land use planning has had only a minor influence.

Since the Second World War successive attempts have been made in the UK by legislation to find an answer to the problem of the unearned increment. The most important of these attempts generated bitter party political controversy and did not survive changes of government. The first such attempt, the *Town and Country Planning Act* of 1947, was in turn a partial implementation of a wartime inquiry into compensation and betterment which came to be known as the Uthwatt Report of 1942. The report made a number of recommendations, most importantly that the development rights in undeveloped land should be vested in the state. All future land required for development would be compulsorily purchased at a value reflecting its existing use and leased back at full market value, thus recovering for the community the increase in value of the land caused by the development. The Labour Government's *Town and Country Planning Act* vested all development rights in the state, introduced a 100 per cent tax on the realised difference between development value and existing use value, made planning subject to central control, made planning permission for all development obligatory, established existing use-value as the basis for compulsory purchase, and set up a global fund of £300m to compensate those people who lost existing development value.

For a number of reasons the land market and development process were stultified following the 1947 Act. The basic problem was that with a 100 per cent development charge the private sector had little or no incentive to develop or to sell their land for development, and the Act had not provided for the public sector to act as developer. On the other hand, it did give the private sector a strong incentive to hold on to their land in the hope that the policy would be changed. And it was. A return to Conservative government in 1951 resulted in the repeal of the 1947 Act and subsequent return to planning controls as the only form of regulation of land use.

The next attempt at betterment taxation (that is, a tax based on the view that gains made from the appreciation of property are in fact 'unearned' in some special sense and, therefore, belong to the community) was introduced in the *Land Commission Act* of 1967, again by a Labour government. This Act provided for a 40 per cent levy on increases in the value of land due to the granting of development permission, payable when it was developed. Apparently learning from the fatal flaw of its 1947 predecessor, the 1967 Act provided for the establishment of a central authority to assemble land banks for prospective development and generally to acquire, manage and dispose of land in the interests of the community. This intervention by the state in the land market was supposed to stabilise land prices and facilitate the release of development land. But the Land Commission did not survive the change of government in 1970, supposedly because it had achieved neither of those objects. Probably the stigma attached (since the 1947 Act) to the betterment tax had more to do with the supposed unpopularity of this Act, combined with naive political expectations that it could achieve a great deal in a short time. The full potential of the Act whereby, acting as a land dealing agency, the Land Commission could apply pressure to recalcitrant individuals and planning authorities for the release of land, assist and subsidise central area residential redevelopment, and override parochial boundaries, was never realised because its life was too short.

Experience in the country which has been most successful in land policy reform, Sweden, suggests that any program of state intervention on the supply side in the land market must be of a long-term nature. In Stockholm as early as 1904 the city purchased 2000 hectares of surrounding development land at a time when the developed area was only 1700 hectares, and three years later legislation was introduced which permitted municipalities to dispose of land only on a leasehold basis, in order to maintain planning control and to discourage speculation. This process continued until almost all the remaining undeveloped land had been acquired, some 12600 hectares by the outbreak of the Second World War. In 1967, continuing the tradition of an active land policy, Sweden decided that local authorities should control all future development land. Local authorities are required to purchase land up to twenty years in advance of need. Despite slow and cumbersome acquisition procedures, advance land acquisition policies appear to have stabilised land values and encouraged coherent planning policies.

This very positive approach to the twin land and planning problems, in which government takes responsibility for providing land for development by the private sector, is usually called development planning (as distinct from statutory or land-use planning). In order to initiate development the government has to buy the land. If it purchases well in advance of its needs then it can acquire land quite cheaply, service it, and put it on the market at a price or rent designed to cover its costs of acquisition and servicing. Because its costs are lower than the costs in the private sector (especially interest payments) it is able to compete effectively with private land developers. If it is able to increase the supply, the price of developed land will also tend to fall, which in turn reduces the price which private developers can afford to pay for undeveloped land. The government, or Land Commission, or municipality may retain ownership of the land through the period of development or it may sell or lease it on the condition that it be developed in a particular way within a specified time.

Development planning thus allows the government to control the volume of development and, within limits, the price of developed land. It is practised in varying degrees in different countries. In both Sweden and The Netherlands the municipalities have been mainly concerned to provide cheap land for low-cost housing and for government services. Private developers have remained important as suppliers of land for high-income housing and for some commercial and industrial development, and private firms have been responsible for much of the work in servicing land in the municipally promoted developments, and for most house construction. In the British new towns and in Canberra, the development authorities own all the land and take all the development decisions, and the market has almost no direct influence in determining land use. But both the new towns and Canberra are only a small proportion of the urban development occurring in the UK and Australia, and the enlightened development planning approach in use in them must be regarded as somewhat of an aberration from the dominant free-enterprise-dictated development process occurring throughout the rest of both countries.

Since one of the objectives of development planning is to avoid the increase in value which occurs in anticipation of urban development it is necessary either to purchase well in advance of the need for land, or to legislate to enable the government to purchase at less than market price. The Swedes have used the first approach, purchasing land since the turn of the century. The British new towns had to purchase their land when the development was initiated, but they were able to acquire it at existing use value. In Canberra the Federal Government purchased most of the site early this century. If a government becomes sufficiently active as a developer of land it can dominate the market and largely determine the general level of prices for both raw and developed land by its control over the supply. In both Sweden and The Netherlands municipalities are now responsible for about two-thirds of all land development and the aim is to provide land, especially for housing and government services, cheaply. To play this leading role in the land market the municipalities need adequate resources, which in both Sweden and The Netherlands are provided by the central government.

In Australia, up to 1972, the competition between land-use planning and the free market for development sites was relatively easily won by the free market forces. In the UK, the effort to employ strong land-use controls, combined with reliance on private sector initiative for nearly all private development, has inevitably resulted in a high price of land for development and property for redevelopment. The attempts of 1947 and 1967 to tax away all or part of the increase in value were unsuccessful, highlighting an inherent contradiction between controlling development through the use of planning restrictions and taxation policies, and relying on private initiatives to produce the volume of development necessary to keep property prices at a reasonable level.

More recently, both Britain and Australia have attempted to overcome this contradiction and pursue a land and planning policy more in line with the successful Swedish model. In the UK, the *Community Land Act* of 1975 attempted to provide a framework for ensuring that ultimately the vast majority of all development would take place on land either in, or which had passed through, public ownership. The objectives were virtually the same as those embodied in the 1947 and 1967 Acts: to enable the community to control the development of land in accordance with its needs and priorities, and restore to the community the increase in value of land arising from its efforts. The methods were different. Public authorities were to be empowered by the *Community Land Act* to buy land at a price excluding development value, but for a transitional period the basis of compensation would continue to be market value. The Government intended that the scheme would make the current system of planning more effective and would ensure that development was more positively planned, with local authorities being required to look up to ten years ahead in the planning of their programs of land acquisition. The implementation of the Act required a rather complex three-stage execution. In stage one, a full duty had not been imposed on authorities to ensure that land passed through public ownership but those authorities were supposed to be considering the desirability of bringing development land into public ownership. In stage two, a full duty was imposed in a particular area to bring land into public ownership but compensation was still at open market value. But the cost to local authorities was reduced by the deduction of the Development Land Tax, which could rise ultimately to 100 per cent. In the final stage, a full duty was imposed on all local authorities throughout the country and compensation for public acquisition prior to development was assessed at current use-value. (It was estimated that by the time that stage was reached an additional 12000 staff would be required to implement the scheme, 4000 of whom would have to be senior qualified staff.)

Was this latest Act likely to solve, once and for all, the UK's land and planning problems? Some observers suggested that this Act was a recipe for its own repeal. It was administratively complex (as was the 1947 Act); it required considerable valuation skill, and could produce both political and professional arbitrariness. There was never a political consensus as to the scheme's acceptability (it was attacked by more radical as well as Conservative opponents), and the Conservative Party leadership had promised to repeal the Act if elected. Its success depended very largely on the resources made available from the public purse, at a time when most public sector spending was being cut back by the Labour Government. However, all of this became irrelevant with the election in 1979 of the Thatcher Government. The Conservative Party honoured its promise: the *Community Land Act* was repealed in 1980 and for the third time in the post-war era the attempt to find a radical solution to the land problem had failed.

For some of the same reasons, the first attempt to solve this problem in Australia—a Land Commission program sponsored by the Federal Labor Government between 1972 and 1975—also met with limited success before it was dismantled by the subsequent conservative government. DURD, created by the Whitlam Labor Government, embodied in its series of urban programs the belief that a solution to the land question was central to a resolution of most of the urban and planning problems identified in the 1972 policy speech. In Chapters 3 and 4 the general constraints on DURD's programs were discussed—in particular its limited control over crucial private sector investment decisions. What must now be considered is the way in which private ownership of land, and the power of finance and property capital, interact to impose severe limits on the possibilities of land policy reform.

There are a number of ways of tackling the land question, from radical to moderate to limited solutions, representing a spectrum of political thought and a continuum of practicability. Under 'radical' proposals one would count all those schemes which aim at achieving a total nationalisation of all land. Moderate reforms would include public acquisition in advance of need for development (which could be thought of as temporary national-isation, for a period sufficient to achieve enough unification of ownership to enable positive and comprehensive planning without debilitating private development agencies), betterment taxes (which, if levied at 100 per cent in fact involve nationalising development rights), release of publicly acquired and serviced land on a leasehold basis, and possibly a capital gains tax on land profits. Limited reforms encompass the whole range of planning controls and taxes familiar even to conservative govern-ments—from zoning and floor space ratio regulations to taxes on the with-holding of land, and so on.

If guides to a successful land policy are being sought, then the third category of limited reforms can be dismissed. Planning controls have proved far too limited. Various attempts at taxing land have been counter-productive, resulting in increases in land prices as the tax is passed on to the consumer. The first category can also be dismissed, not simply because there are no working examples on which a policy could be based, but, because nationalisation is likely to be politically unacceptable and there-fore, impermanent; because the administrative corollary of total and instantaneous nationalisation is the horrendous task of comprehensive and simultaneous valuation of all land and property in the country; and because the need for absolute ownership and the flow of ensuing benefits have yet to be established.

On the other hand, under the moderate reform category there are two existing, successful models from which to choose. The British new towns and Canberra are examples of the public acquisition of all land prior to development, and subsequent release to the public under a system of leasehold tenure. This approach ensures comprehensive planning and enables the lessor (the state) to recover the increases in the value of land through a system of land rents, revised at regular intervals. Conditions written into leases allow planning authorities much more control over the timing of development, over what is built and what buildings are used for, than is possible under normal planning and building regulations. But the legal features of a lease are insufficient by themselves to achieve the advantages of leasehold. They must be supported by the economic feature—land rent—which must be reappraised regularly. In Canberra this was done at twenty-year intervals until eliminated in 1970, mainly because of popular opposition to the large increases which were imposed after every twenty-year reappraisal. Perhaps then, the approach to land development in Sweden and The Netherlands is the most appropriate model for Australia—the policy of public acquisition of land for development well ahead of need. (In South Australia the Housing Trust has been doing this since the late 1930s, for about 40 per cent of new development land, including a good deal of commercial and industrial land.)

But when in early 1973 the Federal Labor Government made public its intention of establishing Land Commissions in each State to try to stabilise and lower land prices it met with very different responses in different States. The Victorian Government was quicker than most other States in its response. At a Cabinet meeting on 16 July 1973, it directed the Victorian Housing Commission (VHC) to become an instant land banking agency and to spend $8m as quickly as possible on broad acres in an effort to be seen to be pre-empting the DURD Land Commission proposal. But the VHC paid urban prices for rural land and wasted $4.5m of public money (see Chapter 8). In the process it bolstered the land boom and protected the interests of property speculators. This was precisely the opposite of what DURD had intended to achieve through the establishment of a Land Commission; the Victorian Liberal Government, however, was acting in accordance with its long tradition of support for and defence of property interests.

In Chapter 4, the increasing importance of property investment to finance capital—to banks, finance companies and insurance companies— was outlined. The figures on the property assets and investment of the insurance companies speak for themselves, as do the figures on the profits made by estate agents, finance companies and property development companies at the expense of the public in the Victorian 'land deals' saga (Sandercock, 1979:41). Clearly, for finance capital, land and property ownership is just another (albeit increasingly lucrative) sector to invest in.

The existence of land-ownership by finance capital is central to political issues of land policy since, although the absolute amount of land owned by these groups is small, it nevertheless dominates the shape of the land market precisely because it is land-ownership by finance capital and, as such, is solely concerned with the maximisation of return on land. The dynamic created through this form of land-ownership has been partly responsible for the spatial problems of urban areas, and specifically for those aspects of the problems to which the *Community Land Act* in the UK and the Land Commission program in Australia were a response. Finance capital buys land and property in order to sell at a higher price. It produces nothing in the process. It speculates on urban dynamism and on the provision of facilities by the community and (metaphorically) takes today the value expected tomorrow. But in so doing, and forcing up land prices, finance capital is forcing up the costs of production for industrial capital and producing conflict within the process of capital accumulation. Perhaps then, as suggested in Chapter 4, the interest of finance capital in the profits of land-ownership is not compatible with the interest of industrial capital in accumulation. But what follows from this politically? Does the existence of this conflict between different sectors of capital provide the political space for reformist manoeuvre? The answer seems to be, yes it does.

It could be argued that the very establishment of a land commission program is a victory for industrial capital, since the stabilisation or reduction of the price of land lowers the costs of production of this sector of capital and thus aids profits. The history of the South Australian Housing Trust's operations in the Adelaide land market supports this argument. Since the late 1930s that organisation has not only provided cheap land for industrialists, but the fact that housing land was also cheap for the productive workers meant that labour costs could be kept down, thus further benefiting the industrial capital which could be attracted away from the eastern States. So a Land Commission is no threat to industrial capital, and may be a positive help to it. As for the different groupings of finance capital, whose main investments are in the central business area and on the urban fringe, Land Commissions threaten to undermine the latter, but not the former property holdings as a source of profit.

There is no doubt that finance capital has the power to halt reforms at the point at which they begin to threaten or undermine the private market. One example of this under the Labor Government of 1972–75 was the success of the campaign mounted by insurance companies to prevent the establishment of an Australian Government Insurance Corporation, a campaign similar, in many respects, to that waged by the banks against the previous Labor Government's attempt to nationalise them in 1947. But in the case of land there is a conflict of interest between the different sectors of capital. For industrial capital, the ownership of land is neither the result of selecting sectors for investment nor the basis of a separate economic or social function. Land is owned because it is a condition of production, and the cheaper it is, the lower the costs of that component of production. For finance capital the ownership of land is based on decisions about the most profitable avenues of investment. The more land prices are inflated the more finance capital stands to profit.

The existence of this conflict of interest may be of great help to land reformers. It may ensure, in the right circumstances, the success of a far reaching Land Commission program. But what are those 'right circumstances'? There are two remaining difficulties that must be dealt with before any optimism can emerge. Firstly, if those arguments about the fiscal crisis of the state bear any approximation to truth, where is the money for a land acquisition program to come from? Secondly, even if the money could be raised, could such a program ever win sufficient acceptance in the conservative States and amongst the majority of Australian people, to guarantee its survival through changes of State and Federal governments? Both these questions involve some consideration of the future role of the Australian Labor Party.

The ALP found itself in an ideological vacuum in 1974–75 when it was confronted with a contracting economy on the one hand, and on the other, a welfare program that demanded increased public spending. While the arguments about the fiscal crisis of the state are quite persuasive, their message of doom involves an assumption of a static political situation. There is only one positive direction for the ALP to take in order to avoid such a fiscal crisis and that direction is a more radical one. If the ALP wants to continue to exist as an agent of reform and social change it must find a way of financing its reforms, and there is now only one way to do that (unless one believes that the next era of capitalist expansion and economic prosperity is just around the corner). That way is through the expansion of democratic public ownership of the means of production, which means the nationalising of productive, profit-making enterprises; not necessarily all of them, perhaps the key companies in each sector of industry.

However, while that seems necessary as an overall strategy for the survival of the ALP as an agent of radical social change in the midst of the increasing fiscal problems of capitalist states, it is less relevant to the specific question of land reform. For while a sizeable initial capital outlay is necessary to finance the early operation of acquisition programs by Land Commissions, those programs ought to become self-financing as long as they are given sufficient opportunity to get underway, rather than being nipped in the bud at the first change of government. DURD's Land Commission program was in fact funded on just that assumption. Money was loaned to the State governments (that is, to those which accepted the idea) at long-term bond-rate interest, repayable over thirty years; but no payments were expected for the first ten years. Both the South Australian Housing Trust and the Swedish municipalities' land acquisition programs are self-supporting and provide working proof that the financing of such an operation is not a great drain on limited public resources.

What then, of the last remaining difficulty—that of political acceptability? What about that 73 per cent of the Australian electorate who are, or are becoming via mortgage repayments, home owners, and who therefore consider themselves to be part of the great property-owning democracy and who then identify with the emotive arguments used by those big property owners to rally support in defence of property rights, when what the big owners really mean is their right to make big profits from their properties? What of the argument that 73 per cent of the electorate itself has a vested interest in the increasing value of their quarter-acre block, even if only as a psychological hedge against inflation? The 73 per cent is a 1968 figure. Home ownership has fallen since then to about 63 per cent, according to the latest private polls. Since figures for older age groups lag on the way down, there must now be massive exclusion of the 'standard' young households. Now these are powerful popular arguments, but they are based on certain misconceptions and false analogies and it is in the sphere of public education about the real nature of the land problem and of property rights that there is a great deal of work to be done.

The first proposition claims that ordinary home owners identify with large property speculators and investors when it comes to proposals that 'threaten property rights'. This attitude may indeed exist, but it is based on a (deliberately fostered) confusion about the nature of property rights. There is, in real life, a world of difference between the property rights attached to my 'quarter-acre' block and those attached, say, to the thousands of hectares held by a speculator, finance company, insurance company, etc. My ownership of my quarter-acre block, in practice, gives me the right to occupy it for my own use (shelter, etc.) for as long as I choose, with a fair amount of psychological security, and to pass it on to my children. It does not give me the opportunity to profit and to exploit others. But if I owned several properties, or several hundred or thousand hectares, then the rights attached to that ownership are precisely the rights to profit, to exploit the labour of others.

Following this line of argument, then, suggests that the second proposition is also misleading—that all home owners have a vested interest in increasing property values. Why should they, when they can never collect or realise the increase in value of their own block because, if they sell in a generally inflating market, they must use all of that income to find another plot to live on and another house to live in?

If these mythical propositions could be displaced from their current position as leading community conventional wisdoms the land struggle would be well on the way to being won. That struggle can be won, democratically, but not without a fight. And if, during that fight, some of the weaknesses in the so-called democratic process and some of the inequalities in Australia's supposedly egalitarian society are exposed, so much the better. That recognition in turn might lead to broader struggles for more radical changes.

In practical terms it is safe to assume that no party on the right of the political spectrum would be interested in ending the land racket and reforming land policy, and that no party to the left of Labor will have any chance to do so in the foreseeable future, given the political complexion of the Australian electorate. What kind of radical or moderate or limited solution to the land question should the Australian Labor Party aim for then? And what combination of short-, medium- and long-term programs might ensure its success?

One can forget about that whole range of 'limited' solutions which include taxes on undeveloped land, betterment taxes and capital gains tax. It is clear from past experience that these taxes are either passed on to buyers, or cause restrictions in the supply of land (and, therefore, also cause prices to rise). The single most drastic solution available—nationalisation—can also be forgotten. That would be politically unacceptable (at least in the short term) unless, or perhaps even if it were achieved by generous compensation. Nationalisation through compensation would not only be absurdly expensive (could the Mint print enough money?) and administratively complex, but would require the intolerable creation of yet another bureaucratic apparatus.

In the past, those reformers who have advocated nationalisation have done so in the belief that ownership itself is the problem, that private ownership, by definition, is a 'bad thing'. But private ownership of land is not inherently evil: it depends on the rights which that ownership confers on the owner. Under Australia's existing system of property rights, private ownership gives people the right to profit from increasing land values and thus to exploit the labour of others. But if the meaning of property rights was changed, through legislation, to confer only the right to security of occupation under the existing use and the right to pass it on to one's children, that would remove the exploitative and inequitable element of ownership without in any way threatening to undermine that deep-seated psychological attachment most Australians seem to have to the idea of home ownership.

The opponents of such a change would be that minority of Australian voters who own more than their residential property and who do so precisely for the purpose of trading in and profiting from such ownership. Aside from those people and perhaps another small group with some expectations of capital gain from their quarter-acre block in old age, most households and most productive users of land should not feel threatened and would not be disturbed by such a change in the meaning of property (land) rights.

Working to change public attitudes to property rights then, should be the first priority, or short-term goal, of the ALP. But at the same time it ought to be pursuing a policy, when in government, of buying up land ahead of the need for urban development, at rural-use value, by compulsory purchase if necessary, and selling it cheaply into urban use. If this is done on a large enough scale it should arrest land price inflation and establish low prices generally for new residential land.

Some form of public agency, along the lines of the South Australian Land Commission would need to be created to implement this policy of state dealing in land. In New South Wales, under the Wran Labor Government, the NSW Land Commission is doing just that (see Postscript). In Victoria, an Urban Land Council created by the (right-wing) Hamer Government sold suburban blocks at about the same price as the going private sector rate, under specific instruction from the Government not to be too competitive. The newly elected Cain Labor Government had not moved to create a Land Commission by late 1982, but by then job creation and public housing had become top priorities, while the property market was in a slump that corresponded to the general financial slump.

But are Land Commissions enough? The answer is no, at least not if they are to be limited to dealing in the production of new residential blocks. For given the declining population growth rate on the one hand,

and the sprawl and scale of Australian cities on the other, the real pressure on land prices for the next twenty years may be focused on inner city and middle distance residential land, the more so if recently devised 'urban consolidation' policies are implemented by State governments. If this turns out to be the case, then one needs to go beyond the idea of a Land Commission that deals only with the conversion of rural to urban land at a fair price. One needs to think, in the medium term, about a public land dealing agency which is also buying whatever already-urban property they need for, say, low-income housing or any other public purpose (including conservation) at existing-use value.

Or, alternatively, consideration needs to be given to the nationalising of development rights. This alternative would be a logical outcome of the short-term program to change public attitudes to property rights. It would mean passing legislation removing the right of the individual to any profit from land transactions. It sounds acceptable in theory, but in practice it would involve considerable bureaucratic expertise and sensitivity and *that* may be harder to achieve than the change in public attitudes to property rights. So, preferably, the medium-term program would be to extend the operations of the public agency (Land Commission) into already-urban property acquisition. But if this is to be done by paying market prices (and it is impossible to see how else it could be achieved while still ensuring political survival), yet leasing or reselling cheaply, then the public agency will be losing money. How should these losses be met? Some part, possibly all of it, may be met by a tax on certain kinds of landed property in that region, or nationwide—say a tax on properties which produce incomes, or on owner-occupied houses valued above a certain level or which stand on land valued above a certain value, per hectare.

But ultimately, the question of where the money for any reform program is to come from is one that the ALP must face up to realistically; it is unlikely that the whole range of (often costly) reforms can be paid for by ever-increasing taxes on individuals. The ALP therefore must, in the longer term, respond to the current 'fiscal crisis of the state' with a policy of nationalisation of key productive enterprises. For reform of land policy is only the first prerequisite for the achievement of all those other urban policies identified so well by Whitlam in 1972. Urban reform is just one of many desperately needed social reforms in this country—all of which cost money. It would be unreasonable and unrealistic to expect that urban problems should have first priority in any future Labor Government. And precisely because of that, solutions to urban reform are inseparable from the more general economic problem of solutions to health problems, the status of Aboriginals, the condition of the education system, and so on. In a no-longer expansionary capitalist economy the state will have to find new ways of financing these programs.

In the long term then, the ALP has no choice (if it is to continue to be the party of reform) but to become a more radical, democratic socialist

**Table 7.1   Total lots produced by NSW Land Commission and their local government area**

| Year | Total lots | Penrith | Campbelltown | Blacktown | Fairfield | Warringah |
|---|---|---|---|---|---|---|
| 1976–77 | 326 | 326 | — | — | — | — |
| 1977–78 | 489 | 422 | 67 | — | — | — |
| 1978–79 | 849 | 439 | 410 | — | — | — |
| 1979–80 | 1064 | 711 | 353 | — | — | — |
| 1980–81 | 4248 | 2241 | 1483 | 29 | 220 | — |
| 1981–82 | 4102 | 1560 | 1321 | 23 | 573 | 35 |

| | Goulburn | Woollongong | Shellharbour | Muswellbrook | Gosford |
|---|---|---|---|---|---|
| 1980–81 | 26 | 237 | — | — | — |
| 1981–82 | — | 7 | 128 | 269 | 186 |

*Source:*   NSW Land Commission.

party, with a determined program of nationalisation of key productive enterprises. In the process, the urban land question will be solved. Land will be owned by its users and occupiers (not confiscated by the socialist state apparatus), or by public agencies. Which is not so far, after all, from what Henry George wanted to see happen 99 years ago.

**Postscript**

The NSW Land Commission (LandCom) began its operations auspiciously in 1976, inheriting from its predecessor, the Urban Land Council, estates in the western and southwestern suburbs of Sydney and in the Illawarra which had been acquired at favourable prices from developers during the previous year. It was able to add to its stock, often at even more favourable prices, during 1977 and 1978.

Beginning with a capital grant of $15 million from the State Government and $17 million in deferred interest loans from the Commonwealth, LandCom set about lot development, slowly at first, but in 1979 producing 1349 lots and in 1981–82, a total of 4102. Table 7.1 indicates the total lots developed each year since 1976–77 and their locational breakdown by local government area (LGA).

Apart from its lean (compared with other statutory authorities) management style, there are two aspects of LandCom's activities that are worth nothing. Firstly, as Table 7.2 illustrates, the average price of a LandCom lot has almost doubled since 1976–77. This is partly explained by rising costs of water and sewerage, but more importantly, by the much higher prices now having to be paid for its raw land. In other words, LandCom benefited from the property market crash of the mid-1970s, but is now paying market prices.

**Table 7.2   Average price of LandCom lots, 1976–82**

|         | $       |
|---------|---------|
|         |         |
| 1976–77 | 9 000   |
| 1977–78 | 9 260   |
| 1978–79 | 10 640  |
| 1979–80 | 12 240  |
| 1980–81 | 14 710  |
| 1981–82 | 17 000  |

*Source*:   NSW Land Commission.

This situation raises questions about the role of the NSW Land Commission, in particular, and the Land Commission ideal, more generally. If a Land Commission is operating in a market where the price of raw land is rising, then its only advantage (over the private sector) in the attempt to produce lots at a 'fair price' is that, theoretically, it does not have to build into its price the profit margins that are the *raison d'être* of the private developer. But if the Land Commission is operating under a government which is short of revenue and sees in the Land Commission's activities an opportunity to enhance its own consolidated revenue, then the whole purpose of providing cheaper land may be undermined. The NSW LandCom has in fact made a profit over the past years, but has been under increasing government pressure both to return some of this profit to consolidated revenue and dramatically to increase its lot production. The target set by the government during 1981–82 for the next three years was 20 000 lots, that is, more than double the production rates of the previous two years.

Perhaps this has become so urgent because the rapidly rising interest rates of 1981–82 have made the process of developing land for the bottom end of the market no longer sufficiently profitable to attract the private sector. In other words, the Land Commission may be stepping in where the private sector no longer wants to tread.

If the average price of LandCom lots in Campbelltown and Penrith over the last twelve months is compared with the average market price of private developers' lots in the same area, the pattern is interesting. Table 7.3 shows that while the (lower) LandCom prices have remained stable in Penrith and risen by 16 per cent in Campbelltown, the adjacent (higher) private sector prices have fallen dramatically, reflecting rising interest rates and the difficulties of people trying to raise loans to enter at the bottom of the land market.

**Table 7.3   Average price of LandCom lot compared with private developers in Penrith and Campbelltown, Nov. 1981–May 1982**

|            | Penrith | | Campbelltown | |
|            | LandCom | Private market | LandCom | Private market |
|------------|---------|----------------|---------|----------------|
| Nov. 1981  | $16 200 | $28 100 | $16 000 | $28 000 |
| Dec. 1981  | $16 350 | $24 900 | no figs. | no figs. |
| Jan. 1982  | $16 350 | $24 000 | $17 700 | $25 600 |
| Feb. 1982  | $16 150 | $24 500 | $16 700 | $22 400 |
| March 1982 | $15 780 | $26 800 | $18 600 | $22 000 |
| April 1982 | $15 750 | $25 700 | no figs. | no figs. |
| May 1982   | $16 250 | $23 900 | no figs. | no figs. |

*Source*:   Bob Hirst, NSW Land Commission.

The property market and land development process are among the more capricious elements of capitalist society and of capital markets. Property booms happen only with the active support of the capital market. Massive shifts of investment into property tend to reflect a lack of alternative investment opportunities, as happened, for example, with the collapse of the mineral boom in the late 1960s and decline of manufacturing industry in the early 1970s. (In Australia it is helped by the lack of a capital gains tax, too.) Above all, movements in the property market since the late 1960s have revealed the extreme openness of Australia to the world capitalist economy and the inherent jerkiness of the capitalist mode of growth.

In *Sydney Boom, Sydney Bust,* Daly (1982) provides the first account of the effect of international capital markets and capital flows on urban property development in one Australian city, highlighting the extreme mobility of property investment and the speed with which capital moves from central city office building, to residential subdivision, to shopping centres and hotels. Australian cities are vulnerable to the vagaries of footloose capital seeking new or more profitable avenues of investment. Yet when that same capital is withdrawn, when economic circumstances change and prospects look better elsewhere, it is usually left to the public sector to cope with the consequences.

With this kind of backdrop, the political economic role of a Land Commission comes to seem rather less radical than earlier claims have suggested. Rather, it would appear that the NSW Land Commission plays a role in the property cycle analogous to that of Keynesian demand management in the business cycle. When there is a downturn, the Land Commission bails out private landholders (albeit at a price far below those owners' expectations) and steps in to perform a function which is socially necessary but no longer sufficiently profitable to attract sufficient involvement from the private sector.

A final comment, related to the previous points, concerns the quality of the suburban environment being produced by LandCom. In recent years criticism has mounted over the failure of the Commission to provide any of the social infrastructure (as opposed to the physical infrastructure of water, sewerage, drainage, etc.) which, social research has argued for the past ten years or more, is essential for new development on the urban fringe, in order to help break down feelings of isolation and provide community support systems for nuclear families. Initially the Commission relied on the Department of Youth and Community Services and councils for advice on community services but it has now established its own community planning unit. Early efforts at community development were confined to the provision of advice and support for embryo resident organisations, and to making its sales counter available as venues for community activity; it later extended to the provision of community houses in collaboration with councils, and mobile kindergartens in conjunction with the Kindergarten Union. The Commission has also accelerated the provision of shopping facilities by itself building and leasing shops well before private enterprises could be induced to make such investments, and being prepared to accept a minimum rate of return on funds so committed.

Section 94 of the *Environmental Planning and Assessment Act* allowed councils for the first time to levy developers to meet the cost of providing community facilities. Some local councils (for example, Blacktown) were angry that LandCom appeared to want to evade its responsibilities. The chairman of LandCom (and others) has argued persuasively that this section of the legislation is unworkable and counter-productive, in that the costs of developers' contributions will be passed on to the home buyer in the higher price of the allotment, thus denying more people access to home ownership. The Commission has consistently advocated that because of the resulting social implications, limits to contributions should be set by the State Government and not left to councils alone, and this view has now been accepted.

Section 94 aside, it does seem that criticism of LandCom for failing to provide community facilities is, to some extent at least, misplaced. Rather, the problem is linked with the larger fiscal crisis in the financing of urban and social services at State level, which is partly a result of changing Federal–State–local financial relations, but more importantly a result of the squeeze on the social consumption expenses in the NSW Budget while an expanding capital works program provides the industrial infrastructure for private resource development (power stations, coal loaders, and so on).

In the 1982 climate of sharp economic downturn, with thousands of jobs being lost each week in NSW, and the three major statutory authorities (electricity, rail and water and sewerage) facing financial crises, it does appear that the Government is intent on urban development on the cheap.

LEONIE SANDERCOCK

# 8 Politics and land deals: the case of Melbourne

One of the most 'sensational' themes in the history of Australian cities has been the story of land speculation and the corrupt behaviour of politicians and public officials in high and low places associated with that speculation. In Melbourne the story began in the late 1830s, repeated itself in the 1850s, and 1880s, and continued into the twentieth century with only one changing emphasis.

It has been argued elsewhere (Sandercock, 1979) that there were three main characteristics associated with the land dealings or scandals of the nineteenth century. They were fuelled by an overabundance of 'building societies', 'land banks', 'land investment companies', 'mortgage banks' and so on, whose main interest was speculation in urban real estate. These ventures were based on a deeply held belief that it was impossible to lose money by 'investing' in land and that it was perfectly proper to profit from such speculative 'investment'. In the 1880s, in particular, they were marked by corrupt behaviour on the part of politicians and public officials, especially (but not only) those connected with the Ministry of Railways, for the ability to influence the location of railways and tram routes was a sure guarantee of a speculative fortune.

During the 1970s there was land speculation just as widespread as that of the notorious 1880s and with the same basic features. Insurance companies, finance companies, commercial banks and building societies have all used money deposited with them (deposited for life insurance, home savings, or superannuation) to speculate in land in the city centre and on the urban fringe. The speculation is still based on the same beliefs about safeness of and right to profit from such 'investment'. But in the twentieth century these beliefs have been backed by collusion between speculators and officials connected with the urban planning process. This collusion has centred around the zoning procedure—the basic tool of the statutory planning process. In fact, ever since zoning powers were introduced at local government level after the First World War, but especially since the introduction of metropolitan planning and the dramatic growth in population and economy after the Second World War, the ability to influence or gain knowledge of zoning decisions in advance has become the key to the twentieth-century land dealer's success. (Just as the ability to influence or gain knowledge of proposed rail and tram routes in the 1880s guaranteed many speculative fortunes in that decade.)

After the Second World War, partly because of the huge expense of providing services to the far-flung speculative subdivisions carved up in previous land booms, the Victorian Government recognised the need for some overall metropolitan planning process. The Melbourne and Metropolitan Board of Works was given planning powers based on the procedure of zoning. Since the 1950s, when population growth began to put increasing pressure on available serviced land, zoning decisions came to have crucial significance because of their effect on land prices.

Any individual or company owning rural land on the urban fringe which was (re)zoned for urban development was the instant recipient of huge profits. This was also the case with those who owned residential land in the urban area rezoned for flat development, or commercial or industrial activities, or land in the city centre with a planning permit to replace two storeys with forty-two.

With such easy profits at stake, some individuals and companies sought the inside running. That is, the system created the incentive to discover from the relevant authorities, before purchasing land, which land would be most likely to be the choice for rezoning to higher, more profitable uses, or which land might be the choice for purchase by a public authority. Or where land was already owned and there was some uncertainty as to whether it might be zoned to a higher, more profitable, use, owners could exercise their democratic right to lobby to influence the decision about the future use of their land. This can make nonsense of attempts at rational planning and efficient public service provision, especially when, within the planning and servicing authorities themselves, people with access to information or the power to influence decisions use that information or power for personal profit.

From time to time an enterprising journalist discovers what appear to be examples of this, and the public is treated to a 'land scandal', which is usually short-lived, often attracts libel writs on the newspaper, and rarely results in any kind of punitive action or policy change.

In Melbourne in the early 1970s a team of investigative journalists, led initially by Ben Hills and later by Tim Colebatch, became extremely skilled at ferreting out the details of such questionable land transactions. And what began as isolated, or one-off reports in 1973 and 1974, eventually grew into the gigantic, connected sequence of events surrounding purchases by and sales of land to the Victorian Housing Commission. This came to be known as the 'land deals' in 1977.

It began in earnest early in 1977 when readers of Melbourne newspapers were treated to stories about huge profits being made by big insurance and finance companies and rural landowners who held land on the fringe of metropolitan Melbourne. One company, Lensworth Finance (Vic.) Pty Ltd, for example, made $1.6m in two months by buying 405 hectares from a Sunbury farmer on 4 October 1973, and selling it to the Housing Commission on 16 December 1973. That land was not zoned for urban development by the metropolitan planning scheme—which raised a number of questions about the deal in the minds of the public. So did several other transactions and potential transactions—at Geelong, Mt Dandenong, and Mt Ridley, for example. The energetic *Age* reporters got to work and began uncovering information about the people and companies involved in these deals and their possible connections with public officials and politicians. By August 1977, they had succeeded in embarrassing the Hamer Government sufficiently to force the Premier to hold a public inquiry into three particular land purchases by the Housing Commission involving land at Sunbury, Melton and Pakenham. While the inquiry sat for three months there were daily press progress reports about the $4.7m profits made by speculators, waste of public money and alleged corruption and bribery. When the findings of the inquiry (the Gowans Report) were published there was a further spate of publicity, in March 1978.

The Gowans Report concluded that the Housing Commission 'paid too much for what it got, so that vendors or their intermediaries achieved rewards in excess of what the community thought was fair, and failed to fulfil the hopes of early land and housing relief which optimistic forecasts had led people to expect' (Gowans, 1978:13). It also recommended the institution of criminal proceedings against two individuals, a middle-level Housing Commission purchasing officer and a real estate agent, who appeared to have conspired 'to commit misbehaviour in a public office' (Gowans, 1978:192). In attempting to discover how these excessive (by $4m) prices were arrived at, who influenced decisions at what stage and for what reasons, the Gowans Report was on almost every page critical (but politely so) of those involved in the process—especially the Minister for Housing, Vance Dickie, and the valuers who had valued the land at or above the price sought by the vendors. But its overall conclusion was that there was insufficient evidence to justify an interpretation that the excessive prices were the result of a conspiracy to defraud the Housing Commission. Rather, they appear to have been caused by 'manifestations of greed and ineptitude'—the latter by the Housing Commission, the former by those dealing with it. The Report could not comment on the wider questions of political responsibility and financial prudence: these were not within its terms of reference. But *Age* editorials did so, on several occasions (26 October 1978; 23 March 1978; 15 October 1977; 5 November 1977) and *Age* 'Insight' articles continued to probe the questions that were left unanswered by the Gowans Report.

Thus, the 'land deals' continued to fester, and came to a new head in October 1978, with further disclosures and allegations relating to Housing Commission purchases excluded from the terms of reference of the Gowans Inquiry. The *Age* (25 October 1978) was again very critical:

> of the Hamer Government's competence and responsibility in its land dealings with speculators and developers... This whole sorry mess calls for a full and satisfactory explanation—if indeed such is possible from a government whose land dealings at excessive public expense and to the undue private profit of the quick and the smart have been a scandal that is still unfolding.

At this point, rumours that there would be an early election began to seem inaccurate. As 'scandal' was piled upon 'scandal' it became clear that Hamer would do better to call the election at the latest possible date, in the hope that the summer holidays and the non-return of Parliament would defuse the powder keg that had been mounting throughout 1978. As it transpired, that was a good tactical decision by the Liberal Party (LP). What some sources had regarded as an election-winning issue for the Australian Labor Party (ALP) did not amount to that. In the election campaign proper the LP did its best to ignore the subject of land deals, while the ALP made far less of it than might have been expected.

An *Age* (30 April 1979) poll taken a week before 5 May indicated that only 1 per cent of the population thought it was the key election issue—although 23 per cent thought that honesty in government was a key issue. The voting results tell the final story. The land deals were not the election winner that the ALP had initially hoped they might be. The following social, economic and political factors may help to explain why this was so.

Firstly, there is no evidence to suggest that the social values which underpinned the land booms and associated scandals of the nineteenth century have undergone any qualitative change whatsoever. In other words [and bearing in mind that a majority of electors (75 per cent of households) are property owners] people still believe that it is impossible to lose and perfectly proper to profit from 'investing' in land, and that those who are not doing it simply envy those who are. Land speculation does indeed deserve to be dubbed 'the national hobby', and, at a time when the rate of inflation of land prices easily outstrips the general rate of inflation in the economy, this attitude is, in narrow economic terms at least, understandable. Thus, there has been no more questioning in the 1970s than there was in the 1870s or 1880s of the ethics of, or philosophy behind, land speculation. One hundred years ago Henry George, in *Progress and Poverty*, argued that the increase in value of land that came about as a result of general economic and population growth did not belong to the individual who happened to own that land. Rather, it belonged to the community. Henry George had little impact in his own time, and those who today try to advocate similar arguments (though usually different remedies) find themselves preaching in empty halls.

What of the corruption often associated with land speculation and large profits? Well, the statue of Tom Bent still stands, just off the Nepean Highway, as a monument to the great Australian indifference to misuse/abuse of public office (Cannon, 1966), an indifference that is less characteristic of either the British or American public. Continued acceptance then, of the national hobby of land speculation, and a certain resignation about corruption in high places, is one way of explaining the failure of land deals as a powerful election issue.

Connected with that point may be the fact that arguments against speculation may be accepted in theory, but not in terms of economic realities (or the hip-pocket nerve, as the press are fond of describing it). Since a majority of Australian households do own, or are paying off, their own homes, they see themselves as property owners and, therefore, as having an interest in inflated land prices. Promises by the Opposition to set up a Land Commission to curb rising land prices may, therefore, only be attractive to that minority of the electorate who are trying to get on to the home ownership escalator. Australians are not renowned for altruistic voting patterns. Not many property owners would knowingly vote for a party that promised to halt escalating property prices.

Thirdly, in political terms, land scandals are obviously of far more concern to urban dwellers than to the rural electorate. One can only speculate about the importance of the land deals in the swinging of metropolitan seats away from the LP. But the ALP increased its rural vote so minimally that it must be concluded that most rural voters either have no interest whatsoever in this issue, or that they possibly have a self-interest in seeing land prices rise.

Finally, it would seem that despite quite extensive press coverage of 'the land deals', the public were not able to see the wood for the trees—in other words, the really harmful consequences of land speculation and associated 'land deals' have not been made clear to the people, either by the press or by the Labor Opposition. It is, therefore, not surprising that 'land deals' failed as a key election issue.

There are four harmful consequences of land speculation: the effects on land prices; on city planning; on the efficient provision of public services such as housing, schools, hospitals, transport and so on; and on the overall level of inflation. Rising land prices are the most obvious consequence of speculators' dominating the land market. (But, as has already been suggested, that majority of households which already own their quarter-acre block do not necessarily see this as undesirable.)

The activities of land dealers, however, also make it extremely difficult for planning authorities to plan the most desirable form of city growth; to stop suburban sprawl, to limit the size of large cities and to limit the amount of high-rise office space in city centres. Schemes drawn up by planning authorities to indicate directions for future urban growth have been used by speculators as form guides for future profits. The planning process has been exploited and its aims have been undermined both by individual speculators and by big companies with political influence and leverage, and the city has suffered as a result.

Further, government authorities providing urban public services have, like the ordinary home buyer, been held to ransom by the activities of speculators buying up land on the urban fringe and then asking inflated prices of those authorities.

Finally, there is the detrimental effect of speculative land dealing on the national economy—which has been described as the 'unacceptable face of capitalism'—for capital invested in property speculation could be far more usefully invested in productive enterprises that would increase national output, help solve balance of payments problems, and create jobs. But capital invested in land, to force up the price, does little or nothing to increase productivity and contributes in no small way to the general inflationary spiral.

Had these harmful consequences of speculative land dealing been demonstrated to the electorate, the issue might have carried more weight in the campaign. The failure of both the media and the Labor Opposition to attempt that task of public education ensured that the electorate simply got bored with the repetitive accusations of 'scandal'. But the stark electoral fact of life remains that any issue which is of purely metropolitan or urban concern will not produce a change of government in Victoria. The Labor Opposition must improve its rural vote if it is ever to win government. That is the lesson of the 1979 election. Conservatism, cynicism or indifference are no more and no less a feature of the Victorian electorate than they are of any other Australian State. The rural gerrymander continues to dominate election results, and as an *Age* editorial (2nd June 1979) pointed out (after the elections):

> In theory, Australia is a democracy in which all people have an equal vote in determining how the country is run. In practice, for a century or more the value of one's vote has depended on where one lives. Governments, both conservative and Labor (but most often the former) have tried to ensure that country areas dominated by their supporters have more MPs than their due, and city areas dominated by their opponents have fewer. This rigging of the electoral system is usually defended with sentimental phrases about protecting the interests of country voters. Yet in these days it is patently intended to protect the interests of the conservative parties themselves. In a close election, the system can cheat the electors' decision—and ensure that a Government remains in power despite the electors' choice.
>
> In Victoria's case the need for electoral reform is particularly clear. Both the Legislative Assembly and the Legislative Council are now so badly gerrymandered that, under Federal law, the electoral commissioners would be able to order an immediate redistribution... The onus is now on Mr. Hamer to come forward with a firm commitment to reform the electoral boundaries within the lifetime of this Parliament along the lines of one vote, one value.

Twenty-four days after the 1979 Victorian State election, Parliament resumed after six months' hibernation. There were plenty of new faces on the benches and a few new ministers, but the same party was running the State, despite what was probably the most 'scandal-ridden' campaign since the 1880s. Only hours after Parliament resumed, the scandals created headlines again and the Hamer Government announced a Royal Commission into Housing Commission administration generally, and its land purchasing practices in particular. The *Age* commented: 'To our knowledge, the only thing which the government knows today which it did not know two months or even six months ago, is that the State election is behind it' (6 June 1979).

'Police probe land deal', ran the *Age* headline on 30 May 1979; 'State calls in the fraud squad'. Accompanying the front-page article, Ron Tandberg's cartoon depicted Premier Hamer and new Housing Minister Brian Dixon on top of a cliff. Hamer's foot is on the clearly crumbling edge, as he says to Dixon, 'Here's some information Victorians must be given'. The next frame shows the two politicians walking away from the cliff edge just before it crumbles off and falls into space, and Hamer finishing the sentence, '. . . now the elections are over.'

Land dealings only become a political issue in Australia when they are associated with scandal. The vagaries of the property market, the boom-and-bust syndrome, and the inequitable distribution of urban land, are regarded as normal and natural. Clearly, the situation needs reform.

MICHAEL BERRY

# 9 Tenant politics

In the weeks prior to the 1976 Victorian election a new political force
appeared to be afoot in inner suburban Melbourne. During that period,
members of the Tenants Union of Victoria (TUV), based in Fitzroy, and
the St Kilda Tenants Union (TUSK), stood tenants' rights candidates in
the St Kilda and Prahran electorates. That campaign and subsequent
developments had a significant local impact at the 1979 and 1982
elections; in particular, consideration of the tenancy issue may explain the
size of the swing against the sitting Liberal member in St Kilda.

**Forced tenants and reluctant landlords**

Historically, the demise of tenancy as a political issue can be traced as far
back as the suburban boom of the 1880s. During this decade Melbourne's
population doubled to about half a million. The bulk of this growth was
absorbed in the rapidly growing 'outer' suburbs falling into what we would
now call the city's 'middle ring' (Hawthorn, Prahran, Camberwell,
Heidelberg, Essendon), where new housing was built almost entirely for
owner-occupation. The great land boom took the form of subdivision of
land for freehold sale and the speculative fever was fuelled by the interlocking vested interests of landowners, developers and politicians, the
rapid extension of public transport, the rise of building societies and other
credit institutions, an increasing marriage rate and the successful pro-
mulgation of 'the suburban dream' to own one's house. These factors
combined powerfully to influence housing aspirations in favour of owner-
occupation, appealing in particular to the upper reaches of the working
class.

Contemporary popular opinion equated home-ownership and good
citizenship. Property ownership was held to be uplifting for the common
man. It gave him a stake in the country and encouraged hard work, thrift
and respectability. More accurately, it gave him a stake in a capitalist
society and narrowed his concerns to security of employment in order to

meet his long-term mortgage commitments. This was well appreciated by conservative and liberal interests who were increasingly concerned by the sharpening class tensions accompanying the rise of the labour movement. Government housing policy, at all levels, has accepted and reinforced the bias towards owner-occupation. In the first decades of this century, government efforts in the housing area were characterised by inaction. The private market was left to deliver and distribute the goods while government intervention was generally confined to marginally adjusting background conditions—building regulations, conveyancing procedures and the like. During the 1930s the Victorian Government was finally forced to make a commitment to public housing and to recognise that the market had failed to provide adequate housing for the poorest sections of the population. However, as the charter and subsequent operation of the newly created Victorian Housing Commission demonstrated, 'public housing' meant 'welfare housing'. Government's role was to house only the most desperate cases while the overwhelming majority (some 95 per cent) were to find their way into owner-occupation or private tenancy. A number of commentators (for example, Apps, 1973; Patterson, 1975) have recently argued that this reduces to a non-choice, since the balance of economic and social advantages including security of tenure, freedom from harrassment, and the potential for accumulating wealth through capital gains, was and is overwhelmingly in favour of owner-occupation. Households which can afford to buy are being 'forced' into owner-occupation through lack of a viable rental alternative, a 'natural' market trend which has been strengthened by the continuing welfare perspective of government towards public housing, the continuing favourable taxation treatment of capital gains and imputed rental income accruing to owner-occupiers, and the tendency of State governments (especially Victoria's) to patch-up rather than replace antiquated landlord–tenant legislation which is strongly biased against the rights of tenants (Bradbrook, 1976).

Historically, government action and inaction in the housing sphere has largely ignored tenancy issues. There are powerful structural constraints operating in Australian society to prevent the placing of tenancy on the political agendas of government. Normative constraints follow from the entrenched ideology of home-ownership. Economic constraints are inherent in the widespread enjoyment of benefits by existing home owners who form a majority of the electorate. Government policy favouring tenants over owner-occupiers would risk a hefty electoral backlash.

Furthermore, by analogy with 'the road lobby', it might be possible to talk about 'the owner-occupation lobby' as that complex of groups and institutions with a common vested interest in the extension of home-ownership; every house sold into owner-occupation benefits builders, banks, building societies, insurance companies, estate agents, solicitors, valuers and government treasuries. This lobby is neither economically nor politically unimportant and must be taken into account by governments when framing housing policies. Finally, some constraints are inherent in the political system itself. In a parliamentary system based on geographical electorates, tenants may be concentrated in the wrong areas. For example, tenants are significantly under-represented in the crucial marginal seats on Melbourne's eastern fringe where much of the city's new residential construction is taking place and where the attention of the large numbers of young families with mortgates is naturally focused on the stances of government on interest rates, deposit gaps and planning requirements. Together, these constraints help explain the relative political neglect of tenancy interests in Victoria and place large obstacles before tenant organisations wishing to mobilise support for significant housing reforms.

**Organising tenants**

In 1975 the TUV was set up by a group of tenants, lawyers, welfare workers and other professionals. The new organisation was based in Fitzroy and depended heavily on volunteers and the resources of established community organisations like the Brotherhood of St Laurence. Its early activities were concentrated in several areas. A phone advisory service was introduced to provide general advice about tenant problems, rights and avenues of complaint. With the Fitzroy legal aid office, the TUV was able to offer free legal aid. The TUV also became involved in a number of action-research projects, such as the one funded under the Australian Assistance Plan in the outer-eastern region of Melbourne. This involved a survey of tenant attitudes and problems (Faulkner and Berry, 1976), the manning of local advisory centres and contact with interested local groups. In the sphere of action, advice and support were provided to tenants wishing to organise rent-rise strikes. Submissions for funds were also made to government agencies and private trusts in order to support TUV activities. Resources were clearly vital for a volunteer organisation dependent on the goodwill of longer established groups. Finally, the TUV assumed an advocacy role on behalf of all private tenants, through media interviews, frequent press releases, public meetings and the forging of links with related groups including the Housing Commission Tenants Union, emergency housing, and other groups loosely linked under Shelter, the new housing lobby.

In the same year a group of local tenants organised to form the St Kilda Tenants Union. St Kilda, with its extremely high population of low- to middle-income tenants and lodgers and significant degree of ownership by institutional and absentee landlords, offered fertile possibilities for mobilisation around tenants' rights issues. Early experience with the TUV advisory service had indicated the high level of legal and illegal abuse borne by tenants in this area. TUSK initially engaged in confrontation with individual landlords and estate agents. Politically, it focused on St

Kilda Council in an effort to reverse that council's traditional property-owner bias. The TUV hoped that the successful politicisation of tenants in St Kilda would provide a model for organising elsewhere so that, eventually, a popular base would emerge from which to fight tenancy issues at the State and Federal levels.

## The 1976 election: St Kilda and Prahran

Early in 1976 the TUV decided to stand candidates at the coming election. The seat of St Kilda was chosen for a number of reasons: it had the largest concentration of tenants in any Australian electorate—68 per cent of dwellings were tenanted while 52 per cent of the total stock were tenanted private flats; TUSK was well established and Brian Dixon, the sitting Liberal Party (LP) member, had undermined his credibility by unsuccessfully attempting to gain preselection for the neighbouring seat of Brighton. Finally, the swing required to unseat Dixon was not large and a tenants' rights candidate could hope to push the decision to preferences. The decision to field a candidate in Prahran was intended to underline the fact that the tenants' rights movement was more than a localised affair; although two candidates hardly added up to a political party it was decided to concentrate limited resources. Prahran was chosen because of its high tenant population (55 per cent) and proximity to St Kilda. In addition, Sam Loxton, the sitting Liberal member, had a weak record on tenancy issues.

Clearly, neither tenants' rights (TR) candidates expected to win. However, it was hoped that significant tenancy reform promises could be wrung from both major parties. To this end the TUV interviewed all candidates in order to determine their respective stances on tenancy issues and delayed its allocation of preferences until the last possible moment. In this limited sense, the campaign proved successful. The Premier promised to review existing landlord–tenant law in Victoria preparatory to bringing down a new Act, and to involve tenants and other interested groups in the review process by calling a 'community forum' after the election. The Australian Labor Party (ALP), sensing political mileage to be made from this late-appearing issue, made braver promises to extend the tenancy question beyond law reform to a general housing policy review. However, Labor's promises on tenancy were understandably hazy; they, like the Government, had but recently discovered the tenancy question in a political culture impregnated with the ideology of home-ownership. Eventually, the TUV allocated TR preferences to the ALP.

The outcome of the election was somewhat less successful. Both sitting members were returned with small majorities on the primary count. The TR candidates returned just over 4 per cent of primary votes in each electorate, a better result than that of other minor candidates.

The picture becomes a little more interesting when these results are disaggregated to the booth level. In St Kilda, TR received less than 2 per cent in each of the three Elsternwick booths, but 8 per cent in Argyle (St Kilda North), 7 per cent in Ripponlea North (Ripponlea) and over 5 per cent in St Kilda (St Kilda Central). The latter three booths fell into the areas with the most dense population of tenants in flats and where the TR campaign was concentrated, suggesting that tenants did respond to the tenants' rights issue more than the overall picture implies. More importantly, it encouraged the hope that future tenant electoral support could be mobilised. Conversely, in Prahran, the TR vote was much more evenly spread, varying from 3.5 per cent in Armadale to 5.5 per cent in Prahran East. It is not possible to accurately gauge the direction of TR preferences since both seats were decided on the primary count. However, Faulkner (1976), using the actual two-party preferred vote for the same booths in the two matching Legislative Council constituencies as a crude base, estimated that, in St Kilda, Labor would have received a substantial majority of the combined preferences of minor candidates, especially at the booths where the TR primary vote was concentrated. Faulkner drew the tentative conclusion that TR preferences would have gone tightly to Labor in St Kilda. Assuming the TR candidate had not simply siphoned off primary votes from Labor, this would suggest subsequent tenant gains might pose an electoral threat to the Liberals. Such was not the case in Prahran where TR preferences did not seem to be tightly grouped. Thus, Loxton had less to fear than had Dixon from a growing tenant movement in his electorate, since he could expect a substantial leak-back of TR preferences.

In summary, the 1976 election demonstrated, albeit to a limited degree, that in spite of the constraints, tenants could be mobilised to exert pressure for reform. Displaying remarkable foresight Faulkner (1976:7) concluded:

> 1979 should see a much stronger vote (for tenants rights) and, presumably, a loss of support for Dixon if the present preference allocation is maintained. If, further, the DLP stand a candidate, then Dixon's primary vote may be very low. 1979 could be crucial in the fight for St. Kilda.

## Between elections

Several months after the election the Government honoured its promise to call a community forum on landlord–tenant law reform. It was represented by three ministers, including Dixon and the new Attorney-General, Haddon Storey, who clearly saw the exercise as a one-off 'community consultation', preparatory to a new Act's being hammered out by an inter-departmental committee deep within the public service. The two-hundred-strong meeting, representing a large number of Melbourne housing and welfare groups, including the TUV and TUSK, had other ideas. A series of motions from the floor decided, first, to widen the debate to look at the Government's total role in housing, and second, to ensure continuing community participation in the evolution of a new Act, which would apply to all tenants, public as well as private. Subsequent developments focused on the second demand.

As a result of the forum and subsequent public meetings, the Community Committee on Tenancy Law Reform (CCTLR) was formed, comprising individual tenants, and lodgers and representatives from such widely divergent organisations as the TUV, the Real Estate and Stock Institute (RESI), the Institute of Applied Economic and Social Research at Melbourne University, and the Women's Liberation Halfway House Collective. The committee worked exhaustively over the next eighteen months in preparing a report with over 150 recommendations which was presented to the Attorney-General in mid-1978 and subsequently published. At the same time an inter-departmental government working party was preparing its own draft report on desirable reforms. A new Residential Tenancies Bill, incorporating some of the community committee's recommendations, was introduced to Parliament in December 1978 and was one of the unfinished pieces of business when Parliament was dissolved for the 1979 election.

The new Bill promised important improvements over the existing law but fell far short of many of the community committee's recommendations. In particular, it did not replace the old bond system, nor require landlords to justify evictions. Thus, the community committee and TUV attempted to mobilise tenant support, both to push for improvements in the Bill and as a counterweight to the lobbying power of property-owners and their representatives who had made a concerted attempt to discredit the community committee and sink the draft Bill. The RESI, which initially supported the Bill, vocally withdrew from the community committee and launched an attack on both the Bill itself and the committee's credibility (Wakefield, 1978).

A second arena of tenant action over this period was in St Kilda, where TUSK opened a shop-front advisory service and continued to lobby council. In the 1977 council elections TUSK stood candidates in each ward. The council's current policy of encouraging strata-titled conversion of rental properties to owner-occupation came under close attack, since it resulted in increasing numbers of evictions and, in the continuing absence of official concern for replacement housing, in hardship for displaced tenants.

Overall the tenants' rights candidates received 25 per cent of the vote (over 40 per cent in one ward) and although failing to win a seat, did establish a credible political presence. This result appears even more impressive in view of the appalling state of St Kilda's electoral roll and the *Local Government Act* which grants automatic voting rights to property owners (including absentee owners) but optional voting status to tenants.

These questions formed the basis of a TUSK campaign in 1978 to pub-
licise the inadequate state of the rolls and the degree of effective tenant dis-
enfranchisement at the local level. TUSK engaged during this period in a
door-knock campaign to get tenants on the council roll, paralleling the
ALP's continuing attempts in the area to get voters on to the State rolls.

During this period public housing once more surfaced as an important
political issue. However, development of the housing issue demonstrates
the relative political impenetrability of tenancy as an issue in a property-
owning democracy. The public housing debate was quickly focused on the
'land deals' scandal and the related issues of government inefficiency and
corruption. The much more far-reaching effects of the new Commonwealth–State Housing Agreement were largely ignored. That agreement
invited State governments to raise public rents to market levels and to meet
individual hardship through a system of means-tested rent rebates. When
similar legislation was introduced in the UK in 1972 the political backlash
was large enough to play an important part in the Conservative Government's downfall two years later. In Victoria the move scarcely raised a
ripple, in spite of attempts by the TUV and the Housing Commission
Tenants Union to mobilise support against the new policy and to delay its
introduction through court action.

The obstacles against tenant mobilisation were also clearly highlighted
during 1978–79 in relation to the battle over funding for the TUV
advisory service. Previously the Government had agreed to provide
$50 000 for the service, $25 000 each from the Housing and Community
Welfare Services Departments. The latter grant arrived, the former did
not. The then Housing Minister, Geoff Hayes, delayed payment after a
number of incidents in which the service offered legal aid and advice to
public tenants opposing the Housing Commission. He was later quoted as
saying that he would view grant requests from groups attacking the
Commission 'less favourably' than otherwise (*Age*, 2 May 1979). Similarly,
in a letter to the *Age* (8 May 1979) the president of the RESI (hardly a
disinterested body) attacked the TUV for using taxpayers' money for
political purposes by deliberately confusing its advisory and advocacy
roles. This confusion is inherent in the attempt by the TUV to couple a
'neutral' advisory role with the militant advocacy of tenant interests. The
political strategy of conservative groups like the RESI will naturally be
aimed at minimising the legitimacy of, and financial support for, tenant
organisations like the TUV, both to limit the effectiveness of advisory
services and to reduce the likelihood that these resources might be used
politically, to challenge, their entrenched vested interests.

## The 1979 election

After discussion the TUV and TUSK decided not to stand candidates in
1979. Instead they opted for the now familiar strategy of interviewing and

publicising the views of all candidates. Again, resources were concentrated in St Kilda, where TUSK distributed 15 000 copies of a pamphlet entitled, *The Tenancy Stakes: A Form Guide to the 1979 Election in St. Kilda*. This summarised the responses to interviews with each of the four candidates, especially their attitudes to eviction, standard fair leases, and bonds, which were seen as inadequately covered in the draft Bill. The Democratic Labor Party (DLP) candidate returned a 'late entry' and was described as a 'rank outsider'. The Australian Democrat (AD) 'weighed in' well on the three issues but was dismissed as having little chance of winning. Dixon was accused of 'delivering empty promises to tenants' in the past and found wanting on the three issues, so 'why back Dixon for another three-year wait?' The ALP candidate satisfactorily answered the eviction, lease and bond questions and was given qualified support—'untried, sounds good on paper'. Summing up, the pamphlet advised: 'tenants have more hope of pressuring the ALP than the Liberals for change'.

Labor attempted to 'ride home' the tenancy bandwagon by stressing the need for 'real' tenancy reform. On the other hand, tenancy issues were downplayed in Dixon's campaign which emphasised his Statewide contributions to community welfare, youth employment, and 'life be in it' programs. Dixon outlined his strategy—and his problem—thus: 'It's very hard to turn my mind to the St. Kilda situation because of the time and pressure in my work. Yet all my work would be lost if I lost St. Kilda.' The respective priorities of the major candidates were reflected in their final advertisements in the pre-election edition of the local newspaper. In Dixon's case, there was only a minor mention of the unpassed Bill, while Hardy chose 'real reform' for tenants along with the poor state of local schools and local traffic problems as his key issues.

The 1979 results are summarised in Table 9.1 and compared to the TR vote in 1976. St Kilda became the State's most marginal seat. Dixon's share of the primary vote fell by 8 per cent and he finally held the seat by less than 100 preference votes, giving the Government its majority of one in the new Parliament. What, then, are the possible reasons for this change?

The most-publicised explanation of Dixon's near demise centres on the anti-abortion campaign of the Right to Life Association (RTLA). On the basis of Table 9.1, the extreme RTLA scenario would go like this: due entirely to the RTLA campaign against Dixon all of the DLP vote (4.9 per cent) resulted from Liberal defections, while the remaining Liberal loss (2.8 per cent) reflected extreme defections directly to Labor for the same reason. In addition, 49 per cent of DLP voters were willing to direct their second preferences to the ALP.

In its extreme form this scenario does offer a possible, albeit unlikely, explanation for Dixon's loss of support. However, it provides only half an explanation for Labor's total gain (5.2 per cent). The difference may well have been due to the accumulated impact of the tenants' rights campaign

**Table 9.1 Percentage distribution of primary votes in 1976 and 1979 Victorian elections, St Kilda**

| Booth | Liberal 1976 | Liberal 1979 | Change | Labor 1976 | Labor 1979 | Change | TR 1976 | DLP 1979 | AD 1979 |
|---|---|---|---|---|---|---|---|---|---|
| *Elsternwick* | | | | | | | | | |
| Elsternwick | 56.4 | 49.4 | −7.0 | 38.2 | 38.9 | +0.7 | 1.5 | 5.7 | 6.0 |
| Elsternwick Sth | 60.0 | 51.3 | −8.7 | 34.5 | 35.9 | +1.4 | 1.4 | 6.2 | 6.5 |
| Gardenvale | 68.6 | 58.1 | −10.5 | 24.7 | 27.9 | +3.2 | 1.7 | 7.9 | 6.1 |
| Elwood | 55.0 | 47.3 | −7.7 | 36.7 | 43.3 | +6.6 | 4.4 | 3.9 | 5.5 |
| *Ripponlea* | | | | | | | | | |
| Ripponlea | 47.8 | 40.1 | −7.7 | 44.7 | 50.4 | +5.7 | 3.6 | 3.6 | 6.0 |
| Ripponlea Nth | 47.2 | 32.3 | −15.0 | 42.4 | 52.9 | +10.5 | 6.9 | 8.4 | 6.5 |
| *St Kilda* | | | | | | | | | |
| Elwood Nth | 49.4 | 43.4 | −6.0 | 43.5 | 46.1 | +2.6 | 4.1 | 3.5 | 7.1 |
| St Kilda | 45.8 | 42.4 | −3.4 | 45.3 | 49.5 | +4.2 | 5.2 | 3.4 | 4.7 |
| St Kilda Sth | 50.0 | 43.6 | −6.4 | 41.3 | 47.3 | +6.0 | 4.6 | 3.7 | 5.3 |
| *St Kilda Nth* | | | | | | | | | |
| Argyle | 42.9 | 35.7 | −7.2 | 45.9 | 53.8 | +7.9 | 7.9 | 4.9 | 5.6 |
| St Kilda Nth | 51.3 | 41.6 | −9.6 | 40.9 | 46.9 | +6.0 | 4.6 | 6.1 | 5.4 |
| *Postal* | 70.1 | 64.8 | −5.3 | 23.0 | 27.6 | +4.6 | 2.3 | 4.0 | 3.6 |
| *Absent* | 58.3 | 42.7 | −15.6 | 30.0 | 39.7 | +9.7 | 3.1 | 8.4 | 9.2 |
| *Total* | 52.6 | 44.9 | −7.7 | 39.1 | 44.3 | +5.2 | 4.1 | 4.9 | 5.9 |

*Source:* Returns released by the Victorian Electoral Office.

in St Kilda over the previous three years. Interestingly, the two booths in which Labor scored its biggest gains, Argyle and Ripponlea North, were precisely those booths which returned the largest TR vote in 1976. In the case of Argyle, Labor's gain in 1979 exactly matched the TR vote in 1976; could this have been a coincidence?

There are obvious and decisive criticisms that can be levelled at the scenario. First, it ignores the donkey vote. Assuming a donkey vote of 2 per cent, this cuts the maximum abortion vote for the DLP back to 2.9 per cent and places further strain on the second half of the argument by awarding 4.8 per cent of Liberal defections to Labor. On the other hand, it strengthens the preference argument since it suggests that more than 90 per cent of 'genuine' anti-abortion votes leaked to Labor.

Second, it ignores the impact of the AD candidate who polled more votes than the DLP. A percentage of Liberal voters may have defected to the Democrats for reasons unrelated to the abortion issue—for example, the unpopularity of the Hamer Government. On the preference front, the 50–50 split might even have reflected a positive leakage to Dixon from Democrat voters approving of his reputedly progressive (for some, soft) line on abortion. Third, it ignores the accumulated effects of ALP State and local efforts during the previous three years.

It also ignores other reasons for voting DLP and for giving second preferences to Labor. In a letter in the *Age*, the DLP candidate in St Kilda outlined some of these reasons: Dixon's failure publicly to oppose Moscow as the next Olympic venue; his membership of 'a scandal-tainted government'; and the ALP candidate's opposition to 'the extreme left, making it a reasonable experiment to prefer him'. He concluded: '. . . . . .the Right to Life scale emerged and had, in my opinion, little or no impact on my vote, unless it reinforced our loyal core voters whose reasons for voting DLP were already, as always, more than abortion alone' (*Age*, 12 May 1979).

Finally, and most importantly, it ignores the full impact of the TR campaign in shifting votes from Dixon. For example, in the case of Ripponlea North (a TR 'stronghold' in 1976), although the DLP vote was in excess of 8 per cent, Dixon's vote fell by 15 per cent. Thus, TR efforts over three years and three elections in St Kilda may have directly and indirectly increased Labor's vote and decreased the Liberal vote. Rather than add to this list of possible factors and explanations, the final nail can be hammered into the RTLA coffin by noting the dubious arithmetic of the extreme scenario, which implicitly assumes an unchanging electoral population. In fact, St Kilda has Victoria's highest transient population.

**The 1982 election: lead-up and outcome**

The uncertain career of tenancy law reform continued after the 1979 election. Following a period of public debate and comment, the Government substantially amended the 1978 draft Act in favour of landlord interests. In particular, in the December 1979 Bill, grounds for eviction were eased, tenancy issues were left with the Courts instead of being transferred to a new tribunal as suggested in the 1978 Bill, and the possibility of tenants' taking out an insurance policy as an alternative to the bond system dropped. After further minor changes a third draft was presented to Parliament—the Residential Tenancies Bill, 1980—and passed in November 1980.

In the period between the first and final drafts a number of interested groups lobbied hard. The CCTLR carried out a questionnaire survey of more than 300 welfare and housing related groups in Victoria and received overwhelming support for their original recommendations; they also presented the Attorney-General with a petition calling for the abolition of bonds. RESI, as noted above, had disassociated itself from the CCTLR by early 1979 and made direct representation to the Attorney-General opposing key features of the new legislation; it also wrote to members and all local government authorities criticising the Bill and advising them not to co-operate with the CCTLR's survey. At about the same time, TUSK and the Women's Liberation Halfway House Collective withdrew from the CCTLR and, together with the TUV, pushed more radical demands for reforms on the Government. In February 1979, the Property Owners Association (POA) was formed primarily to oppose the new Bill; POA was initially funded by Brick Security Ltd, a property investment firm that acts for landlords. This group lobbied directly and by way of public seminars, newsletters and letters to the newspapers. The Law Institute of Victoria also publicly opposed the Bill, calling for more conservative reform.

However, the major housing issue in the early 1980s developed in another direction. Between mid-1979 and mid-1982, first mortgage interest rates rose by 3–4 per cent at a time when average real wages fell (see Chapter 11). The extra financial burden was felt most by recent home buyers, many of whom had borrowed heavily, fully extending themselves at the lower interest rates. These households were strongly concentrated in the outer suburbs of the capital cities, the most marginal State and Federal electorates. Governments came under increasing electoral pressure to aid these households and ease the plight of home owners generally. It was not merely the implicit electoral threat posed by disgruntled home owners which concentrated the attention of governments in this area. The housing construction industry and unions, suffering the worst recession for twenty years, lobbied for government policies which would stimulate demand for new housing; this effectively meant policies which would increase owner-occupation among lower-middle to upper-middle income households who had traditionally moved to the new housing estates on the urban fringe. Tenants who were also suffering under the clamp applied by rising housing costs and falling real wages were not as strategically well placed to demand ameliorative policies. Melbourne's private tenants were, arguably, much worse off than most home owners as the rental vacancy rate fell to an all-time low, reflecting the cessation of new house construction and the increase in households unable to gain alternative access to owner-occupation. Public tenants, existing and prospective, bore the brunt of further large cuts in Federal expenditure on public housing and the phased introduction of market rents detailed in the 1978 Commonwealth – States Housing Agreement. However, in spite of the continuing plight of tenants, it was owner-occupiers and, especially, the ubiquitous 'first home buyer' who dominated the public stage in the months leading up to the Victorian election in April 1982.

The Liberal Party opened the campaign with two mortgage interest subsidy schemes as the central features of their housing policy. The first scheme offered means-tested subsidies to first home buyers over the first three years of their loans and was costed at $60 million. The second scheme—uncosted—involved subsidies on 2400 new house – land packages negotiated with private developers. The Liberals also promised a $400 stamp duty rebate to first home buyers. In reply, Labor offered a $10 million 'housing income guarantee scheme' to offset rising interest rates, an extra $35 million for low interest loans through co-operative building societies, control on maximum building society interest rates and matched the Government with alternative schemes for stamp duty rebates and interest subsidies for first home buyers. However, unlike the Liberals, the ALP also made a commitment to increasing the public housing stock, including the construction of 1200 new rental units in the first year of office, and amending the Residential Tenancies Bill in keeping with the original recommendations of the CCTLR.

Nevertheless, in spite of Labor's 'even-handed' policy, attention focused securely on the competing schemes for mortgage interest relief. A week after the Liberal Party policy speech, the Federal Government announced that bank mortgage interest rates would rise a further 1 per cent to 13.5 per cent, softening the blow by introducing a limited tax rebate on mortgage interest paid by recent first home buyers. The Victorian Liberal Party responded by scrapping its previously announced interest subsidisation scheme for first home buyers and 'reallocating' the funds to meet the extra rise in mortgage payments of all affected home buyers not covered by the Federal rebate. One newspaper reporter commented: 'The Victorian Government yesterday appeared to be thrown into a near-panic over the rise in interest rates' (*Age*, 19 March 1982).

However, in spite of their last minute attempts to both dissassociate themselves from the Fraser Government's housing and general economic policies and retrieve lost ground through widening mortgage interest relief throughout the electorate, the Victorian Liberal Party lost the 3 April election with an average swing to Labor of about 5 per cent on a two-party preferred basis. Labor picked up most of its gains in the middle-income home-ownership belt of electorates in the southern and eastern suburbs of the metropolitan area, though it also won St Kilda and held Prahran. Although the issue of mortgage interest rates clearly figured as one of the main reasons for Labor's victory, the same cannot be said for the tenancy issue. The new Cain Government's commitment to public housing and further tenancy reform was formally stated in the Party's policy document, *ALP Housing Policies*, released in December 1981, but was not well publicised prior to the election, especially in the hectic campaign period dominated by the mortgage interest question. It was only in St Kilda that tenancy maintained its saliency as an important local election issue, an exceptional situation dependent on special factors stretching back to the mid-1970s. The issues relating to tenancy had maintained their political significance in St Kilda as a result of the particular institutional and historical developments focused there over the preceding six or seven years; the 1982 election result in St Kilda is a special case, proving the rule that tenancy issues are inherently difficult to organise on to the political agenda in property-owning democracies like Australia.

The Labor candidate in St Kilda was Andrew McCutcheon, a well-known Melbourne architect and planner, ex-Mayor of Collingwood, ex-Board of Works Commissioner, member of Shelter and general housing activist. His campaign effectively ran for two years leading up to the election and was heavily concentrated on housing, especially tenancy, concerns. Labor's strategy was based on working with local housing groups and generating an awareness of housing issues among local voters. Tactically, the ALP focused on Dixon's poor record and commitment to tenancy issues while Minister for Housing—reflected in the delayed and watered-down provisions of the new Act—by comparison with McCutcheon's demonstrable interests and expertise in this field. The election result, summarised in Table 9.2, attests to the success of this strategy and the undoubted saliency of tenancy as a local political issue in an election uncomplicated by the cross-cutting concerns which arose in 1979. Thus, although McCutcheon's vote gain approximated the Statewide swing to Labor, Dixon's loss was substantially greater than the average swing

**Table 9.2  Percentage distribution of primary votes in 1982 Victorian election, St Kilda**

|       | 1979 | 1982 | Change        |
|-------|------|------|---------------|
| ALP   | 44.3 | 48.8 | 4.5 (4.7)     |
| LP    | 44.9 | 39.2 | −5.7 (−3.14)  |
| DLP   | 4.9  | 3.0  | −1.9 —        |
| AP    | —    | 0.6  | — —           |
| AD    | 5.9  | 4.3  | −1.6 (−0.1)   |

Note:  Figures in brackets represent changes in the statewide percentage shares of primary
       votes captured by the major parties at the 1979 and 1982 elections; AP represents
       Australia Party.
Source:  Returns released by the Victorian Electoral Office: *Age*, 20 April 1982.

against the Liberal Party (5.7 as opposed to 3.1 per cent). Once again, Labor's main gains were concentrated in the booths with the highest concentrations of tenants and where tenant organisations had focused their actions.

In the months since its election the Cain Government has proceded cautiously in the housing area, as in all areas, in an attempt to avoid being compared with the Whitlam Government and its 'big-spending' reformist policies in the early 1970s. Initiatives in emergency housing, the upgrading and self-management of public housing and the purchase of vacant housing from other government authorities, as well as the continuation of programs like the spot purchase of public housing introduced by the previous Government have passed largely without public comment. More importantly, the 1982 Budget increased expenditure on public housing by a substantial 80 per cent, about the same rate of increase as direct financial aid to home buyers, redeeming Labor's major election promises. Movement on the private tenancy front has been slower. At the time of writing the Government is about to introduce amendments to the Residential Tenancies Bill which will prevent the wholesale eviction of the State's remaining protected or rent-controlled tenants. However, no clear commitment has yet been given as to whether and when the more far-reaching demands of the CCTLR and radical housing groups like the TUV and Shelter, will be met. Government action in these areas will run up against the political-economic and institutional constraints described at the beginning of this chapter and reflected in the sorry progress to date of the tenancy law reform movement. There is no guarantee that a Labor government, especially one facing a declining local economy, will be any more willing or able than its conservative predecessor to move beyond these constraints.

MICHAEL BERRY

# 10   Whose city? the forgotten tenant

In this chapter the inter-related economic, social and political disadvantages inflicted on tenants as a group, and on poor tenants in particular are to be considered. The analysis is based on a survey of tenant perceptions and problems in the outer-eastern region of Melbourne (Faulkner and Berry, 1976). Although some social scientists, policy advisers and politicians are becoming aware of the patterns of inequality embedded in the operation of housing markets in Australia, almost no attempt has been made to view the system from the bottom, to comprehend the disadvantages and deprivations suffered by the housing underdogs.

## The economic disadvantages of tenancy

The 1972 national poverty inquiry clearly demonstrated the impact of the distribution of housing costs on the incidence of poverty. For most disability groups the proportion of households below the poverty line fell after housing costs were accounted for. Due to the relatively high incidence of home-ownership at all levels in Australian society, low income is partly offset by low real housing costs. This is particularly true for the home-owning aged, many of whom have paid off mortgages and are enjoying low and even negative real housing costs. However, this situation is reversed for the low-income renter. Tenants in Australia, and particularly private tenants, are more prone to poverty *after* than *before* housing costs: after rent has been deducted they are the least likely of all housing groups to have sufficient income to meet the other necessities of life.

From Table 10.1 it can be seen that 15.3 per cent of income units who fully own their houses are very poor *before* housing, and this group comprises 39.3 per cent of all income units in this category. Since this housing group accounts for only 26.2 per cent of all income units, its members are significantly over-represented in the 'very poor before housing' category, as are those who rent from public housing authorities,

156

**Table 10.1 Poverty in Australia by type of occupancy**

| Type of occupancy | Total no. of income units (000) | Percentage of total income units | No. of income units very poor before housing (000) | Percentage very poor before housing | Percentage of total units | No. of income units very poor after housing (000) | Percentage very poor after housing | Percentage of total units |
|---|---|---|---|---|---|---|---|---|
| Full ownership | 1026 | 26.2 | 157 | 39.3 | 15.3 | 38 | 14.5 | 3.7 |
| Buying | 1139 | 29.1 | 34 | 8.5 | 3.0 | 45 | 17.2 | 4.0 |
| Rents from Housing Commission | 183 | 4.7 | 26 | 6.5 | 14.2 | 18 | 6.9 | 9.8 |
| Rents privately | 839 | 21.4 | 86 | 21.6 | 10.3 | 107 | 40.8 | 12.8 |
| Rent free | 126 | 3.2 | 31 | 7.8 | 24.6 | 10 | 3.8 | 7.9 |
| Pays board | 378 | 9.7 | 18 | 4.5 | 4.8 | 18 | 6.9 | 4.8 |
| Board free | 225 | 5.7 | 47 | 11.8 | 20.9 | 26 | 9.9 | 9.3 |
| *Total* | 3916 | 100 | 399 | 100 | 10.2 | 262 | 100 | 6.7 |

*Source:* Adapted from Commission of Inquiry into Poverty, *Poverty in Australia: First Main Report*, April 1975, AGPS, Canberra, 1975, Table 10.2, p.159.

and, to an even greater extent, those who live rent- or board-free. The reasons are clear enough. Old people, many of whom are living on pensions or low savings accumulated in pre-inflation days, are themselves over-represented in the full house-ownership group. Housing Commission tenants have had (initially) to meet a fairly stringent means test. People living rent- or board-free are often the partially dependent children or aged relatives of couples treated as separate income units. On the other hand, private tenants are neither under- nor over-represented—they comprise 21.4 per cent of total income units, and account for 21.6 per cent of income units very poor before housing. People buying—that is, partly owning— their houses are significantly under-represented in this category. Although they comprise 29.1 per cent of all income units, only 3 per cent of this group are very poor before housing, accounting for 8.5 per cent of all units falling into this category. The fact that this housing group includes many younger and middle-aged people, at or approaching peak income-earning points in their careers, is relevant here, as is the built-in tendency of the financial sector to sift out low-income applicants for housing loans. Increasingly, access to housing finance is being closed to low and lower-middle income earners.

However, the situation is reversed once housing costs have been deducted. Whereas only 3.7 per cent of full house owners are very poor *after* housing, 12.8 per cent of private tenants and 6.7 per cent of all income units fall into this category. Private tenants make up 40.8 per cent of all income units very poor after housing, although comprising only 21.4 per cent of the total population. In other words, private tenants are twice as likely to be in serious poverty as are other housing groups. Relatively high housing costs, as well as low income, combine to keep an eighth of private tenants in Australia below an austere poverty line, and probably keep a similar proportion marginally poor.

The poor economic position of tenants was also apparent in the outer-eastern survey. Tenants were asked what proportion of their family income they spent on rent, and the results are summarised in Table 10.2.

Almost 60 per cent of the tenants were paying a quarter or more of their family incomes in rent. Credit institutions will normally only lend up to the point where loan repayments reach one-quarter of the *principal income earner's* income, although sometimes a portion of the second income earner's income will be included in the calculation. In other words, a majority of tenants in the survey were paying at, or in excess of, the maximum repayment rate allowed by most institutions financing home purchase, a fact which presumably accounts in large part for their continued status as tenants.

Blue-collar tenants and, in particular, those unemployed, on pension and in home duties, were over-represented in the group paying a quarter or more of their income in rent. Routine white-collar workers were significantly under-represented, indicating that the more affluent tenants in the

**Table 10.2   Proportion of income spent on rent**

| Proportion of income | Number | Percentage |
| --- | --- | --- |
| less than a fifth | 40 | 18.4 |
| about a fifth | 48 | 22.0 |
| about a quarter | 67 | 30.7 |
| about a third | 40 | 18.4 |
| between a third and a half | 7 | 3.2 |
| about a half | 12 | 5.5 |
| more than a half | 4 | 1.8 |
| *Total* | 218 | 100 |

*Note*:    35 tenants were not sure and 16 tenants did not answer.

region will find it much easier to move into home-ownership.

Tenants were also asked the number of rent increases incurred in the past year. Forty-seven per cent had incurred no increase, 52 per cent had incurred one or more increases, and 16 per cent had incurred two or more. In the highest number of cases (47), landlords or agents did not give any reason for the increase, thus bearing out the general experience of the Tenants Union of Victoria. In cases where reasons were given the most common were increased rates, inflation and increased maintenance costs. It is worth noting that in the past few years it has become increasingly common in Melbourne for leases to have additional clauses incorporated, automatically raising rents in line with quarterly changes in the Consumer Price Index. This escalating cost is, of course, avoided by the full home owner, and partly avoided by the part-owner whose mortgate interest rates have generally not risen as rapidly (although this appears to be no longer true in the early 1980s).

In only 6 per cent of cases did tenants receive more than one month's notice of rent increases; a quarter received a week or less, and 11 per cent received less than a week which, incidentally, implies a breach of the Victorian law, since in no circumstances is less than a week's notice to quit valid. The reaction of tenants to the rent increases is summarised in Table 10.3.

As the table demonstrates, almost two-thirds of tenants did not agree with the rent increases, but in all but one case they felt constrained to pay.

The claim by landlords that rising rents are necessary to cover rising maintenance costs is interesting in the light of the recent and substantial criticisms by tenants and tenant organisations concerning repairs and maintenance in general. Victorian law and standard leases do not require landlords to keep their properties in a reasonable state of repair. The largest single disadvantage of dwellings perceived by tenants in the survey (23 per cent) was that the 'place needs repair or is in poor condition',

**Table 10.3   Reaction to rent increase**

| Category | Number | Percentage |
|----------|--------|------------|
| Yes I paid—and thought increase fair | 52 | 36.4 |
| Yes I paid—did not have any alternative | 66 | 46.2 |
| Yes I paid—after I was told to pay or leave | 3 | 2.1 |
| Yes I paid—but did not agree with increase | 21 | 14.6 |
| No I did not pay—or agree to increase | 1 | 0.7 |

*Note:* For 118 tenants this question was not applicable, and 8 tenants did not answer.

followed by 'rent too high' (19 per cent). Moreover, of the 77 tenants who were promised repairs before moving in, 26 per cent did not have them attended to, and a further 16 per cent had to wait two months or more. In addition, in 11 per cent of cases, repairs judged necessary by tenants were refused by the landlord or agent. Partly as a result of the poor repair situation, a significant number of tenants (45 per cent) had carried out repairs to the dwelling for which they were not recompensed. The mean value of self-repairs was $54, and in 16 per cent of cases the value reached or exceeded $100. When this figure is added to the bonds paid, rent in advance, fees for the connection of basic services, etc., the tenant, particularly on a low income, can be severely disadvantaged.

The economic position of tenants *vis-à-vis* owner-occupiers is further eroded by various 'hidden' subsidies enjoyed by the latter. Capital gain on properties owned, the implicit rental income 'earned' by a house for its owner, and the very favourable taxation treatment of both, serve to minimise the owner-occupiers' real housing costs. Apps has dramatically demonstrated the magnitude of these advantages and the magnitude of the gap between the real housing costs of tenants and of owner-occupiers in otherwise equal situations (Apps, 1973). Moreover, the value of these 'subsidies' varies positively with the value of the house, size of mortgage loan and taxable income. 'Almost anyone who opts, by choice or necessity, for not being an owner-occupier, is almost invariably acting in a way which is demonstrably irrational in terms of his own long-term scope for maximising real wealth and income' (Patterson, 1975:28).

It was apparent from the survey that tenants were aware of the economic and other disadvantages of tenancy. When asked whether they would prefer to buy or rent their dwellings if they could afford to do either, 85 per cent of tenants opted to buy; only 12 per cent chose the rental alternative, while 3 per cent were undecided. Tenants were also clearly aware of the financial constraints on purchasing a house; when asked how long they intended remaining as tenants, only 12 per cent said less than a year, 53 per cent said over a year, 30 per cent said over three years, and 35 per cent were not sure.

Preferences to buy varied slightly with occupational status. White-collar tenants were marginally more in favour of purchase than blue-collar tenants. The group most likely to prefer renting was that comprised of tenants in home duties, on pensions or unemployed. This is not surprising since many aged tenants in the sample were in this group, and preference to buy or rent is strongly related to age (see Table 10.4).

The dividing line regarding tenure preference appears to be 40 years of age, since up to this point tenants were strongly in favour of purchase, while beyond it preference to rent climbed steeply. It seems that older tenants are much more willing to trade-off economic benefits in favour of freedom from the responsibilities of ownership and management. Alternatively, they may have a lower ability to realistically appraise their interests.

**Table 10.4   Preference to buy or rent related to age (%)**

| Age group | Prefer to buy | Prefer to rent | Not sure | Total |
|-----------|---------------|----------------|----------|-------|
| 15–20     | 90            | 10             | —        | 100   |
| 21–25     | 96            | 4              | —        | 100   |
| 26–30     | 92            | 6              | 2        | 100   |
| 31–35     | 96            | 4              | —        | 100   |
| 36–40     | 91            | 9              | —        | 100   |
| 41–50     | 65            | 22             | 13       | 100   |
| 51–60     | 53            | 34             | 13       | 100   |
| over 60   | 62            | 35             | 3        | 100   |

Preference to buy or rent was also related to family composition. Married couples and single-parents were over-represented, and single people were under-represented, among those preferring to buy. It is clear that stage in the life cycle is an important determinant of the decision to rent or buy.

Interestingly, no significant differences were found between Australian-born and overseas-born tenants with respect to preference to purchase. This tendency was fairly constant throughout the study. Ethnicity, at least when measured in such a crude way, does not appear to have been a significant factor in the outer-eastern region. This is possibly due to the higher proportion of Anglo-Saxon migrants living on or near the urban fringe of Melbourne (Burnley, 1974), and the relatively long average period of residence in Australia (eleven years) of the overseas-born tenants who were interviewed.

The poor economic position of tenants in urban Australia is largely the result of the operation of the housing and credit markets, and the reinforcing effects of public policies. Inherent imperfections in the housing market fall heaviest on low-income tenants. Rental housing is a 'low order' use of urban land. Whenever conditions change in the housing market—for example, whenever interest rates or building costs rise, government planning strategy alters, or legislated minimum physical standards rise—the profitability and supply of new rental accommodation is significantly affected. Baker (1975) has argued that such changes account for the virtual cessation of construction of new rental accommodation in Melbourne over the past few years. However, as Jones (1976) argues, the rental supply from the existing housing stock is also inherently unstable. Whenever investors/landlords are faced with declining profitability in the rental sub-market, they can sell their properties for home-ownership with relative ease or develop their land for higher density residential or, even better, non-residential use. In all cases, the supply of rental housing falls and rents rise accordingly. This market pressure has recently become especially strong in the inner suburbs of the capital cities, traditionally working class areas offering poorer residents a bundle of locational advantages, but increasingly catering for higher-income residents and white-collar commercial developments (Commission of Inquiry into Poverty, 1975).

Jones has also pointed out that 'filtering'—the process whereby new, expensive housing is constructed, freeing older existing houses for lower-income use—does not work well in the housing market (Jones, 1976). Older housing often filters up, rather than down, particularly when situated in valued locations, or it filters 'sideways' as the children of middle- to high-income parents leave home and, with parental help, purchase their first home. Given the high economic returns to home ownership, those who can afford to, overspend on housing, resulting, as Ross King has demonstrated,in significant under-crowding at one end of the housing scale and over-crowding at the other (King, 1973).

The distribution of a tenuous stock of rental housing is also influenced by more personal factors—by what Pahl has termed the 'gate-keepers'—in particular, the estate agent profession (Pahl, 1975). Price is not the only rationing factor. Discrimination based on family composition, age, ethnic background, sex and class can also be important. In the outer-eastern survey, tenants were asked, without further specification, whether they had ever been discriminated against. Fifteen per cent answered in the affirmative. Unskilled blue-collar workers and those in home duties, unemployed or on a pension, were significantly over-represented in this group, as were single-parents and groups sharing accommodation. In the case of single-parents, 30 per cent claimed discrimination. White-collar workers were under-represented, and no significant differences attached to ethnic background.

In summary, tenants in Australia are, both individually and as a group, economically powerless. They are at the mercy of wider economic forces which effectively determine, as a residual, the amount and quality of housing available to them.

**The social disadvantages of tenancy**

Tenants also suffer from severe social disadvantages—insecurity of tenure, lack of privacy, a legally sanctioned absence of basic rights, and social stigma. The poor legal position of tenants is anchored both in State legislation and standard form leases.

Tenants on a lease do have limited security of tenure—until their lease runs out. Prior to the 1980 Residential Tenancies Bill, tenants in Victoria not on leases could be served with two or four weeks' notice to quit (without reason), depending on whether or not they paid rent monthly. The Tenants Union of Victoria and the Sackville Report on poverty have argued persuasively that this is insufficient time for tenants to find and move to alternative accommodation, and particularly so for low-income tenants whose choice is tightly constrained financially. In our survey we asked tenants how long they would require to move. Only 13 per cent said less than a month. Forty-seven per cent required two months or more, with 18 per cent requiring over three months. If undecided respondents are ignored, 58 per cent of those expressing a preference required two months or more. This would seem to provide support both for Bradbrook's (1975) recommendation that two months be the minimum period of notice, and for the claim by the Tenants Union of Victoria for a three-month minimum.

Although tenants on leases have some security of tenure, this is normally secured by signing away most other basic rights (Bradbrook, 1975). In our survey, 39 per cent thought that their lease protected their rights completely, and 58 per cent thought it was equally fair to both tenant and landlord. Although these proportions are fairly high, it is apparent that there were significant numbers of tenants who were dissatisfied with their leases on these general grounds. This dissatisfaction is even greater when answers to more specific questions are considered: 96 per cent of tenants said that landlords should not enter without notice, and 93 per cent said reasons should be given for entry. It is interesting to note that in the survey, of the tenants able to specify their leases, over 80 per cent were on the RESI lease which specifically grants landlords or their agents right of entry at 'any reasonable time' without the necessity for giving notice or reason. In theory, tenants can refuse to sign standard leases, but the alternatives are restricted by the almost universal use of these leases. Finally, 73 per cent of tenants expressed support for a standard fair lease to protect the rights of tenants (16 per cent were undecided).

A major area of tenant discontent centres on bonds or security deposits. The most common problems relate to the amount of money demanded in advance (which can cause hardship to poor families or even prevent them from renting), and lack of protection against 'bond-snatching', the landlord practice of unfairly refusing to return all or part of the bond at the end of the tenancy for spurious reasons. In the survey, 77 per cent had paid a bond on their current dwelling, more than three-quarters of this group paying $100 or more. Sixteen per cent of the total sample stated that, at some time, part or all of their bond had been withheld, and 84 per cent of this group considered that it had been withheld unfairly. Similarly, 17 per cent of tenants considered that the amount of the bond demanded had, at some time, prevented them from renting the dwelling concerned.

As a minority grouping in property-owning Australian society, tenants are often stigmatised:

> In a country where home-ownership is the national dream and home-owners are seen as the paradigm of the model citizen, the status of the tenant inevitably suffers. Tenants are commonly regarded as transitory or as failures, people who have little commitment to property or community. (Commission of Inquiry into Poverty, 1975:164)

This is particularly true of public tenants whose landlords, the State housing authorities, have generally been peculiarly adept at clearly labelling their clients 'inferior' through a combination of means-test, distinctive building styles, physical concentration and centralised, paternalistic management and attitudes. Although most glaringly present in the high-rise developments of the 1960s, such images and judgments relate, according to the inquiry on poverty, to large Housing Commission estates in general.

**The political disadvantages of tenancy**

The continued deprived position of tenants rests not only on the internal dynamics of the housing market in a class-stratified society, but also on the institutional distribution of power constraining its operation. Tenants, as a group, are politically powerless. The Australian political system is, objectively, 'inpenetrable' to tenancy issues; the perpetual 'non-decision' to ignore tenancy as a public issue reinforces the subjective acceptance of powerlessness (Crenson, 1971).

In a parliamentary democracy based on geographic electorates, where a large majority of voters either own or aspire to own their homes, public policy will 'naturally' discriminate in favour of home owners, regardless of which party is in power. Moreover, tenants live in the *wrong* electorates. They are concentrated in the inner ring of suburbs of the major cities, normally safe for one major party, and spread thinly over the marginal electorates on the urban fringe. Thus, in the region covered by the survey, which incorporates several of the most marginal Federal seats in the country, tenants account for only 12 per cent of the population, little more than a third of the national average. As a consequence, many of the housing policies of governments are not merely neutral in their effect on tenants, they further widen the gap between them and home owners. An example is the home-interest mortgate deduction scheme introduced by the Whitlam Federal Labor Government. The benefits flowing to lower-middle-income home owners were not matched by corresponding tax-relief measures for lower-middle-income tenants. Similarly, whenever policies aimed at narrowing this gap are suggested, governments are quick to oppose. In 1975 the Priorities Review Staff (PRS) merely raised the possibility of taxing the imputed rental income of owner-occupied housing on equity grounds, only to immediately dismiss it as politically unrealistic (Priorities Review Staff, 1975); the then Labor Minister for Housing, Joe Riordon, publicly attacked the PRS for even *considering* the possibility.

When government policies are explicitly directed towards tenants, they tend to be ineffective or counter-productive. In the outer-eastern survey we asked tenants whether they had ever heard of the (Victorian) Fair Rents Board; 58 per cent answered 'yes' and, in response to a further question, only 5 per cent stated that they had used the Board. This low rate of usage is due partly to lack of knowledge of the Board, and partly to its poor record of success. The then Victorian Attorney-General, V. Wildox, stated in Parliament that in the year to October 1974, the Board had dealt with 308 cases: in five cases the rent was reduced, in 265 cases the rent was increased, in ten cases the rent remained unchanged, and the remaining cases were adjourned or withdrawn (Victorian Parliamentary Debates, 1974:3472).

It was also found that only 43 per cent of tenants in the sample were registered to vote at local government elections. The practice by councils of not automatically including all tenants (and spouses) on the electoral roll, as property owners are, effectively disenfranchises many tenants at the local level.

Geographic dispersion and isolation are reinforced by deeper class and ethnic divisions among tenants. Tenants are not a homogeneous group. Although a large majority share common deprivations and a desire to move into home-ownership, differences exist as to likelihood of owning, general life chances and life styles. Even where geographic dispersion is not a problem, differences of resources and outlook embedded in class, ethnic background, age or stage of life cycle, pose massive obstacles to mobilising tenants. These problems are apparent, for example, in the high-rise Housing Commission estates of Sydney and Melbourne, where twenty or more ethnic groups of all incomes and ages are concentrated, some trapped due to low income, some working and saving furiously to buy their own houses—often from their current landlord. Both groups are to some extent subject to fear: the trapped, facing an ever-present reserve army of unhoused, fear eviction in the face of no private alternatives; the mobile fear eviction before they have accumulated access to private alternatives (Faulkner, 1974). Fear is also reinforced by repressive and unfair laws and the manner of their application. Fear, individual victimisation, poor communication and divergences of resources, outlook and aspirations, backed by government neglect or worse, form the obstacles which tenant organisations must overcome to advance the position of tenants in Australia.

In the outer-eastern survey only 26 per cent of tenants had heard of the

Tenants Union of Victoria, but 85 per cent stated that there was a need for such a body. Furthermore, 12 per cent of tenants specifically supported the payment of interest on all bonds held by landlords to the Tenants Union to fund a tenants' advisory service. These signs, although hardly staggering, do suggest that organisations like the Tenants Union of Victoria and local tenants groups can expect to mobilise further support (see Chapter 9).

Stretton (1974) has argued persuasively that housing is a bundle of productive resources, a process or activity rather than a commodity, or, in Turner's words, a verb rather than a noun (Turner, 1972). The way in which people use their housing resources will materially affect their welfare and real incomes, and those of their children. Sociologists should look at housing as they do education—in particular, they should seek to relate access to housing to structured inequality. In what ways do housing inequalities reinforce class divisions in Australian society? In what ways do housing and educational inequalities interact? When sociologists turn their attention to these questions, they will almost certainly find that tenants fare even worse then they had expected.

# Part Four   INTO THE EIGHTIES

LEONIE SANDERCOCK & MICHAEL BERRY

# 11    Cities without jobs? Prospects for the 1980s

In the Sydney of 1982 an unemployed father of six kids under the age of eight leaves his wife because she is then better off, on a supporting parent's benefit and lower Housing Commission rent, than if he stayed. A seventeen-year-old lad, unemployed since he left school, and increasingly hassled by unsympathetic parents, leaves home and joins the ranks of the 15 000 homeless people in this town. At the Matthew Talbot Hostel for homeless men at Woolloomooloo he joins other fourteen- and fifteen-year-olds who sleep on mattresses on a concrete floor because the 480 beds are always full.

A young married couple have saved $10 000 as a deposit for their first home. With both their incomes pooled, they can only afford a weatherboard or fibro cottage somewhere beyond Bankstown—unless they want to be next door to a container terminal, underneath the flight path, or just down the road from the council tip, in which case they could live, for the same $45 000 price, in inner St Peters. The $35 000 loan would have to be financed through a financial institution, if they have a good credit rating. And they will have to make repayments at $115 per week. Their alternatives are stark—a grotty inner city terrace or detached cottage in Penrith would both rent at approximately $90 a week.

Another couple, not so newly married and with three kids, are struggling to meet the weekly payments on their building society home loan of $30 000, as interest rates have risen from 10.5 per cent in 1979 when they finally got the long-awaited loan, to 13.5 per cent in 1982, a yearly repayment extra of well over $1 000. They must both work, which means childcare for the three children. They cannot get them into a long day care centre (at $43 a week each) because the queues for government-funded long day care stretch to the horizon. So they've organised their own patchwork of childcare. He works Sundays so he can have one weekday off to mind the kids. For two days of the week the wife's mum travels (by taxi) to mind them, and for the other two days they are left with a neighbour. Another couple, in a similar dilemma, travel sixteen kilometres, although there's a local *private* service available, in order to have their kids attend a funded centre. And their troubles have not ceased—interest rates and house prices have continued to climb in 1982.

A teenage girl, unable to find work since she left school (like 26.5 per cent of her peers) picks up some local babysitting occasionally, then decides she may as well have her own babies, since there's nothing else to do—thus compounding her own problems, the Housing Commission's problems, and so on. Two-thirds of the women with kids of pre-school age surveyed in the outer Sydney suburb of Kings Langley would go to work if childcare were available—assuming, of course, that jobs are available. In the outer suburbs of Adelaide, Melbourne and Sydney, the 'moonlight flit' is becoming increasingly common—couples or families disappearing in the middle of the night, walking out on their home loans, and TV and furniture and lawnmower hire purchase debts.

These anecdotes are not isolated instances. Life on the urban fringe—where young and not so young people/couples/families/households are struggling to establish themselves—is getting increasingly difficult [and not just on the urban fringe, either (*Sydney Morning Herald*, 6–8 July, 13 August, 24–26 August 1981)].

Housing has become expensive everywhere in the metropolitan area, although more so in Sydney and Melbourne than anywhere else, and for a variety of reasons. These include the effects of the speculative market (project developers claim that 30 per cent of their clients now are 'investors', buying and hanging on for the necessary period of twelve months to avoid capital gains tax, then reselling for profit); the effects of shortages on the supply side of serviced land, in Sydney (but not Adelaide or Melbourne); but above all, because of changed financial circumstances. The demands of financing the (predicted) investment boom mean that home buyers are now having their first taste of what it is like to have to compete for loan funds with mining companies. (A *first* taste, because home loan interest rates are still well below the market price for money.)

In 1967, with the average weekly income on $66 and bank interest rates at 5.7 per cent, it was possible for a single-income family to buy an average house in all but nine of Melbourne's 55 local government areas. By 1972 when the average weekly wage had risen to $98 and bank interest to 7 per cent, two more areas had been added to the list of suburbs beyond the reach of average income earners. By 1977, however, there was only one municipality in Melbourne where an average home could be purchased by a single-income family on the average wage. That area was Footscray. The average wage stood at $200 but bank interest was up to 10.5 per cent and house prices had more than doubled over the previous ten years (Labor Resource Centre, May 1981). A second income has become essential for ordinary families wishing to participate in the great Australian dream. Australia's home-ownership rate appeared to peak at about 75 per cent in the early 1970s and, given the increasingly harsh financial climate of the past few years, would seem to be headed for substantial decline. However, the picture is more complex and uncertain than this. There are a number of built-in checks to declining home-ownership. Firstly, political pressure on government intensifies, encouraging *ad hoc* policies designed to shore-up areas of likely collapse—witness the scramble of late among Federal and State governments to be seen to be easing the interest burden of 'first home buyers'. Secondly, the process of new household formation is crippled—kids who would otherwise have set up house in the outer suburbs on a manageable mortgage now stay on at home with mum and dad or group together with their mates sharing rent payments and dole cheques. And thirdly, some lucky kids draw on the wealth and credit-worthiness of their families: parents or aunts or god-parents pass on their wealth before they die in the form of a deposit for their children's house, often remortgaging their own houses to find the balance. Clearly these processes introduce new and novel means of further unequalising housing costs among Australians.

This has two implications for the quality of urban life: firstly, an ever-widening gap between home owners and renters, and secondly, increasing hardship for renters. In Sydney, soaring rents are now the key factor in the widening compass of poverty. In certain parts of the city those groups already most vulnerable—single-person households, one-parent families, the unemployed, and especially unemployed young people—are the victims, paying from 60 to 75 per cent of their meagre incomes on rent, as Table 11.1 reveals (*Sydney Morning Herald*, 25 August 1981).

Sydney's high rents have helped make Sydney's poor the poorest in Australia. But the problem is by no means confined to Sydney. The Housing Industry Association forecasted average rent rises of 20 per cent throughout Australia in 1982 (*Weekend Australian*, 24–25 April 1982).

A significant aspect of the rent problem is the diminishing public sector

**Table 11.1   Percentage of income paid in rent, according to household group**

| Area | Percent of income paid in rent | Percentage in each household group | | |
|---|---|---|---|---|
| | | Single-person household | One-parent families | Two-parent families |
| Metropolitan area | 46 | 42 | 32 | 26 |
| City | 50 | 84 | 6 | 10 |
| Woolloomooloo | 55 | 83 | 7 | 10 |
| Marrickville | 63 | 30 | 40 | 30 |
| Surrey Hills | 50 | 86 | 8 | 6 |
| Campbelltown | 29 | 6 | 56 | 38 |
| Mt Druitt | 27 | 7 | 58 | 35 |

*Source: Sydney Morning Herald* 25 Aug. 1981

presence in the rental market. The huge reduction in Federal funds for welfare housing since the mid-1970s has meant a halving in the number of dwellings completed by the NSW Housing Commission in 1980–81, compared with the previous four years. In that same period the number of families on its waiting list doubled to 40 000. In Victoria, following the 1981 Federal Budget's further cutbacks to this area of public spending (from $285m to $250m in twelve months), the State (*Liberal*) Minister for Housing called on the Federal Government to increase housing funds by $400m, stressing the 'long term human costs' involved in such cutbacks (*Sydney Morning Herald*, 2 September 1981).

The housing problem has been compounded by other cutbacks in public spending that make the lives of ordinary people increasingly difficult (while leaving the better off unaffected)—less money for public transport, for childcare, hospitals, schools, women's refuges, community health centres, community youth support schemes, and so on (Jones, 1979:41).

Since the demise of the last Federal Labor Government, public investment in the cities has been slashed (Scotton and Ferber, 1978, 1980) making that Government seemingly, and the Department of Urban and Regional Development specifically, the last of the big spenders on urban problems. But lest this be seen as a purely party political issue, it is interesting to note that in the State of NSW, education, health and housing face 30 per cent cuts in expenditure. Only 11.3 per cent of the State's capital works funds were spent on education and health combined, in 1980–81—the lowest for a decade, and expected to drop further. Water and sewerage funds have been declining since 1973–74. According to a secret government report on the impact of the resources boom which was leaked to the *Sydney Morning Herald* in July 1981, these cutbacks in social expenditure in the city were to compensate for massive State expenditure on capital works programs for power generation, port facilities and rail electrification schemes to aid private investment in resource development. According to this report, 25 per cent of the State's entire capital works program was earmarked to boost power generation, largely to supply the energy-hungry aluminium smelters that were to be constructed in the Hunter Valley.

Here, then, is one of the two key reasons why Australian cities are experiencing, and will continue to experience hardships and declining standards of public services—more public sector capital is being channelled into so-called 'productive' infrastructure facilities for private enterprise and less, therefore, is available for the so-called 'non-productive' infrastructure, or social expenditure (that is, housing, schools, hospitals, childcare etc.). This is the crowding-out effect of the 'resources boom'. The second reason is more 'philosophical': rooted in the conservative backlash against thirty years of the welfare state and government intervention in the economy and provision of a range of subsidies, benefits and services.

The philosophical and political backlash against the welfare state and the whole edifice of Keynesian economic policy which underpinned it, took off in most of the advanced capitalist countries in the mid-1970s as a direct response to their rapidly rising levels of both unemployment and inflation. Social democratic governments floundered and were defeated, as their traditional Keynesian economic policy tools proved incapable of dealing with these twin problems. Conservative parties were re-elected on the strength of their appealingly simple explanation of and remedies for the situation.

The villain was identified as big government. Underpinned by monetarist economic doctrine as expounded by Professor Milton Friedman, conservatives argued that all the troubles being experienced were rooted in too much government spending and too much government regulation. Both were stifling private enterprise, the real generator of economic growth. Both were causing inflation; and high inflation automatically produced unemployment.

The remedies for ailing economies were, therefore, presented as a scientific, monetarist package: public spending cuts, tax cuts, 'tight' money and 'rolling back government regulation'. The reality is somewhat different. Some tax rates have effectively fallen, notably those in the corporate sector increasingly benefiting from generous investment allowances and other deductions and the unwillingness of the Fraser Government to close subtle and not so subtle loopholes. The personal tax rates of high income earners have probably also fallen, thanks to the lucrative avenues for tax avoidance. In compensation, other taxpayers have had to pay higher taxes, especially ordinary wage and salary earners; inflation and a move towards indirect taxes have seen to that. On the expenditure side, health, housing and the like have been cut mercilessly, all in the interest of monetary restraint and fiscal responsibility, while spending which socialises (subsidises) private sector production costs (power stations, port facilities, etc.) has increased. Government deregulation has proceeded only at the level of rhetoric. There is much talk of deregulating the banking, airline and telecommunication systems, for instance, and of relaxing such regulatory measures as environmental standards—but little action. There is even less talk and action on ending tariff protection. In fact, the Fraser Government has sought and partly achieved a substantial decline in real wages and 'the social wage' in favour of rising profits and increasing economic inequality. Such a strategy is certainly anti-Keynesian but it also has little to do with monetarism, at least as Milton Friedman conceived it. Nevertheless, monetarism *has* performed a vital ideological function in legitimising tight monetary policies and the attack on social expenditure.

The impact of the new conservatism on urban life is becoming all too painfully obvious, especially in the UK, but also in Australia. Monetary policy works by restricting bank and other lending and by rationing the credit so allowed by high interest rates. It will be apparent to most that those who receive the high interest rates—banks and individuals with loanable cash—do not suffer from such rates. Neither do affluent citizens who do not need to borrow money; or cash-rich corporations that are similarly situated; or those (like large monopolistic firms) which, though they borrow, have the market power and position that allow them to pass the higher costs of money along to the public.

But, as one passes down the income scale, there comes those who suffer from the deprivation and restraint that it is the purpose of monetary policy to induce: those who must borrow money for their business, to find housing, to replace a car. In Britain the effect of high interest rates has produced the largest failure rate among small businesses in half a century. But the really disastrous effect is yet further down the income scale. For monetary policy works against endemic inflation not through some technically neutral nexus that relates the money supply to prices; it works against inflation in highly organised societies like the US, the UK and Australia only as it creates enough unemployment so that this restrains trade union claims, and enough idle plant capacity so that price increases are forgone, discounts initiated and the unions resisted.

As the Federal Treasurer has brought down a succession of 'monetarist' budgets—axing cash for housing, for the Community Youth Support Scheme (CYSS), for health, education and so on—there has been a tendency to see this policy as a technical exercise and to ignore its social consequences as somehow unworthy of practical thought. Or the proponents of monetarism move directly from the money supply to the effect on inflation without consideration of the intervening process and the pain associated therewith (for example, the doubling of waiting lists for public housing). It is short-sighted, too, if riots in British cities are interpreted as a lashing out against deteriorating living conditions and opportunities and rising social and racial tensions.

Australian cities, then, have felt the sting of Liberal Party policies through dramatic cutbacks in urban social services. But obviously this affects each city's poor, rather than its more affluent residents, for the latter are not nearly so dependent on public support schemes. The more affluent may have less disposable income as a result of having to pay for these services in the market place, but at least they *can* pay. The unemployed, old age pensioners, low-income households of whatever variety, cannot. And their problems are being exacerbated, in the low-income neighbourhoods of all Australian cities, by the effects of public policy, the resources boom, and of Australia's changing role in the international capitalist system.

What we are now living through is no less than a major restructuring (which some have called the de-industrialising) of the Australian economy in line with changing international investment patterns, energy costs and sources, and a changing international division of labour. This has two major effects on Australian cities.

Firstly, the 1970s have seen the decline of manufacturing industry in the traditional 'industrial triangle' of south-eastern Australia (from Newcastle through Sydney and Wollongong to Melbourne, Geelong, Adelaide and Whyalla) with associated unemployment for workers in the textile, car, ship-building and iron and steel industries (Stilwell, 1980). The dominance of multinational and monopoly capital in key manufacturing industries has facilitiated the relocation of production in those industries. Plant has been moved to Third World countries where labour is cheap, plentiful and docile, at the expense of workers in the advanced capitalist countries who had often struggled successfully through strong unions for higher wages. This has left both inner and outer zones of Australian cities with a dwindling pool of jobs in car, textile and associated industries.

Secondly, Australia's abundant energy supplies and raw materials (it is now one of only four net energy exporters of the 29 countries in the OECD) have made it increasingly attractive to big foreign investors in resources. Record levels of foreign capital inflow over 1980–81 attest to this.

The Fraser Government's economic strategy has relied heavily on the so-called resources boom to regenerate growth in the private sector after the recession that began in 1974–75. That strategy has had formidable implications for the future well-being of city dwellers because most of the public sector spending for capital works for the rest of the decade is being committed to the provision of infrastructure for private sector resource development projects outside the major cities.

Almost all States are heavily involved in a huge infrastructure borrowing program geared toward the exploitation of mineral resources (as in WA and Queensland) or to support for the processing of minerals based on cheap electricity pricing policies (as in NSW and Victoria). In June 1980, $1700 million worth of infrastructure borrowings were approved by the Loan Council and in 1981 the States submitted a further $4500 million worth of new projects. Most of the capital expenditure on ports was allocated to those serving the coal industry; on power stations, to those being constructed to meet the heavy electricity demands of the aluminium processing industry; and on public transport to the electrification of lines outside the metropolitan area (for example, to Port Kembla, serving the needs of the coal industry). In NSW alone, as much as 25 per cent of all major capital works beyond 1981–82 could be spent on the building of power stations geared toward the aluminium industry. In Victoria, the undeclared amount which the State Government was to spend on transmission lines to an extension of facilities at Portland, where Alcoa began building an aluminium smelter and associated pricing subsidies was further indication of the massive drift of public resources away from the major cities for the subsidising of private developments (Logan, 1980).

Multinational aluminium companies seek Australian sites because of its cost advantages: cheaper power, locally available bauxite, and less strict environmental standards (Australian Conservation Foundation, 1981). These same companies may be able to manipulate pricing by selling aluminium to a subsidiary outside Australia at a low price which gives no apparent profit, and so is not liable for tax here. So why are these subsidies being offered?

It appears that interstate rivalries have yet again led to the situation where each State is competing to attract big investors by offering larger incentives. What is missing is some form of Federal intervention to protect taxpayers from the capacity of multinationals to play off the States against each other. But there is an even more basic question. If the employment and income benefits and long-term profit benefits of private resource based industry are to be confined to a small section of the total community, to what extent does the community interest—located mainly in the cities—warrant the diversion of public sector funds to provide the infrastructure needed for private sector resource development (AIUS, 1980:17)?

There is a further relevance in these events for the future well-being of city dwellers in their effects on existing inequalities both within and among Australian cities. Not all States are equally well endowed with sought-after resources and abundant energy supplies, and this has powerful effects on the prospective fortunes of the different State capitals. Perth is likely to experience strong growth through mineral projects, aluminium smelting and the North West gas shelf, and through communications with Southeast Asia and Singapore. In Tasmania, however, most of the hydro-electric resources have been tapped, there is little scope left for cheap power, and growth prospects are modest. The proposed Gordon below Franklin dam would only provide 180 Megawatts of power and at great environmental cost. The local economy of Hobart will be relatively static and the greatest concern will be finding funds to improve the existing urban fabric and to protect the built environment (AIUS, 1980:11).

Sydney seems to be developing as the head office for business interested in the Asian and Pacific region and there is likely to be strong growth in the Gosford–Wyong area, poised between the coal-rich Hunter Valley and metropolitan Sydney. Pollution, congested local transport and pressure on land and house prices (later in the decade, from resource-rich companies seeking other avenues to invest their profits) are likely to increase. Adelaide's economy is particularly fragile, dependent as it has been since the Second World War on growth in car and consumer durables manufacturing (AIUS, 1980:10–11). Future growth prospects may hinge on the controversial Roxby Downs area (uranium mining) and the Redcliffs petrochemical plant, both of which have been opposed by environmental activists.

Melbourne, too, has been more heavily dependent than Sydney on cars, textiles and clothing and consumer durables industries, and has been going through a noticeable economic slowdown. Thus, the metropolitan area lost almost 40 000 factory jobs during the 1970s (*Age*, 10 July 1980). One indicator of this was the relatively sedate rise in house prices compared with Sydney's soaring values in 1979 and 1980 in established areas.

Central Queensland's resource base ensures that State's expanding export income, but also involves demands for large-scale infrastructure investment outside its existing major urban centres, notably for power stations, railways and port facilities. Crises in the provision of social facilities (housing and schools especially) in Gladstone, a northern focus of resource developments, has already attracted considerable attention (Commonwealth Parliamentary Debates, 1981:88–91).

It does seem, therefore, that real inequalities may be created in the next decade *among* Australian cities. People in Perth, Sydney, Brisbane and perhaps Melbourne have some chance of benefiting *eventually* (although not necessarily) from the 'filter down' effect of resource developments in their hinterlands. The prospects of Adelaide and Hobart are far grimmer, and may depend on whether or not the Federal Government, through the Commonwealth Grants Commission, chooses to redistribute some of the expected benefits of the boom to the newly 'disadvantaged' States.

In the absence of government intervention, further inequalities will develop within each State and each capital city in the new industrial environment of the 1980s. The groups with most economic bargaining power, in the wake of the Arbitration Commission's abandonment of wage indexation in July 1981, will be those unions involved in the resources boom. Skilled professions, technicians and tradesmen, and the organised labour groups in resources, transport, and infrastructure—the builders of power stations, smelters, refineries, pipelines, transmission lines, roads and bridges, and miners—will be the winners. Employers involved in the boom are willing to pay much higher wages than those ruling in the seaboard cities and towns. Many were already doing so under private deals (before the end of wage indexation) which never went to the Arbitration Commission because of the guidelines. The losers, the unions which fall behind, will be mainly in city-based, white collar industries such as retailing, clerical work, the public service, and service industries, and city blue collar groups in manufacturing and unskilled labour, not aligned with the boom.

Thus the next decade may see a widening of the gap, on the one hand, between these very well off groups and those on more modest incomes and, on the other hand, between the employed and those on social welfare. The latter group will be acutely disadvantaged as the major cities suffer from a declining proportion of the state's public expenditure allocation; and from the Fraser Government's 'new federalism' policy, whereby the provision of urban services has become the responsibility of State governments which are (Catch-22) largely dependent on the Commonwealth for their funds. The Commonwealth is exercising 'fiscal restraint' to reduce the relative size of the public sector and is seeking to discourage States' public authority borrowings in the capital market, arguing that this is 'crowding out' private investors. In the light of the need of private investment for public infrastructure provision, this must surely be one of the most glaring contradictions of contemporary Australian capitalism.

If the temptation to defer action in response to emergent issues is succumbed to, and Australian cities are left to fend for themselves until the anticipated profits from resource developments start flooding in, the urban consequences will be dramatic. Widening inequalities and socioeconomic segregation; further distortion of the land and housing market; social divisiveness and industrial militancy; increasing wage and salary demands to offset urban deficiencies; rising rents in the private market as the public housing sector contracts; inadequate maintenance of public works and services, leading eventually to higher repair and replacement costs; the further rundown of urban public transport, causing longer commuter journeys and more pollution; and inadequate responses to changing employment patterns and locations, leisure needs, energy conservation and an ageing population (AIUS, 1980:60–1).

What this scenario assumes, of course, is that the growth benefits of the resources boom will actually materialise and trickle-down, however unevenly, to urban interests. However, as the decade wears on, the very notion of a resources boom is becoming problematical. In the latter half of 1981 the total capital committed to major resource developments fell by $3 billion (*Age*, 14 April 1982), an apparent reflection of declining international commodity prices in the wake of intensifying crisis in the major capitalist countries. If this trend were to continue, along with progressive de-industrialisation, the inequalities and social costs noted above will grow as the Australian economy descends into a generalised depression, causing the bargaining position of State governments (in particular) *vis-à-vis* multinational capital, to deteriorate even further and 'labour discipline' to increase. Idle capital released from resources development and unable to be absorbed in the declining Australian manufacturing sector will tend to be switched back overseas or into increasingly unproductive and speculative local activities, including that historic standby—urban real estate. A new property boom in central city office development and luxury housing is unlikely to reduce existing urban inequalities, although it may result in the creation of some jobs in the building industry.

As yet it is not clear whether a change from a conservative to a Labor federal government will make much difference. So the future of the cities is uncertain. Birth rates and immigration flows have declined markedly, while structural economic change and a global recession have pushed unemployment rates to their highest since the 1930s Depression. In this situation social problems in the cities will be more widespread but opportunities for planners to intervene are likely to be fewer, because the total resources available for improving the cities—where most people will continue to live—will be fewer and the constraints on planners greater.

We are no longer, in the words of Les Murray's poem, 'travelling luxury class in our drift to the cities'.

# Bibliography

Alcaly, R E and Mermelstein, D eds (1977) *The Fiscal Crisis of American Cities* New York: Vintage Books

Alonso, W (1964) *Location and Land Use* Cambridge, Mass.: Harvard University Press

Ambrose, P and Colenutt, R (1975) *The Property Machine* Harmondworth: Penguin

Amery, C and Cruickshank, D (1975) *The Rape of Britain* London: Elek

AMP Society (1976) *Annual Report* Sydney

Amsden, J (1979) Historians and the Spatial Imagination *Radical History Review* 21, Fall

Apps, P (1973) *Tenure, Real Housing Costs and House Price Inflation* Ian Buchan Fell Research Project, Paper No. 5, Sydney: University of Sydney

Archer, R (1967) Market Factors in the Redevelopment of the Central Business Area of Sydney, 1957–1966, in Troy, P ed. *Urban Redevelopment in Australia* Canberra: Urban Research Unit

Aungles, S and Szelenyi, I (1979) Industrial Decline and Urban Crisis: Structural Conflicts between the State and Monopoly Capital—The Case of Whyalla *Australian and New Zealand Journal of Sociology* 15, 1, March

Australian Conservation Foundation (1981) *Newsletter* 13, 6, July (Melbourne)

Australian Institute of Urban Studies (1980) *Urban Strategies for Australia: Managing the Eighties* Canberra: AIUS

Baker, K (1975) The Rental Crisis—Initiatives for Action, paper presented to Proceedings of Cost Rental Housing Seminar, University of Melbourne, July

Bate, WA (1962) *A History of Brighton* Melbourne: Melbourne University Press

—— (1978) *Lucky City: The First Generation at Ballarat, 1851–1901* Melbourne: Melbourne University Press

Ball, M (1976) Owner Occupation in *Housing and Class* London: Conference of Socialist Economists

Baran, P, and Sweezy, P (1968) *Monopoly Capital* Harmondsworth: Penguin

Beed, C (1981) *Melbourne's Development and Planning* Melbourne: Clewarra Press

Bell, C (1977) On Housing Classes *Australian and New Zealand Journal of Sociology* 13, 1

—— (1978) Towards a Political Economy of Housing, in Wheelwright, E L and Buckley, K eds *Essays in the Political Economy of Australian Capitalism* Vol. 2, Sydney: Australia and New Zealand Book Company

Berry, M (1977) Whose City? The Forgotten Tenant *Australian and New Zealand Journal of Sociology* 13, 1, February
_____ (1978) Collective Consumption, Devalorisation and State Intervention, paper presented to the Ninth World Congress of the International Sociological Association, Research Committee on Urban and Regional Development, Uppsala, Sweden, August
_____ (1979) Marxist Approaches to the Housing Question, Centre for Urban and Regional Studies, Research Memorandum 69, University of Birmingham, February
_____ (1980) History, Anyone? *Australian and New Zealand Journal of Sociology* 16, 1, March
_____ (1983) Urbanisation and Social Change: Australia in the Twentieth Century, in Encel, S *et al. Australian Society: Introductory Essays* 4th edn, Melbourne: Longman Cheshire
Bowles, S and Gintis, H (1976) *Schooling in Capitalist America* London: Routledge and Kegan Paul
Bradbrook, A (1975) *Poverty and the Residential Landlord–Tenant Relationship* Australian Commission of Inquiry into Poverty, Law and Poverty series, Canberra: AGPS
Breugel, I (1975) The Marxist Theory of Rent and the Contemporary City in *Political Economy and the Housing Question* London: Conference of Socialist Economists
Briggs, A (1963) *Victorian Cities* London: Odhams
Broadbent, T A (1977) *Planning and Profit in the Urban Economy* London: Methuen
Broadbent, T A and Catalano, A (1975) *Notes on Office Development by Major Property Companies 1960–1975,* Working Note 426 London: Centre for Environmental Studies
Budget Paper No.9 (1975) *Urban and Regional Development 1975–6* Canberra: AGPS
Burnley, I H ed. (1974) *Urbanisation in Australia: the Post-War Experience* Cambridge: Cambridge University Press
_____ (1980) *The Australian Urban System* Melbourne: Longman Cheshire
Butlin, N G (1964) *Investment in Australian Economic Development 1861–1900* Cambridge: Cambridge University Press
_____ (1970) Some Perspectives of Australian Economic Development, 1890–1965, in Forster, C ed. *Australian Economic Development in the Twentieth Century* London: George Allen and Unwin
Byrne, D and Bierne, P (1975) Toward a Political Economy of Housing Rent, in *Political Economy and the Housing Question* London: Conference of Socialist Economists
Cannon, M (1966) *The Land Boomers* Melbourne: Melbourne University Press
Cardew, R, Langdale, J and Rich, D eds (1982) *Why Cities Change* Sydney: George Allen and Unwin
Carr, E H (1964) *What is History?* Harmondsworth: Penguin
Cass, B (1978a) A Critical Evaluation of the Concept of Consumption in Urban Sociology, paper presented to SAANZ Conference, Brisbane, May
_____ (1978b) Women's Place in the Class Structure, in Wheelwright, E L and Buckley, K eds *Political Economy of Australian Capitalism,* Vol. 3, Sydney: Australia and New Zealand Book Company

Castells, M (1977a) *The Urban Question* London: Edward Arnold
_____ (1977b) Towards a Political Urban Sociology, in Harloe, M ed. *Captive Cities* London: John Wiley and Sons
_____ (1978) *City, Class and Power* London: Macmillan
Catley, R (1978) Socialism and Reform in Contemporary Australia, in Wheelwright, E L and Buckley, K eds *Essays in the Political Economy of Australian Capitalism* Vol. 2, Sydney: Australia and New Zealand Book Company
Catley, R and McFarlane, B (1974) *From Tweedledum to Tweedledee* Sydney: Australia and New Zealand Book Company
_____ (1975) Technocratic Laborism—the Whitlam Government, in Wheelwright, E L and Buckley, K eds *Essays in the Political Economy of Australian Capitalism* Vol. 1, Sydney: Australia and New Zealand Book Company
Centre for Urban Research and Action (1976) *The Displaced* Melbourne
_____ (1979) *Landlords and Lodgers* Melbourne
Childe, V G (1923) *How Labour Governs: A Study of Workers' Representation in Australia* London: Labour Publishing Co. Ltd
Clark, D (1975) Australia: Victim or Partner of British Imperialism? in Wheelwright, E L and Buckley, K eds, *Essays in the Political Economy of Australian Capitalism* Vol. 1, Sydney: Australia and New Zealand Book Company
_____ (1976) Marx Versus Butlin: Some Comments on the Snooks-Rowse Debate *Labour History* 30, May
Cloher, D (1975) A Perspective on Australian Urbanisation, in Powell, J and Williams, M eds, *Australian Space, Australian Time* Melbourne: Oxford University Press
Cochrane, P (1976) Australian Finance Capital in Transition *Intervention* 6, June
_____ (1980) *Industrialisation and Dependence: Australia's Road to Economic Development* St Lucia: University of Queensland Press
Collins, J (1978) Fragmentation of the Working Class, in Wheelwright, E and Buckley, K eds *Essays in the Political Economy of Australian Capitalism* Vol. 3 Sydney: Australia and New Zealand Book Company
Commission of Inquiry into Poverty (1975) *Poverty in Australia: First Main Report* Canberra: AGPS
Commonwealth Parliamentary Debates (1981) Canberra: AGPS
Community Committee on Tenancy Law Reform (1978) *Reforming Victoria's Tenancy Laws* Melbourne: Victorian Council of Social Service
Connell, R W (1977) *Ruling Class, Ruling Culture: Studies of Conflict, Power and Hegemony in Australian Life* London: Cambridge University Press
Connell, R W and Irving T H (1980) *Class Structure in Australian History: Documents, Narrative and Argument* Melbourne: Longman Cheshire
Conner, J (1980) The State of Planning Education in Australia: Can Past Investments Yield Future Pay Offs? in Domicelj, S and Zehner, R B eds *Planning Education in Australia: Excellence and Relevance* University of Sydney: Planning Research Centre
Coutras, J and Fagnani, J (1978) Femmes et Transports en Milieu Urbain *International Journal of Urban and Regional Research* 2, 3
Crenson, (1971) *The Un-politics of Air Pollution* Baltimore: Johns Hopkins University Press
Crisp, L F (1960) *Ben Chifley* Melbourne: Longmans
Crompton, D (1961) Book Review *Town Planning Review*, XXXII
Cusack, D and Dodd, J (1978) *Outwork: An Alternate Mode of Employment?*

Melbourne: Centre for Urban Research and Action

Daines, D (1978) The Penalty of Exclusiveness *Royal Australian Planning Institute Journal*, February

Daly, M (1982) *Sydney Boom Sydney Bust* Sydney: George Allen and Unwin

Davies, L (1981) The Future of Practice *The Planner*, 67, 1

Davison, G (1978a) Sydney and the Bush: An Urban Context for the Australian Legend *Historical Studies* 18, 71, October

_____ (1978b) *The Rise and Fall of Marvellous Melbourne* Melbourne: Melbourne University Press

_____ (1979) Australian Urban History: a Progress Report *Urban History Yearbook* 100–9

Dear, M and Scott, A J (1981) *Urbanisation and Urban Planning in Capitalist Society*, London: Methuen

Dennis, N (1972) *Public Participation and Planners' Blight* London: Faber and Faber

Diamond, D and McLoughlin, B eds (1973) *Progress in Planning* Vol. 1, Oxford: Pergamon

Donnison, D (1980) *The Good City* London: Heinemann Educational

Edel, M (1976) Marx's Theory of Rent: Urban Applications, in *Housing and Class in Britain* London: Conference of Socialist Economists

_____ (1979) Review of D Massey and A Catalano, 'Capital and Land: Land-Ownership by Capital in Great Britain' *International Journal of Urban and Regional Research* 3, 2

Eversley, D (1973) *The Planner in Society: the Changing Role of a Profession* London: Faber

Faulkner, A (1974) Tenant Power: Some Thoughts Prior to the Event *Ecstasis* 8

_____ (1976) Tenants' Rights Campaign in St. Kilda, unpublished manuscript, Melbourne: Centre for Urban Research and Action

Faulkner, A and Berry, M (1976) *Tenancy: The Need for Reform* Melbourne: Centre for Urban Research and Action

Fitzpatrick, B (1941) *The British Empire in Australia: An Economic History, 1834–1939* Melbourne: Melbourne University Press

Fodor, R (1978) Day-care Policy in France and its Consequences for Women: A Study of the Metropolitan Paris Area *International Journal of Urban and Regional Research* 2, 3

Gamarnikow, E (1978) 'Introduction' to Women and the City Symposium, *International Journal of Urban and Regional Research* 2, 3

Gans, H (1968) *People and Plans* New York: Basic Books

Geddes, P (1915) *Cities in Evolution* London: Williams and Morgate

Gibson, K and Horvath, R (1980) Aspects of a Theory of Transition Within the Capitalist Mode of Production, unpublished manuscript, Sydney: Department of Geography, University of Sydney

Giddens, A (1973) *The Class Structure of the Advanced Societies* London: Hutchinson

_____ (1979) *Central Problems in Social Theory* London: Macmillan

Gillen, K (1978) New Capitalism, New Marxism, paper delivered at SAANZ Conference, University of Queensland, May

Glynn, S (1970a) *Urbanisation in Australian History, 1788–1900* Melbourne: Nelson

_____ (1970b) Approaches to Urban History: the Case for Caution *Australian Economic History Review*, X, 2, September

Gollan, R A (1963) *The Coal Miners of New South Wales: A History of the Union, 1860–1960* Melbourne: Melbourne University Press

Goodman, R (1972) *After the Planners* London: Pelican

Gordon, D (1978) Capitalist Development and the History of American Cities, in Tabb, W and Sawers, L eds *Marxism and the Metropolis: New Perspectives in Urban Political Economy* New York: Oxford University Press

Gowans, G (1978) *Report of the Board of Inquiry into Certain Land Purchases by the Housing Commission and Questions Arising Therefrom* Victoria: Government Printer

Habermas, J (1976) *Legitimation Crisis* London: Heinemann

Hall, P (1981) The Limitations of Marxist Urban Studies *New Society* 10, 9

Hapgood, K E and Getzels, J (1974) *Planning, Women and Change* Washington, D C: U S Department of Housing and Urban Development

Harloe, M ed. (1977) *Captive Cities: Essays in the Political Economy of Cities and Regions* Introduction, London: John Wiley and Sons

Harloe, M, Issacharoff, R and Minns, R (1975) *The Organisation of Housing* London: Heinemann

Hargreaves, K (1975) *This House is Not for Sale* Melbourne: Centre for Urban Research and Action

Harvey, D (1973) *Social Justice and the City* London: Edward Arnold

_____ (1974) Class Monopoly Rent, Finance Capital and the Urban Revolution *Regional Studies* 8, 3

_____ (1975) The Geography of Capitalist Accumulation: a Re-construction of the Marxian Theory *Antipode*, 7, 2, September

_____ (1978) The Urban Process Under Capitalism: A Framework for Analysis *International Journal of Urban and Regional Research* 2, 1

Hayden, D (1981) *The Grand Domestic Revolution: A History of Feminist Designs for American Homes, Neighborhoods and Cities* Cambridge, Mass.: Massachusetts Institute of Technology Press

Heywood, P (1981) The Future of Planning Education *The Planner* 67, 1

Hirsch, F (1978) *The Social Limits to Growth* Cambridge, Mass.: Harvard University Press

Hobsbawm, E J (1972) Karl Marx's Contribution to Historiography in Blackburn, R ed. *Ideology in Social Science* Bungay, Suffolk: Fontana

Hoinville, G and Jowell, R (1972) 'Will the Real Public Please Stand Up?' *Official Architecture and Planning* 35

Hunt, A (ed) (1977) *Class and Class Structure* London: Lawrence and Wishart

Jones, E (1979) Fraser and the Social Wage *Journal of Australian Political Economy* 5, July

Jones, M A (1972) *Housing and Poverty in Australia* Melbourne: Melbourne University Press

_____ (1976) *Housing Policy in Australia: Future Directions for Reform* Melbourne: Swinburne College of Technology, Centre for Urban Studies

_____ (1979) Australian Urban Policy *Politics* XIV, 2, November

Jacobs, J (1961) *The Death and Life of Great American Cities* New York: Random House

Kelley, M ed. (1978) *Nineteenth Century Sydney: Essays in Urban History* Sydney: Sydney University Press

Kemeny, J (1978) Home Ownership and Finance Capital *Journal of Australian Political Economy* 3, September

_____ (1979) Reply to Tony Ward *Journal of Australian Political Economy* 4, March

Kiddle, M (1961) *Men of Yesterday* Melbourne: Melbourne University Press

Kilmartin, L and Thorns, D (1979) *Cities Unlimited* Sydney: George Allen and Unwin

King, R (1973) *The Dimensions of Housing Need in Australia* Ian Buchan Fell Research Project, Paper No. 3, Sydney: Department of Architecture, University of Sydney

Labor Resource Centre (1981) *Labor Resources* Melbourne: Australian Labor Party, May

Lamarche, F (1976) Property Development and the Economic Foundations of the Urban Question, in Pickvance, C ed. *Urban Sociology: Critical Essays* London: Tavistock

Lambert, J, Paris, C, and Blackaby, B (1978) *Housing Policy and the State* London: Macmillan

Larcombe, G (1981) Economic Recession and Restructuring of the Australian Economy, 1974–1980: A Case Study of Newcastle and the Hunter Region, unpublished Masters in Urban Studies thesis, Macquarie University

Lawson, R (1973) *Brisbane in the 1890s: A Study of an Australian Urban Society* St Lucia: Queensland University Press

Leavitt, J (1981) Women in Planning: There's More to Affirmative Action than Gaining Access, in Wekerle, G Peterson, R and Morley, D eds *New Space for Women* Boulder: Westview Press

Logan, T (1980) *Urban and Regional Planning in Victoria* Melbourne: Shillington House

Lojkine, J (1976) Contribution to a Marxist Theory of Capitalist Urbanisation' in Pickvance, C ed. *Urban Sociology: Critical Essays* London: Tavistock

_____ (1977) *Le Marxisme, l'etat et la Question Urbaine* Paris: Presses Universitaires de France

McCarty, J W (1970) Australian Capital Cities in the Nineteenth Century *Australian Economic History Review* X, 2, September

_____ (1973) Australia as a Region of Recent Settlement in the Nineteenth Century *Australian Economic History Review* XIII, 2, June

_____ (1980) Melbourne, Ballarat, Sydney, Perth: the New City Histories *Historical Studies* 19, 74, April

McLoughlin, B (1969) *Urban and Regional Planning: a Systems Approach* London: Faber

Mandel, E (1968) *Marxist Economic Theory* London: Merlin

_____ (1975) *Late Capitalism* London: New Left Books

Markusen, A (1978) Class, Rent and Sectoral Conflict: Uneven Development in Western U.S. Boomtowns *Review of Radical Political Economics* 10, 3, Fall

_____ (1980) City Spatial Structure, Women's Household Work and National Urban Policy *Signs* 5, 3

Marriot, O (1967) *The Property Boom* London: Pan

Marris, P and Rein M (1973) *Dilemmas of Social Reform* New York: Aldine Books

Massey, D (1977) The Analysis of Capitalist Land Ownership: An Investigation of the Case of Great Britain *International Journal of Urban and Regional Research* 1, 3

Massey, D and Catalano, A (1978) *Capital and Land: Landownership by Capital in Great Britain* London: Edward Arnold

May, A L (1968) *The Battle of the Banks* Sydney: Sydney University Press

Moore, B (1972) *Reflections on the Causes of Human Misery* London: Allen Lane

Mullins, P (1973) Neighbourhood Perception and the Effects of Forced Residential Mobility *Australian and New Zealand Journal of Sociology* 9, 2

—— (1977) The Social Base, State and Urban Effects of a Brisbane Urban Social Movement *Australian and New Zealand Journal of Sociology* 13, 1

—— (1981) Theoretical Perspectives on Australian Urbanisation: 1. Material Components in the Reproduction of Australian Labour Power *Australian and New Zealand Journal of Sociology* 17, 1 March

Murie, A, Niner, P and Watson, C (1976) *Housing Policy and the Housing System* London: George Allen and Unwin

National Mutual (1977) *Annual Report* Sydney

Nell, E (1972) The Revival of Political Economy, in Blackburn, R ed. *Ideology in Social Science* Suffolk: Fontana

Neutze, GM (1978) *Australian Urban Policy* Sydney: George Allen and Unwin

Nowicki, H and Tsoklas, K (1979) Finance Capital and the Australian Ruling Class *Intervention* 13, October

O'Connor, J (1973) *The Fiscal Crisis of the State* New York: St. Martin's Press

Orchard, L (1982) Social Theory and Interventionist Policy: a Study of DURD, unpublished paper presented to CEUS Seminar Series, Macquarie University, October

Pahl, R E (1975) Poverty and the Urban System, in *Whose City?* 2nd edn, Harmondsworth: Penguin

Painter, M (1974) Urban Government, Urban Politics and the Fabrication of Urban Issues: The Impossibility of Urban Policy *Australian Journal of Public Administration* XXXVII, 4, December

Paris, C (1977) Review of Pahl and Pickvance *Urban Studies* June

Parker, R S and Troy, P N eds (1972) *The Politics of Urban Growth* Canberra: Australian National University Press

Pascoe, R (1979) *The Manufacture of Australian History* Melbourne: Oxford University Press

Paterson, J (1975) Home Owning, Home Renting and Income Redistribution *Australian Quarterly* December

Pickvance, C (1976) *Urban Sociology: Critical Essays* London: Methuen

Priorities Review Staff (1975) *Report on Housing* Canberra: AGPS

Ravallion, M (1975) Urban Problems, Public Policies and Social Structure *Australian Quarterly* 47, 4

—— (1977) Urban Problems and Urban Policies, or Merely Urban Assumptions?— a Review of Recent Urban Research in Australia *International Journal of Urban and Regional Research* 1, 3

Rex, J and Moore, R (1967) *Race, Community and Conflict* London: Oxford University Press

Rivers, L and Hyde, J (1975) The Dominance of Finance Capital *Arena* 39

Roberts, M (1974) *An Introduction to Town Planning Techniques* London: Hutchinson Educational Ltd

Rose, H (1978) In Practice Supported in Theory Denied: An Account of an Invisible Urban Movement *International Journal of Urban and Regional Research* 2, 3

Rothblatt, D, Garr, D and Sprague, J (1979) *The Suburban Environment and Women* New York: Praeger

Royal Town Planning Institute (1972) Town Planners and Their Future: Implications of Changes in Education and Membership Policy: A Further Discussion
Paper, London

Sandercock, L (1975) *Cities for Sale* Melbourne: Melbourne University Press

_____ (1976) *Public Participation in Planning* Adelaide: South Australian Government Printer

_____ (1978) A Socialist City in a Capitalist Society? Property Ownership and
Urban Reform in Australia *Journal of Australian Political Economy* 3, September

_____ (1979) *The Land Racket* Sydney: Silverfish

_____ (1982) Producing Planners or Educating Urbanists in Murray-Smith, S ed.
*Melbourne Studies in Education* Melbourne: Melbourne University Press

Saunders, P (1978) Domestic Property and Social Class *International Journal of
Urban and Regional Research* 2, 2

_____ (1979) *Urban Politics: A Sociological Interpretation* London: Hutchinson

_____ (1980) *Urban Politics* Harmondsworth: Penguin

_____ (1981) Is There a Weberian Sociology? A Critique of the New Marxist
Orthodoxy in Urban Studies and an Outline of an Alternative Approach, unpublished Urban Research Unit Seminar Paper, Canberra

Schedvin, C B (1978) Review of R.V. Jackson: Australian Economic Development
in the Nineteenth Century *Australian Economic History Review* XVIII

Scotton, R B and Ferber, H (1978) *Public Expenditure in Social Policy in Australia*
Vol. 1, Melbourne: Longman Cheshire

_____ (1980) *Public Expenditure in Social Policy in Australia* Vol. 2, Melbourne:
Longman Cheshire

Self, P (1972) The Planner's Future *Town and Country Planning*, 40:3

Sennett, R (1973) *The Uses of Disorder: Personal Identity and City Life* Harmondsworth: Penguin

Signs (1980) Special Issue: Women and the American City *Journal of Women in
Culture and Society* 5, 3 Spring

Simmie, J (1974) *Citizens in Conflict* London: Hutchinson Educational Limited

Skeffington, A M (1968) *People and Planning* Committee on Public Participation,
London: HMSO

Spagnoletti, C (1977) *Women and Planning: An Annotated Bibliography* Adelaide:
South Australian Housing Trust

Spearritt, P (1978) *Sydney Since the Twenties* Sydney: Hale and Iremonger

Stannage, C T (1979) *The People of Perth* Perth: Perth City Council

Stedman-Jones, G (1972) History: the Poverty of Empiricism, in Blackburn, R ed.
*Ideology in Social Science: Readings in Critical Social Theory* London: Fontana

Stilwell, F J B (1978) Competing Analyses of the Spatial Aspects of Capitalist
Development *Review of Radical Political Economics* 10, 3, Fall

_____ (1980) *Economic Crisis, Cities and Regions: An Analysis of Current Urban and
Regional Problems in Australia* Sydney: Pergamon

Stone, M (1978) Housing, Mortgage Lending and the Contradictions of
Capitalism, in Tabb, W K and Sawers, L eds *Marxism and the Metropolis* New
York: Oxford University Press

Storer, D (1975) *But I Wouldn't Want My Wife to Work Here* Melbourne: Centre
for Urban Research and Action

Stretton, H (1969) *The Political Sciences* London: Routledge and Kegan Paul

_____ (1970) *Ideas for Australian Cities* North Adelaide: the Author

_____ (1974) *Housing and Government* Boyer Lectures, Sydney: Australian Broadcasting Commission

_____ (1978) *Urban Planning in Rich and Poor Countries* Oxford: Oxford University Press

Szelenyi, I (1977) Class Analysis and Beyond: Further Dilemmas for the new Urban Sociology, unpublished paper, Flinders University, Adelaide

_____ (1978a) The Relative Autonomy of the State or State Mode of Production? paper presented at SAANZ Conference, University of Queensland, May

_____ (1978b) Social Inequalities in State Socialist Redistributive Economics *International Journal of Comparative Sociology* 1 and 2

Tabb, W K and Sawers, L (1978) *Marxism and the Metropolis* Oxford: Oxford University Press

Topalov, C (1973) *Capital et Propriere Fonciere* Paris: Centre de Sociologie Urbaine

_____ (1974) *Les Promoteurs Immobiliers* Paris: Mouton

Troy, P (1978) *A Fair Price, the Land Commission Program 1972–1977* Sydney: Hale and Iremonger

_____ ed. (1981) *Equity in the City* Sydney: George Allen and Unwin

Turner, J (1972) Housing as a Verb, in Turner, J and Fichter, R eds *Freedom to Build* New York: Macmillan

Victorian Parliamentary Debates (1974) Melbourne: Government Printer

Wakefield, K (1978) Tenancy Laws Spell Doom *Age* 14 December

Walker, R (1978a) Two Sources of Uneven Development under Advanced Capitalism: Spatial Differentiation and Capital Mobility *Review of Radical Political Economics* 10, 3, Fall

_____ (1978b) The Transformation of Urban Structure in the Nineteenth Century and the Beginnings of Suburbanisation, in Cox, K R ed. *Urbanisation and Conflict in Market Societies* Chicago: Maaroufa Press

Ward, J (1978) Comment on Jim Kemeny's 'Home Ownership and Finance Capital' *Journal of Australian Political Economy* 3, September

Ward, R (1958) *The Australian Legend* Melbourne: Oxford University Press

_____ (1978) 'The Australian Legend Re-visited *Historical Studies* 18, 71, October

Wekerle, G, Peterson, R and Morley, D eds (1980) *New Space for Women* Boulder: Westview Press

Whimster, S (1980) The Profession of History in the Work of Max Weber: its Origins and Limitations *British Journal of Sociology*, 31, 3, September

Wilson, R K (1978) Urban and Regional Policy, in Scotton, R B and Ferber, H eds *Public Expenditures and Social Policy in Australia Volume 1: the Whitlam Years 1972–75* Melbourne: Longman Cheshire

Women's Electoral Lobby (1975) Submission to the Victorian Status of Women Committee, mimeo

Women's Liberation Halfway House Collective (1977) Housing Discrimination: the Role of Real Estate Agents, mimeo, Melbourne

Woodruff, W (1973) The Emergence of an International Economy, 1700–1914, in Cipolla, C M ed. *The Fontana Economic History of Europe* Vol. 4, Part 2, Glasgow: Fontana/Collins

Wright, E O (1978) *Class, Crisis and the State* London: New Left Books

Zehner, R B (1980) The Survey of Tertiary Education Institutions, in Domicelj, S and Zehner, R B *Planning Education in Australia: Excellence and Relevance* Sydney: Planning Research Centre, University of Sydney

# Index